THE DIAL OF
VIRTUE

A Study of Poems on
Affairs of State in the Seventeenth
Century

BY RUTH NEVO

For from the Monarch's vertue Subjects take,
Th'ingredient which does publick vertue make.
At his bright beam they all their Tapers light,
And by his Diall set their motion right.

PRINCETON, NEW JERSEY

PRINCETON UNIVERSITY PRESS · 1963

Copyright © 1963 by Princeton University Press
All Rights Reserved
L.C. Card: 63-9995

———

Publication of this book has been aided by
the Ford Foundation program to support publication,
through university presses, of works in the
humanities and social sciences

———

Printed in the United States of America
by Vail-Ballou Press, Inc., Binghamton, N.Y.

For Adam A. Mendilow

PREFACE

The research for this book was begun in 1955, when a generous grant from the Anglo-Jewish Association of London enabled me to spend a year in England. I am as indebted to the AJA for that year as I am to Professor H. Jenkins of Westfield College for his advice and encouragement during the year, and to the librarians of the British Museum library for their unfailing courtesy and efficiency.

Dr. D. Krook, formerly of Cambridge, now of the Hebrew University, Jerusalem, read the manuscript and made most valuable suggestions. I am greatly indebted to Professor G. deF Lord of Tate for calling my attention to an important book. Miss R. Toeg and Mr. D. Silk helped me immensely in preparing the manuscript and checking troublesome references and footnotes, a task which was triumphantly concluded by Mrs. G. Richard Price of the Princeton University Press. Mrs. Inge Straus' typescript was a model of accuracy despite the disheartening vagaries of seventeenth century spelling. A brief word about the line references for the poetry quoted may be in order: in each case the reference is to the first line quoted.

The guiding spirit throughout the long period of composition was the scholar, critic, and friend to whom the book is dedicated. He accompanied its development step by step with unflagging patience, unfailing critical insight, and unstinting scholarship. In its final stages he defied ill-health and the pressure of innumerable duties to help me with comment and criticism never less than in the highest degree illuminating and suggestive. My debt to him is incalculable, as it is also to my husband Natan, to whose uncomplaining powers of endurance the book is a tribute and without whose dogged selflessness it would never have been written at all.

The Hebrew University   RUTH NEVO
Jerusalem
1963

[vii]

CONTENTS

[ix]

Contents

THE DIAL OF VIRTUE

*A Study of Poems on Affairs of State
in the Seventeenth Century*

INTRODUCTION

IN CONTRADISTINCTION to the scattered or sporadic political comment which is pervasively present in Elizabethan and Jacobean literature, and to the political studies contained in the drama, political verse as such comes of age with the work of John Cleveland in the 1640's. Nor is this surprising when one considers that the period which saw the prelude to the civil wars, the civil wars themselves, the Commonwealth, and the Restoration was one which brought the angers, decisions, defeats, complexities, and victories of politics home to men's business and bosoms more closely than ever before. Of the well-known writers of the time, there were few indeed who were not directly involved in the political ferment. "Some intrigued at Court, some planned *coups d'état*, some when war came raised troops of horse, many distinguished themselves in the field and more in the dangerous parts of spies and messengers." [1] Some were executed; others were exiled, imprisoned, or had their property sequestrated. Two held high office in the new state, several were notable parliamentarians. And throughout the period the war of the pen was allowed, even "in a maner obliged" to accompany that of the sword,[2] continuing indeed with unabated vigor after the sword was sheathed.

In 1881 Professor A. Beljame [3] found it possible to assert that Dryden, in *Absalom and Achitophel*, "without models, without precursors . . . created the political poem." By 1910,

[1] C. V. Wedgewood, "Cavalier Poetry and Cavalier Politics," *English Critical Essays, Twentieth Century*, 2nd Series (Oxford, 1958).

[2] Abraham Cowley, Preface to *Poems* (1656). In Spingarn, *Critical Essays of the Seventeenth Century*, Vol. II (Indiana, 1957), p. 83.

[3] *Men of Letters and the English Public in the Eighteenth Century* (London, 1948). First published 1881.

however, Professor Previté Orton [4] summed up the results of more recent study of the period with the claim that Cleveland, forty years earlier, was "the founder of a new department of English literature." He was, that is to say, "the first English writer of partisan verse, purely political in his aims." These two contradictory opinions are not quoted here in order to ferment dissension among scholars, nor in the interests of a petty haggling over pride of place among poets, but to draw attention to the fact that an interesting field of study in the seventeenth century has been, perhaps, unduly neglected.

Of Cleveland's right to the title of first or at least most notable political poet, there would seem to have been little doubt in the seventeenth century itself. He was recognized as such by his contemporaries, among whom he was most popular and in many ways most influential. Frequent piratings, false ascriptions and re-editions of his work,[5] appearing at moments of high political tension—1659, 1677—are sufficient witness to this. Anthony à Wood acclaims him as "the first Champion that appeared in verse for the King's Cause against the Presbyterians," [6] and David Lloyd went so far as to announce that Cleveland's "smart satyrs" were "blows that shaked triumphing Rebellion." [7] Yet research into what were entitled in 1689 by exultant Whig anthologists "Poems on Affairs of State" [8] reveals a vigorous and variegated body of material. And when poems are included which were not exactly grist to the Whig mill (the two chief poets, Cleveland and Dryden, already mentioned, were certainly far enough from being that), the spectrum and the scope increase greatly. Many of the poems, both those included in the "state affairs" anthologies and those not included, have been studied before, either in histories of satire

[4] *Political Satire in English Poetry* (London, 1940).
[5] There were eight editions of his poems, or poems attributed to him, or imitations using his name, between 1651 and 1677. The bibligraphical scholarship is best presented by J. M. Berdan in his edition of the poems (New York, 1903).
[6] *Athenae Oxonienses* (1691).
[7] *Memoirs of the Lives . . . of Noble Personages* (1668).
[8] There were several editions of the original collection by this name and others along similar lines between 1689 and 1698. In 1703–1707 a 4-volume collected edition appeared.

or of political satire, or together with the other works of their authors, but, so far as I know, never all together as "panegyric and philippic," [9] an independent category of literary activity. Seen thus, the pieces throw light upon one another and illuminate the quotidian political mind of the age in a way perhaps more intimate and revealing than that of the more formal, fully-set-out political thesis or theory.

It is the nature of political poetry to deal with public causes. Yet it does not employ the systematic treatment of the historian. Political poetry gives us history, as it were, between the lines. And there is a sense in which this is what history is, before it becomes "history." As the editor of the second volume of *Poems on Affairs of State* puts it: ". . . the Design of Collections of this kind, is to afford some assistance to History; the Spirit of the several Parties in the Nation being to be discover'd hereby, as much, if not more, than from any other sort of Writings." [10]

In addition to thus illuminating the political disposition of the age, study of the panegyric and the philippic discloses stylistic problems peculiar to this branch of literature, though not unrelated to problems of style and the evolution of styles in general. With regard to this, the more purely literary aspect of the inquiry, the interest of the state poems lies chiefly, perhaps, in the rare opportunity they afford the historian of style. They enable one to trace, through the medium of many hands and many minds, the evolution of forms, of satisfactory media for the serious literary treatment of material not already equipped by tradition with its own forms.

Thirty years before *Absalom*, there had been produced a great ode which is a political poem *par excellence*. It qualifies as such not alone because of its "fearless political grasp" but also because Marvell has managed "to compress (into the *Horatian Ode*) a whole political theory as well as an extremely striking *aperçu* of the situation." [11] There was in fact through-

---

[9] The phrase is used by Marvell, *The Rehearsal Transpros'd* (1672), p. 39.
[10] 1703–1707 edn., Vol. II, A2 v.
[11] C. V. Wedgewood, "Cavalier Poetry. . . ," *op. cit.*

out the early Stuart, Commonwealth, and Restoration periods a continuous effort to find ways of writing serious verse, whether panegyrical or satiric, about political events or political issues; and the enterprise was accompanied by a good deal of critical discussion. Of "models" and "precursors" for Dryden there was no lack. Many were tentative, uncertain, unsuccessful; several modes were struck out, and there was confusion between them. Yet Dryden's achievement must be seen as the final, perfected tuning of a complex instrument already in existence rather than as the new creation which Beljame suggested.

The finding of ways to write serious verse about political events, personalities, or issues was a highly complex, even complicated task. Great difficulties were encountered when such literary traditions as were available were applied to contemporary material; and these difficulties were aggravated by the connection, found in practice to be inevitable, between two such opposing impulses and such opposing styles as the panegyrical and the satiric.

Political verse is generally thought of as being confined to satire. Certainly the corrective motive plays a large part in the impulse to deal with political topics, and this period is rich indeed in straightforwardly aggressive invective and lampoon. Yet so to limit the conception of political verse is greatly to falsify it. Satire is not the only channel for the political impulse, since there is always a cause, or a personality, to be fought for, as well as against. The result is the combining of panegyric with satire, either in a single work or in separate poems by the same author. The dual category, therefore—panegyric and philippic—is not arbitrarily determined; it reflects the inescapable relation between the two aspects of the poetry which concerns itself with public causes. At the very outset of the period Anthony à Wood praises Cleveland for his "high panegyrics and smart satyrs," [12] and the link is indissoluble throughout the century through all the modifications and modulations undergone by each of the modes themselves.

But this relation, if inescapable, is nevertheless not easily

[12] *Athenae Oxonienses* (1691).

achieved, not easily brought into proper focus in a literary work. The characteristically seventeenth century version of the problem centered in the fact that the Renaissance conception of satire contained within itself a double motivation, while Renaissance literary theory did not allow for the treatment of both the contemporary and the universal, or epic, or heroic, on anything like the same level. Satire's high end was, as Lloyd put it,[13] "to draw all good intentions to virtue" on the one hand, and "to shame the ill from vice," on the other. This had been the professed morality of the first determined efforts by Hall and his contemporaries to establish verse satire as a genre in English literature. But so long as satirists such as Marston and Hall were concerned merely with the rhetoric of contempt, complaint, and condemnation, the other aim, never long forgotten by the Renaissance artist, nevertheless did fade unnoticed into the background of attention. Once satire ceased to be an academic exercise in a fashionable humanistic program and began to respond to the stresses and pressures of actual events in a political context, the inculcation of the right views was felt to be truly as important and necessary as the demolition of the wrong ones, and in a newly urgent way. Then it was that the inherent difficulty of the accepted Renaissance doctrine of satire, and of Renaissance literary theory regarding the separation of the styles in general, made itself felt. For it is not easy to present the deformed image of vice and the fair face of virtue at one and the same time. Above all, it was found not easy to do so with reference to the local and the contemporary, at a time when there were in existence strong literary prescriptions as to how these were to be treated.

Greek theory restricted comedy and satire to contemporary issues, and determined the subjects of epic and tragedy as related to historical or legendary figures and events. The difference lies in the subject's magnitude and importance, both moral and social. The Renaissance renewed this classical tradition of the separation of the styles [14] as one of the most basic founda-

[13] *Memoirs* . . . (1668).
[14] The most important and instructive treatment of this topic is to be found in E. Auerbach's incomparable study, *Mimesis* (Princeton, 1953). First published in Berne, Switzerland (1946).

tions of its art. Even where the traditional "ridiculous" and the traditional "sublime" tend to merge in the broadly human drama of Shakespeare, his comedy is nevertheless for the most part not only localized in socially inferior figures but pervaded by satire of topical and local reference, as opposed to the distanced universality of the historical or legendary or Arcadian figures. Cases in point are Touchstone, the Fool, the Porter, Autolycus, Dogberry, Trinculo, and their like. The temporal and social disparities stand out: "high" distanced and "low" immediate characters and topics constitute virtually different modes, however subtly, in Shakespeare, they may be interrelated and counterpointed.

Thus, as the satirists of the seventeenth century set out from the premises of Renaissance didacticism to make political material yield to their high aims, they encountered problems of an hitherto unsuspected and untoward kind, and of a difficulty greater than that met by the Elizabethan satirists, whose ostensible object had been the drawing of moral doctrine and right reason even from the rough and grinning "satyr." Their aim was to assimilate topical satire to the epic manner and intention of heroic poetry, while dealing with the highest and most serious affairs of state. Where the panegyrist will present great exemplars of virtue in all their glory for emulation, they will reveal great exemplars of ill-doing in all their wickedness and deformity. But the satirist whose concern is with urgent political issues, unlike his academic predecessor, must, to be effective, address himself to a wide audience. Popular appeal tempted to a lowering or degrading kind of ridicule. Moreover, the Cavalier poet's attacks upon the heterogeneous crew of Anabaptists whom he conceived his political opponents to be, were too often cast in the form of grotesque or crude portrayals of a stereotyped image—a creature vulgar, absurd, or brutish, since this kind of portrayal accorded not only with the political orientation of the author but also with neo-classical prescription for the right comic treatment of the socially inferior. The satirist was in danger, therefore, of trampling the bays of the heroic poet in the mire of mere denigration. Alternatively he might fall to a shrill railing, becoming the more shrill and the more venomous in proportion as he realized that his outraged indignation tended to magnify rather than diminish the importance of the *enemy*—a result in conflict with his partisan purpose. The satirist of the Puritan or parliamentary side, on the other hand, tended to restrict himself to an excessive, hyperbolically abusive diatribe unspiced by the preservative of literary wit or craftsmanship.

Automatic aristocratic disdain and the fulminations of outraged virtue struggled, as it were, throughout the period to coalesce into a viable satire. Cleveland and Milton are the chief earlier figures to transcend these limitations, each in his degree and kind; but there could as yet be no agreed standard of style in a country so radically divided. From the 1640's onward it remained the unceasing endeavor of the political satirist to combine "jest and reprehension," in Milton's phrase, in such a way as not to lose the dignity of serious intention nor the advantage of derision. What he was seeking, though nowhere was this clearly recognized until Dryden's *Discourse upon Satire* in 1693, was a "mixed style" in an age of neo-classical separation of styles; a new union of popular and literary speech such as the drama at its best had achieved, and lost; a vehicle which would be able to modulate between the poles of high seriousness and mockery, and which, meant for a wide audience, would speak with the tongues of men and of angels. In the seventeenth century, and in the particular field of the state poem, this meant finding a way to take the conventionally low comic seriously enough to contemplate it on the same plane as that which excites epic "admiration"; or, alternatively, making use of the techniques of colloquial comedy and burlesque in an issue whose seriousness and importance is agreed to be of the highest.

These issues are fought out, in practice and theory, and in verse and prose, during the Restoration period. Opposing opinions are aligned under the rubric Railing versus Raillery—key terms in a dispute of far-reaching significance. It is during this period that the idea of the absurd undergoes a transvaluation which makes the Augustan achievement possible. The skeptical rationality of the Restoration period enabled the criterion of the absurd to shift, at least in part, from the socially inferior to the logically untenable, and the criterion of high seriousness from the sphere of moral doctrine to that of rational coherence. Butler is the completely transitional figure in this development, since, rationalistic as he is, he is still mainly concerned with the absurd and contemptible presumption of his ridiculed butts. He is himself transitional, and he is also the cause of transition in others. Marvell, for instance, whose constant endeavor in satire had been towards an effective "mixed style," deploys the formidable resources of his wit quite differently before and after the advent of *Hudibras*.

But the final achievement, the perfected "mock-heroic," is, of course, Dryden's *Absalom and Achitophel*. It relinquishes no jot of the icy disdain for vulgar presumption which is so effective a weapon; it is cuttingly analytical; its epic allusiveness appeals to neo-classical taste, yet it remains racily idiomatic in its contemporary reference. Above all, it discovers the exact perspective from which to focus upon the opponent, its quarry: neither flooding its object with the too-bright light of melodramatic villainy, nor blurring it with the too-dim light of a contemptible nonentity. It is the answer to the author's own reiterated demand for satire which shall have "majesty . . . finely mix'd with . . . venom," the "fine raillery" of Horace as well as the vehemence and vigor of Juvenal, the sublimity of expression that belongs properly to the heroic, and that capacity to make a malefactor die sweetly which belonged to Jack Ketch.[15] It is this for which the century had been searching. But an account of the conditions which made it possible in terms of the history of philippic in the seventeenth century would be incomplete without the complementary history of the panegyric, with which it is so closely linked.

The study of the panegyric opens with the situation as it was at the outset of the period. The first appearance of the formal term "panegyric" in English literature coincides with the accession of James of Scotland to the throne, and it is more than

---

[15] "Discourse Concerning Satire" (1693), in *Poetical Works*, ed. Noyes (Harvard, 1950), pp. 313, 319. References are to this edition unless otherwise indicated.

coincidence that the flourishing of the form was a Stuart and not a Tudor phenomenon. The dynastic break, the end of the long period of tension concerning Elizabeth's successor, the unaccustomed personality of the new king and his court—all contributed to a heightened awareness of the nature and function of the monarch and a need to re-affirm and reformulate the quality of the subject's allegiance. Monarchic world order with its natural deduction—the king as origin, source, and prime exemplar of virtuous nobility—these are the themes of Stuart panegyric, and by the time of the second Stuart their expression was well established as part of the compliment and ritual of the court. Material thus completely contemporary was assimilated far more easily than satire to the conscious purpose of heroic poetry (the center of poetic ambition in the seventeenth century), for that purpose had always been conceived as the persuasion to virtue through admiration for virtue's noble paradigms. "For there is in Princes," said Hobbes, "and men of conspicuous power, anciently called *Heroes*, a lustre and influence upon the rest of men resembling that of the Heavens. . . ." [16] It was the business of the panegyrist to articulate and make manifest that lustre and that influence, and to immortalize them in lines worthy of fame, serving thus the cause of good order and virtuous discipline in the kingdom. As T. W. Russell succinctly puts it in another connection:

"Neoclassic critics evolved two great conceptions which dominated their thinking: the five-act tragedy, limited and concentrated by the rules of the three unities, and the didactic epic. Emphasis was on the epic poem as the genre most capable of rendering an author and his nation immortal, and the epic, it is clear, was thought to include tragedy within its compass. The function of the epic was conceived to be the glorification of the established government, the education of the prince and nobles and the inspiring of respect and restraint in the people. [17]

The problems and difficulties encountered by the panegyrist during the course of the seventeenth century, however, were no less taxing than those encountered by the satirist, though they

[16] "Answer to the Preface to Gondibert," in Spingarn, p. 55.
[17] *Voltaire, Dryden and Heroic Tragedy* (New York, 1946), p. 10.

have to do, not with the ends and means of a literary style, but with the ideological complexity of the subject matter itself.

When Davenant in 1651 asked: ". . . is it not lawfull for vertuous men to be cherish'd and magnify'd with hearing their vigilance, Valour, and good Fortune . . . commended and made eternall in Poesy?" [18] he was on the face of it expressing no more than the traditional rationale of heroic poetry, including panegyric. But for the panegyrist who had encountered three major contradictory and irreconcilable manifestations of "heroic vertue" in his day; whose basic premises were thus kept under constant reappraisal as Usurper followed King and King Protector across the stage of history; for him Davenant's question may well have stood for the most painful and arduous of his colloquies with himself. For what was "lawfull," what "vertue," what, indeed, "Fortune"? These were no longer, as in the earlier Stuart period, the platitudinously obvious attributes of princes but the burning questions of the day. For Cromwell, the usurper, the regicide, was no Richard III. Many a royalist was ready enough to make the comparison, but it was only the extreme, uncompromising, and utterly intransigent royalist for whom the clear categories of villainous Machiavellian fortune-hunter and sweet royal rose could suffice. The more realistic or objective royalist was forced to a double awareness. He had to admit Cromwell's qualities of greatness, his "admirable sagacity and circumspection . . . (his) most magnanimous resolution" as Clarendon himself puts it; [19] his claim, that is, to share the classic heroic virtues as a creator and restorer of order. Furthermore, he was forced to recognize those sources of his power which lay in the moral convictions and beliefs of half a population, rather than in the capricious play of chance, circumstance, or Fortune—the traditional allies of ambitious upstarts on the make so long as Providence did not intervene to lower their overweening pride. The concepts of classical or Christian heroic virtue, or amoral Machiavellian *virtu*, of Fortune and Providence, thus came under closer

[18] "Preface to Gondibert," in Spingarn, p. 37.
[19] *History of the Rebellion*, Selections from Clarendon, ed. G. Huehns (Oxford, 1955), p. 356.

scrutiny than ever before, while the dialectic, traditional in the history plays of the preceding era, of the prerogatives of rule against the realities of power, acquired new force and a new irony in actuality. "What's a Protector?" is the bitter question of the royalist, and in his answer are reflected these recognitions in the distorting mirror of an outraged hierarchical class-consciousness:

> What's a Protector? He's a stately thing
> That apes it in the non-age of a King:
> A tragic actor, Caesar in a clown;
> He's a brass fathing stamped with a crown:
> A bladder blown, with other breaths puffed full;
> Not the Perillus, but Perillus' bull:
> Aesop's proud Ass veiled in the Lion's skin;
> An outward Saint lined with a Devil within: *1 — reveal*
> An echo whence the royal sound doth come,
> But just as a barrel-head sounds like a drum:
> Fantastic image of the Royal head,
> The brewer's with the King's arms quartered . . .
> In fine, he's one we must Protector call;
> From whom the King of Kings protect us all.[20]

For the royalist, whether he remained the intransigeant spokesman of *jus divinus* or whether he came to accept at least Cromwell's domination of the rage of sects, the problem remained within the sphere of a personalized conception of history: the belief, that is to say, that the events of history are determined, within the limitations of precarious Fortune, and under inscrutable Providence, by the actions and decisions of rulers. He inherited "the ancient's way of viewing things; (which) does not see forces, it sees virtues and vices, successes and mistakes." [21] It was for the republicans, the revolutionary party climbing to power, to develop the idea of "forces" in history. Aided by Old Testament intuitions of history as a continuous revelation of God's plan and purpose for mankind, they were to see their Cromwell's "right," not as his "might"

---

[20] *Cavalier Poets*, ed. Clarence M. Lindsay (New York, 1901), p. 135.
[21] Auerbach, *Mimesis*, p. 33.

alone, not as successful power alone, but as a providential election to the millennial task of total reform. In more secular minds these views escaped the mesh of theological formulations and became the first intimations of a social determinism such as was to dominate the thought of a much later age. For the seventeenth century panegyrist on the parliamentary side, however, the instrumentality of Cromwell, which was the very source of his zeal, his fervor, and his sense of purpose, constituted a serious problem in the performance of the poetic task. For the panegyrist is to cherish and magnify his Great Man by the recital of his vigilance, valor, and good fortune. It proved extremely difficult to do this with the career of Cromwell without having him slip back, as it were, into the category of mighty conqueror. It is a perennial difficulty, as the "personal heresies" of our own time have shown us. Certainly there were few among these early republicans prescient enough and wise enough to keep their vision of the *res publica* untarnished by an extravagant worship of the age's greatest *homo publicus*. Andrew Marvell, alone among the poets, can envisage for a time a truly republican reconciliation between the value and significance of Cromwell's personal power and his historic instrumentality. And his view is prophetic, explicitly messianic, and, as it was to turn out, fragile, in proportion as the republican idea was in fact, in his day, still premature. Charles II returned to a population which was, high and low alike, still basically royalist in sentiment and mentality. The panegyrics which welcome Charles home express intense relief not only at the expected end of conflict in the body politic but also at the possibility of a return to the time-honored patterns of thought, which were now elaborated and extended with redoubled energy. But the respite was brief.

When Dryden describes what he considers "the most beautiful and most noble kind of satire" [22] he is referring to the mockheroic. The term—an invention of the period—is significant. The mode, if not originated during the period, certainly became a characteristic product of the Restoration once it began

[22] "Discourse Concerning Satire," p. 319.

to be closely pursued and consistently developed. But it was not in the form known to the eighteenth century that it first occurred. Its genesis in England is to be found in the crisis which overtook the idea of the heroic during the Restoration, and it passed through several phases before it settled into its final Augustan form.

The late 1660's were a time of crisis both for mockery and for the heroic, the former reaching a nadir of irrational and ribald venom, the latter undergoing a further reappraisal more radical and destructive even than that of the Commonwealth. For the first phase of mock-heroic is the bitter iconoclasm of a people shocked, disappointed, and disillusioned by the political failures and dissolute levities of their returned heroes, Charles II and his courtiers. The reaction was all the more acute since it came so close upon the tremendous baroque assertions which had triumphantly welcomed King Charles home. Never had that conception of the heroic which has its roots in court culture and the politics of monarchy been affirmed in more gradiose, superhuman, and absolute a fashion. When these affirmations conflicted with the realities of impoverished exchequers, inconclusive trade wars, and the chicaneries of international diplomacy, the heroic image became the subject of revengeful mockery and derision.

But if the epic of royalty thus turned towards its decline, the epic of the republic had just begun upon its long ascendancy. Seeds sown during the Commonwealth continued their growth in manifold and subterranean ways. The revolutionary sense of historical purpose which had been articulated then by the Puritan republicans produced its own heroes, its own heroic virtues. It had its own vision of the *vita nuova*, of the last who shall be first and the first last. It opposed the themes and heroes of scripture to those of the pagan classics; evolutionary Providence to hierarchical world-order; and, at its furthest reaches, the inner drama of humble and simple lives to the pomp and circumstance of grand ones. Under its impact the aristocratic Renaissance relegation of the common people to the style of the comic or the grotesque wavered. Bunyan's tinkers are

[15]

heroes of an epic high seriousness, indeed, yet they are the same figures who have been so consistently derided and despised in the anti-Puritan verse of the century.

At the Restoration the privileged and articulate closed their ranks, as it were, and the neo-classical separation of styles was now enforced more consciously and with greater vigor than before. But the breach had been made. Henceforth there arose a rival view of the nature of the heroic and of the course of history. Something of its spirit can be caught in the praise of patriot poets which prefaces the *Poems on Affairs of State:*

". . . a Collection of those Valuable Pieces, which several great Men have produc'd, no less inspir'd by the injur'd Genius of their Country, than by the Muses . . . already receiv'd, and allow'd the best Patriots, as well as Poets . . . there is no where a greater Spirit of Liberty to be found, than in those who are Poets; . . . *Catullus* in the midst of *Caesar's* Triumphs attack'd the vices of that great Man, and expos'd 'em to lessen that Popularity and Power he was gaining among the *Roman* People, which he saw would be turn'd to the destruction of the Liberty of *Rome*." [23]

It is as yet far from fully formulated, or fully operative; traditional aristocratic literary and political patterns were tenacious, and the Whig appeal to the liberty of Rome is a far cry from the Levellers' dream of manhood suffrage. Yet it proved sufficient to shift the political center of gravity permanently from King to parliament, however corrupt and unrepresentative; it spoke for the moment with the powerful voice of city merchants, and Puritan bankers, ex-colonels of the new model army and newly risen landowners of the country party. The breach had been made. If tinkers would not, in any numbers, reach serious literature for many years to come, tradesmen very soon did.

It was the genius of Dryden to see what Butler in *Hudibras* had failed to see: that the source of the heroic view of life and of the sublime in literature had shifted from the chivalry of the dying court culture to the prophecy of the scripture-reading Puritans. This enabled him to establish another phase

[23] 1697 edn., A3 ff.

or version of mock-heroic. *Absalom and Achitophel* is the deflation of the opposition hero in terms of the latter's own heroic; and the difference between Dryden's lampoons and those of his predecessors is a matter not only of skill but also of the level of seriousness he is prepared to grant the objects of his satire.

On the one hand, the state poem is a transient phenomenon; on the other, it is part of a continuous literary stream whose sources are to be found in the Renaissance revival of interest in the classical theory of the epic, and in the break-up, under the impact of new social and economic forces, of the medieval concepts of order and degree, and the chivalric codes of medieval courts. For the period of its existence it registers a response to a time of revolutionary political change and stress; it is for this reason that so minor a tributary of literature, when in sudden spate, can carry with it so much of crucial significance. Its further flow is towards a *débouché* into the forms and preoccupations of the middle-class epic of the eighteenth century, the novel. For when, by the end of the century, the political ferment settled and the new culture of the capitalistic middle classes became more firmly entrenched, the social and literary forces whose growth and liberation so many seventeenth century poems on affairs of state reflect, found their proper issue in that characteristic middle-class form. On the one hand Fielding elaborates his theory of the comic epic in prose, while Richardson transfers the "sublime" of classical tragedy to the depiction in prose of the contemporary bourgeois scene. Lillo's plebeian *London Merchant* brings the stage into the orbit of the same historical process. Only in the heroic poem itself does aristocratic neo-classicism prove stronger than the aftermath of the revolutionary republicanism of the seventeenth century. But the mock-heroic satire of the eighteenth century cut its connection with contemporary history in the interests of an aristocratic Augustan critique of contemporary manners, while the heroic panegyric of eighteenth century Whig mercantilism eulogizes an apostasized hero in Britannia, or Empire, or Liberty, or Trade. No longer does satire hammer out its form and style and content upon the

anvil of social and political change; and no longer does panegyric wrestle, like Jacob with the angel, among the perplexities
and antinomies of divine right and divine providence, Protector and King.

For this study I have tried to cover the bulk of the century's
political verse still extant and I have also canvassed statement
or polemic of a broadly political nature in prose where it
seemed relevant to do so; but I have excluded the popular
broadside. The broadside ballad did not seem eligible for an
inquiry of this kind since it has its traditional unchanging
forms; and it is important, interesting, and voluminous enough
in bulk to merit separate consideration. The line of division,
however, in many cases, has not been easy to determine. For
the most part the use of the couplet or the ode rather than the
ballad meters provided a rule-of-thumb criterion, but there
remain some instances which have demanded a fairly arbitrary
judgment of level of style and performance for their inclusion
or exclusion here.

From the beginning of the period there are to be found
state poems, panegyric or satire, which, in addition to their
relevance in the historical perspective referred to above, are of
importance in the formal history of the emergence of the
closed heroic couplet. They are generally the poems of the
moderates of the period, less partisan than philosophical and
reflective. Denham's *Cooper's Hill* is perhaps the best-known
example, but Cowley's *On the Late Civil War* and his *The
Puritan and the Papist* are, among many others, cases in point.
Their object is to achieve a critical statement of general principle rather than an effective attack or defense. They play an
important part in keeping the state poem to a serious generalizing level which still does not sacrifice the vividness and sting
of immediate application; and they keep the couplet in tune,
as it were, extending its possibilities of concise and flexible
antithetical statement.

In connection with the "slow rise of the closed couplet to
dominance" during the period under discussion, Douglas Bush
remarks that it "implied in some measure the rise of a col-

lective sense of political, social, and philosophical order. In literature that sense of security was attained partly by turning back from troubled explorations of the individual soul to the accepted sententiousness of public occasions and general experience." [24]

These chapters present a thesis which would interpret at least the antithetical quality of the couplet as the reflection of an acute sense of dialectical opposites, as that form most fitted to express the alignment of the nation into irreconcilable camps, at loggerheads to the point of civil war at first, and irreducible nonconformism later. However, there is a level at which the two interpretations do not conflict, since throughout the century a yearning for order was shared by both sides, and the achieved Augustan couplet may indeed represent the binding of the antithesis, the taming of the mutually repellent principles in a structural unity.

A study which is interested both in what *Poems on Affairs of State* calls "a just and secret History of the former Times," [25] and in the evolution of literary forms which express that just and secret history, is fortunate in its choice of the seventeenth century. For among writers upon state affairs at one time or another during that troubled time—Cleveland, Waller, Denham, Cowley, Davenant, Milton, Marvell, Butler, Oldham, Rochester, Dryden—there are to be found enough of the century's excellent poets, even of its very greatest, to provide ample material of qualitative significance.

[24] *English Literature in the Earlier Seventeenth Century* (Oxford, 1945), p. 169.
[25] 1697 edn., A3 ff.

CHAPTER ONE

"Cities their lutes, and subjects hearts their strings"

THE "FORTIS ACHILLES AND THE PIUS AENEAS"

IN THE SENSE in which it is used in the state poems of the seventeenth century, the formal term "panegyric" first appeared in English literature in 1603 in the title of a poem by Samuel Daniel, *A Panegyrike Congratulatorie . . . to the King's Most Excellent Majestie*. The Oxford Dictionary defines the term thus: "a laudatory discourse, a formal or elaborate encomium or eulogy." Of eulogy for the reigning monarch there had been no lack during the time of Elizabeth; but it is different in form and quality from that which flourished during the reign of the Stuarts. The very tendency of Elizabeth to become Gloriana—that is to say, her significance to her people as a supreme symbol in a total system of values, religious, national, ethical, and sociological—militated against the formal separation of royal panegyric from other kinds of literature. She is pervasively present in prose, verse, and drama. And it is not until the break in the dynasty, ending the period of anxiety regarding the succession, and bringing to Whitehall the very different personality and the very different court of the Scottish King, that the need is felt for a formal and specific expression of the subject's allegiance and of the values which command it. This separation is perhaps the first symptom of a central feature of seventeenth century history—the growing breach between the culture of the court and the newly articulate culture of large sections of the population outside the orbit of the court.

The main features of the earlier Stuart panegyric are its

exclusive focus upon the person of the King (or his immediate family), its romantic chivalry, its classicizing tendency, and its dependence upon a static view of divinely ordained world-order. The romantic chivalry disappears when the young Prince becomes the most problematic of kings; but the remaining features, despite modifications, remain characteristic of royalist panegyric throughout the period, as does its status as a legitimate and honorable "kinde," and a most proper vehicle for the expression of the art and skill, as well as the loyalty, of the poet. "The greatest instance of Wit is to commend well," is Dr. Tillotson's statement, quoted by Fenton much later, of the most general grounds for a rationale of panegyric: "Wit . . . is a keen instrument, and everyone can cut and gash with it: but, to carve a beautiful image, and polish it, requires great art and dexterity. To praise any thing well is an argument of much more Wit. . . ." [1]

Upon the occasion of the Prince's courtship of Henrietta in 1623, Edmund Waller wrote a poem entitled *Of The Danger His Majesty (being Prince) Escaped in the Road at Saint Andero*. There is no contemporary comment upon this poem, but Elijah Fenton in his Observations to the 1729 edition of Waller's works—looking back, that is to say, over the whole range of the seventeenth century court panegyric, and speaking from the point of view of the fully formulated neo-classical doctrines which that panegyric had played its part in shaping —regards it as a model. "This Poem," he writes, "may serve as a model for those who intend to succeed in Panegyric; in which our Author illustrates a plain historical fact with all the graces of poetical fiction: as will appear by comparing it with the subject, as the writers of that age have left it recorded." [p. iv]

The poem (pp. 1–6) can be divided into three parts: the setting forth of the ships on their journey to France, where Henrietta's "conquering eyes / Have made the best of English hearts their prize"; the heroic bearing of Prince Charles during the storm; and the rescue. The poem is motivated by the theme of heroic love:

---

[1] E. Fenton, ed. *The Works of Waller* (London, 1730), p. iii. Citation of the poems of Waller is from this edition.

That noble ardour, more than mortal fire,
The conquer'd ocean could not make expire;
Nor angry *Thetis,* raise her waves above
Th'heroic *Prince's* courage, or his love:
'Twas indignation, and not fear he felt,
The shrine shou'd perish, where that image dwelt.

The Prince's heroic love is for a lady whose heart has been moved by noble Fame's accounts of his prowess, "haughty, brave, and bold"; the chivalric theme is decorated with similitudes of classical reference and the greatest magnitude in order to give the presentation an epic proportion:

The gentle vessel, (wont with state and pride
On the smooth back of silver *Thames* to ride,)
Wanders astonish'd in the angry Main,
As *Titan's* car did, while the golden rein
Fill'd the young hand of his advent'rous son,
When the whole world an equal hazard run
To this of ours . . .

Great *Maro* cou'd no greater tempest feign,
When the loud winds usurping on the Main
For angry *Juno,* labor'd to destroy
The hated reliques of confounded *Troy* . . .

The romantic-heroic themes of Magnanimity, Love, Courage are all focussed in the figure of *"Charles* and his virtue," the ship's sacred load:

So near a hope of crowns and sceptres, more
Than ever *Priam,* when he flourish'd, wore;
His loins yet full of ungot Princes, all
His glory in the bud, lets nothing fall
That argues fear . . .
God-like his Courage seem'd, whom nor delight
Could soften, nor the face of Death affright:
Next to the pow'r of making tempests cease,
Was in that storm to have so calm a peace.

The poem ends with a bow to Virgil and an hyperbole drawn from the conception of world-order as an immutable and hierarchical chain of being. It is to this metaphysic that the monarchical view is chiefly indebted, and it continued to lean upon it during the century's repeated assaults.

> Well sung the *Roman* bard; "all human things
> "Of dearest value hang on slender strings."
> O see the then sole hope, and in design
> Of Heav'n our joy, supported by a line!
> Which for that instant was Heav'n's care above
> The chain that's fixed to the throne of *Jove*,
> On which the fabric of our world depends;
> One link dissolv'd, the whole creation ends.

The same features, with the exception, naturally, of the love and beauty motif, characterize *To the King on His Navy*, 1627.[2] Fenton notes particularly that "the turn of the Poem is happy to admiration: the first line, with all that follow in order, leads to the conclusion; all bring to the same point and centre . . ."

> Should Nature's self invade the world again,
> And o'er the centre spread the liquid Main,
> Thy pow'r were safe; and her destructive hand
> Would but enlarge the bounds of thy command:
> Thy dreadful Fleet would style Thee Lord of all,
> And ride in triumph o'er the drowned Ball:
> Those Tow'rs of oak o'er fertile plains might go,
> And visit mountains where they once did grow.
> The world's restorer once cou'd not indure,
> That finish'd *Babel* shou'd those men secure,
> Whose pride design'd that fabric to have stood
> Above the reach of any second flood:
> To thee his chosen more indulgent, He
> Dares trust such pow'r with so much piety.

[2] 1627, according to Thorn Drury; 1632, according to Rymer; 1636, according to Fenton.

"Here," Fenton continues, "is both *Homer* and *Virgil;* the *fortis Achilles* and the pius *Aeneas* in the person he complements; and the greatness owing to his virtue." [p. xvii]

GOD IN THE PERSON OF CAESAR

Fenton, in 1729, is concerned with the correct morality, and with the decorum of the classical modeling. What is no less interesting, however, is the degree to which the all-capable virtue of the King-hero is already beginning to take precedence over the limiting and universal notion of bounds, naturally and divinely instituted, and binding, of course, upon the King himself, together with the rest of creation. A comparison with Ulysses' degree speech in *Troilus and Cressida* will make the difference instantly apparent. The images of disorder are now used hyperbolically, to show the hyperbolic supremacy of the King over them. Though, in 1656, Blount[3] defined panegyric as "a licentious kinde of speaking or oration, in the praise or commendation of kings, or other persons, wherein some falsities are joined with many flatteries," "flattery" is an insufficient explanation for such a development. The fear of collapse and disruption of Shakespeare's Ulysses, fears shared by many contemporaries in a time of political and dynastic unrest, were not instantly realized. There was an interim stage before the crisis of the civil wars during which the sense of cosmic order was narrowed down and entrenched in a more mundane conception. Order came to be derived not from the stars in their courses, but from the court and its satellites. Malcolm MacKenzie Ross, in his *Poetry and Dogma*, has devoted considerable space to an analysis of the way in which the universalistic and suprapersonal Elizabethan symbol of the crown, which possessed a validity and significance greater than the particular head which wore it, gave way, in the Stuart period, to something like a deification of the reigning monarch. The shadow of the coming schism has everything to do with the change. In the person of the monarch greatly endowed, royalist political thought centered its hopes. "By the reign of Charles I," says Ross, "the crown is no longer a symbol of a tight, island

[3] *Glossographia* (1656).

'Christendom-in-little.' It is the badge of an embattled party." [4]
And that party grew more and more ideologically dependent
upon the most concrete possible rendering of the idea of divine
right. Thus Waller's *Of His Majesty's receiving the News of
the Duke of Buckingham's Death*, 1628, a poem which finds the
King's magnanimity and self-command such that even "Bold
Homer durst not so great virtue feign," ends with an explicit-
ness scarcely veiled by the classical allegory:

> Such huge extremes inhabit thy great mind,
> God-like, unmov'd; and yet like woman, kind!
> Which of the antient Poets had not brought
> Our *Charles's* pedigree from Heav'n; and taught
> How some bright dame, comprest by mighty *Jove*
> Produc'd this mix'd Divinity and Love?   [p. 8]

Again, in the poem *Upon His Majesty's repairing of St. Paul's*,
1635,[5] he presents the royalist view of "order and concent"
as springing by direct influence from the person of the King
rather than from the universal system of divinely created nature. That central doctrine of medieval theology may recede
into the background of consciousness while its ancient and
powerful metaphors remain vivid in the mind. They are then
easily transferable from the doctrine of cosmic concord to
that of royal fiat. Thus where Ulysses had warned, "untune
that string, / And hark what discord follows," Waller directly
invokes the Pythagorean harmonies themselves in praise of the
King's "regiment":

> He, like *Amphion*, makes those quarries leap
> Into fair figures, from a confus'd heap:
> For in his art of regiment is found
> A pow'r, like that of harmony in sound.
> Those antique minstrels sure were *Charles*-like Kings,
> Cities their lutes, and subjects hearts their strings;
> On which with so divine a hand they strook,
> Consent of motion from their breath they took . . .
>
>   [p 11]

---

[4] *Poetry and Dogma* (Rutgers, 1954), p. 119.
[5] By Fenton's dating. But the reference to it in *Cooper's Hill* ("the
late theme") in 1642 suggests a later date.

Cowley's first juvenile effort at panegyric carries the theme to a point little short of idolatry. What Ross calls "the Cavalier trick of paying tribute to God in the person of Caesar" (p. 120) is clearly to be seen in *On His Majesty's Return out of Scotland,* 1633,[6] which concludes:

> Great Charles! Let *Caesar* boast *Pharsalia's* Fight,
> Honorius praise the *Parthians* unfeign'd Flight,
> Let *Alexander* call himself *Jove's* Peer,
> And place his Image near the Thunderer,
> Yet while our CHARLES with equal Balance reigns
> 'Twixt *Mercy* and *Astraea;* and maintains
> A noble Peace, 'tis he, 'tis only he
> Who is most near, most like the Deity.

The poem as a whole is ritualistic in intention, and hypnotic in effect. The exordium labours to dramatize awe:

> Great *Charles,* there stop, ye Trumpeters of Fame,
> (For he who speaks his Titles, his great Name,
> Must have a breathing Time) *Our King;* stay there,
> Speak by Degrees, let the inquisitive Ear
> Be held in Doubt, and e're you say, *Is come,*
> Let every Heart prepare a spatious Room
> For ample Joys; then *lo* sing as loud
> As Thunder shot from the divided Cloud.[7]

The ritual continues with the mythological strewing of the way, in imagery which is quite adventitious except to the hypnotic effect:

> Let *Cygnus* pluck from the *Arabian* Waves
> The Ruby of the Rock, the Pearl that paves
> Great *Neptune's* Court . . .
> Let spotted *Lynces* their sharp Talons fill,

[6] Cowley, *Works,* ed. Tonson, 3 vols. (London, 1721). This poem appears in Vol. III, pp. 30–32 (Juvenilia) and was omitted from the collected works.

[7] Both the Amphion of Waller and the "divided cloud" of Cowley are echoed by Marvell in his republican panegyrics. The echo points up the significance of the latter's variation on the theme. See Chapter 4 below, pp. 101, 111.

With Chrystal fetch'd from the *Promethean* Hill . . .
Let the self-gotten *Phoenix* rob his Nest,
Spoil his own Funeral Pile, and all his best
Of Myrrh, of Frankincense, of *Cassia* bring,
To strew the Way for our returned King . . .

In such poems the process of applying to a secular monarch the absolute encomia hitherto sacred to the divinity is well advanced.

THE PANEGYRIC AS A SPECIES OF HEROIC POETRY— "SACRED TO PRINCES, AND TO HEROS"

The idealization and idolization of the King were not, however, the only functions of the Stuart panegyric. It served, in addition, a didactic purpose: the inculcation of virtue in the hearts of princes and subjects alike. Much space in the poems is given to analysis of the King's own resplendent virtue, which is not only the proof and manifestation of his divine authority, but also the medium through which his beneficent influence operates upon the hearts of his subjects.

The nature of his virtue is generally consistent with the chain-of-being conception of world-order. It is defined by upper and lower limits, such as bind every creature into the interlocking scheme of things:

> Two distant Virtues in one Act we find,
> The Modesty and Greatness of his Mind.[8]

It is the King's modesty which keeps his greatness within human and proper bounds, and his greatness which guards his modesty from passivity—the "contentedness" of which Davenant complained, in his analysis of heroic poetry, when he presents the view that the Court and the Camp are the most effectual schools of morality through the shining example of their "Chiefs": ". . . for good men are guilty of too little appetite to greatness, and it . . . proceeds from what they call contentednesse (but contentednesse when examin'd doth mean

[8] Waller, "Upon His Majesty's repairing of St. Paul's," p. 11.

[27]

something of lasynesse as well as moderation). . . ." [9] By a similar process of thought, the King's "ships and building" become, in *Upon His Majesty's repairing of St. Paul's*

> Emblems of a Heart
> Large both in Magnanimity and Art.

The perfection of the King's virtue is given an Aristotelian formulation by Cowley in *On his Majesty's Return Out of Scotland:*

> Who is there where all Virtues mingled flow?
> Where no Defects or Imperfections grow?
> Whose Head is always crown'd with Victory
> Snatch'd from *Bellona's* Hand, him Luxury
> In Peace debilitates; whose Tongue can win
> *Tully's* own Garland, Pride to him creeps in.
> On whom (like *Atlas* Shoulders) the propt State
> (As he were *Primum Mobile* of Fate)
> Solely relies; him blind Ambition moves,
> His Tyranny the bridled Subject proves.
> But all those Virtues which they all possess'd
> Divided, are collected in thy Breast; . . .[10]

It is this last passage that most clearly reveals the ethical function of the panegyric, that which gave it its status as a branch of literature's chief and noblest kind—heroic poetry.

That the function of the heroic poem was a moral one—the fashioning of a gentleman or noble person in virtuous and gentle discipline—was a Renaissance commonplace. But Davenant's definition of the chief object of heroic poetry is specifically ". . . for vertuous men to be cherish'd and magnify'd with hearing their vigilance, Valour, and good Fortune . . . commended and made eternall in Poesy"; [p. 37] and his contention that ". . . Princes and Nobles, being reform'd and made Angelicall by the Heroick, will be predominant lights,

---

[9] "Preface to Gondibert: an Heroick Poem" (1651), in Spingarn, pp. 14–15.
[10] Tonson edn., Vol. III, p. 31.

which the people cannot chuse but use for direction, as Glo-
worms take in and keep the Suns beams till they shine and
make day to themselves . . ." [p. 45] brings the task of that
noblest kind, designed to "form the mind to heroic virtue by
example" considerably nearer to the eulogistic practice of the
Cavalier panegyrists.

What better example of heroic virtue could be found than
the supreme exemplar of heroic virtue? What more stimulating
invitation to the ambitious panegyrist than Hobbes' dictum in
The Answer to the Preface to Gondibert: ". . . whatsoever
distinguishes the civility of *Europe* from the Barbarity of the
American savages, is the workmanship of Fancy but guided by
the Precepts of true Philosophy. . . . He therefore that undertakes an Heroick poem, which is to exhibit a venerable &
amiable Image of Heroick vertue, must not only be the Poet,
to place and connect but also the Philosopher, to furnish and
square his matter. . . ." [p. 60] Thus Fenton finds the didactic
theory of heroic poetry to be the very mainspring of Waller's
work: ". . . it was his (Waller's) principal intention to rec-
ommend with all the ornaments of poetry the brightest ex-
amples of his own age to the imitation of all that should succeed; and even desir'd that every verse might be expung'd which
did not imply some motive to virtue . . ." [p. iii]

Indeed there is no record of dissent from the doctrine that
the panegyrics of princes are an important and legitimate
species of heroic poetry, from the time of their first flourishing
prior to the civil war until the period when the domination of
court literature can be said to cease. Dryden, himself a consistent practitioner, gives the idea its fullest formulation in
1672: "Heroic poesy has always been sacred to princes, and
to heroes. . . . It is indeed but justice, that the most excellent
and most profitable kind of writing should be addressed by
poets to such persons whose characters have, for the most part,
been the guides and patterns of their imitation; and poets, while
they imitate, instruct. The feigned hero inflames the true; and
the dead virtue animates the living. Since, therefore, the world
is governed by precept and example, and both these can only

have influence from those persons who are above us; that kind of poesy, which excites to virtue the greatest men, is of the greatest use to humankind." [11]

The court of Charles II was the last court in England which was, or thought itself to be, the cultural center of the nation and the source of all civilized standards. The disappearance of the court in this sense coincides with the disappearance of the didactic conception of heroic panegyric.

The High Seriousness of Denham and Cowley

That which is excellent and profitable in the panegyric is perhaps most fully exhibited in the long reflective poem of Denham, *Cooper's Hill,*[12] which was composed in 1642 but not printed in an authorized edition until 1655. In it the heroic couplet, the stately measure of Waller, attains a balance and equanimity universally praised in its own day and since then for "sweetness" and "majesty." These are the qualities miraculously combined in the person of the King himself; but in Denham's poem, unlike those of the more partisan panegyrists, the King's meekness and majesty, his "friend-like sweetnesse, and [his] King-like aw" (in the 1642 version) are related through the landscape imagery to a conception of the entire harmony of things. The King—"the best of Kings"—is example, not creator of cosmic order, and it is Nature who knows that

> the harmony of things,
> As well as that of sounds, from discords springs.
> Such was the discord, which did first dispense
> Form, order, beauty through the Universe;
> While driness moysture, coldness heat resists,
> All that we have, and that we are, subsists.
> While the steep horrid roughness of the Wood

[11] Dedication (to the Duke of York) of *The Conquest of Granada* (Mermaid edn.), Vol. I, p. 23.

[12] *Poetical Works*, ed. T. H. Banks (Yale, 1928), p. 63. The introduction deals with the question of the variant texts. Quotations are from the 1655, that is, except for minor variations, the 1668 edn.

Strives with the gentle calmness of the Flood.
Such huge extreams when Nature doth unite,
Wonder from thence results, from thence delight . . .

[l. 203]

Earl Wasserman, in *The Subtler Language* has trenchantly
pointed out how much Denham's poem owes to the doctrine
of *concordia discors*, a doctrine and a mode of conception
which his verse, with its chiastic antitheses, parallels, and in-
versions, skilfully enacts. He shows how the same principle
shapes the poem as a whole, and defines the political and historical analyses. The three hills: Windsor, with its royal residence; St. Anne's, with the ruins of Chertsey Abbey; and St.
Paul's, with the rebuilt cathedral towering above the swarm-
ing city, are symbolic, he says, of three "different relations of
sovereign and populace, religion and activity. The central hill,
Windsor, being the residence of Charles, is the perfect harmonious balance and interaction of the two powers. . . . The
other two hills . . . illustrate the dangerous and unnatural
imbalance of royal solicitude and popular zeal on the one hand,
and of royal tyranny and public apathy on the other." [13]

In the absence of this harmony of discords, all sways back
and forth in a dialectic of opposite excesses:

Then did Religion in a lazy Cell,
In empty, airy contemplations dwell;
And like the block, unmoved lay: but ours,
As much too active, like the stork devours.
Is there no temperate Region can be known,
Betwixt their Frigid, and our Torrid Zone?
Could we not wake from that Lethargick dream,
But to be restless in a worse extream?
And for that Lethargy was there no cure,
But to be cast into a Calenture?
Can knowledge have no bound, but must advance
So far, to make us wish for Ignorance?

[13] *The Subtler Language* (Johns Hopkins, 1959), p. 66.

And rather in the dark to grope our way,
Than led by a false guide to erre by day? [l. 135] [14]

The poem, then, is the perfect formal expression of the poet's mature, judicious, and temperate attitude to the political issues of his time. In this, as well as in the use of topographical emblems for political definitions, Denham is cousin germane to the Marvell of the Nun Appleton poems. Windsor and the Thames are his main emblems, forming the kind of static allegory that Marvell in his turn was to call a "Mask":

Windsor the next (where *Mars* with *Venus* dwells,
Beauty with strength) above the Valley swells
Into my eye, and doth it self present
With such an easie and unforc't ascent,
That no stupendious precipice denies
Access, no horror turns away our eyes:
But such a Rise, as doth at once invite
A pleasure, and a reverence from the sight.
Thy mighty Masters Embleme, in whose face
Sate meekness, heightned with Majestick Grace
Such seems thy gentle height, made only proud
To be the basis of that pompous load,
Than which, a nobler weight no Mountain bears,
But *Atlas* only that supports the Sphears. [l. 39]

The Thames becomes an emblem of greater complexity, standing first for the benefits of monarchy and becoming finally a similitude for political power and the mutual confines of monarchy and democracy, as moderate spirits were increasingly to see them. The benefits of monarchy are presented with a metaphorical finesse matching the fine balance of limits which characterizes his views:

[14] These formulations strike the note that will be characteristic of the moderate and skeptical minds of the second half of the century as they address themselves to the problem of the political *via media*. In *The Progress of Learning* (1641), Denham had begun his analysis of Reason and Enthusiasm in the skeptical tradition, and had struck out a phrase which was to be remembered by more than one critic of the times:

Almost as many minds as men we find . . .
Legions of Sects, and Insects come in throngs . . . [l. 156]

. . . survey his shore;
Ore which he kindly spreads his spacious wing,
And hatches plenty for th'ensuing Spring.
Nor then destroys it with too fond a stay,
Like Mothers which their Infants overlay.
Nor with a sudden and impetuous wave,
Like profuse Kings, resumes the wealth he gave.
No unexpected inundations spoyl
The mowers hopes, nor mock the plowmans toyl:
But God-like his unwearied Bounty flows;
First loves to do, then loves the Good he does.
Nor are his Blessings to his banks confin'd,
But free, and common, as the Sea or Wind;
When he to boast, or to disperse his stores
Full of the tributes of his grateful shores,
Visits the world, and in his flying towers
Brings home to us, and makes both *Indies* ours; . . .
O could I flow like thee, and make thy stream
My great example, as it is my theme!
Though deep, yet clear, though gentle, yet not dull,
Strong without rage, without o're-flowing full.

[l. 168] [15]

[15] These famous lines were added only in 1655. Wasserman (pp. 84–85) has a brilliant analysis of the verse technique of these lines as an embodiment of the idea of *concordia discors*. Wasserman has notably added to our understanding of this poem, but I feel impelled to take issue with him on the matter of the Thames and its meanings. He claims that the poem disconcertingly redefines the river's significance when, instead of symbolizing "Nature's ideal art of creating contraries and harmonising them" it suddenly becomes part of an enlarged scene (ll. 217 et. seq.) consisting of mountains, plain, and river, and consequently only one factor in the total harmonious state. If Mr. Wasserman is basing his view upon the 1655 improved text, he would seem to be pushing his meanings too hard, seeking a one-for-one allegorical significance in a poem whose symbolism, like that of "Upon Appleton House" inhabits a no-man's-land between description and interpretation, between "eye" and "fancy" (as Mr. Wasserman himself notes). Figures of this order train the reader to follow glimpsed, veiled allusion in a truly reflective, rather than dogmatic, act of the mind. The emblem books would have suggested such a double vision of concrete particulars. Thus, "benefits of monarchy," economic and civil, seems to me sufficiently to indicate the river's figurative intent throughout its course in the poem. Narcissus would

The stress and clash of the opposing forces of the time, the upsurge and final outbreak of violence, are powerfully rendered in the last section of the poem:

> Thus Kings, by grasping more than they could hold,
> First made their Subjects by oppression bold:
> And popular sway, by forcing Kings to give
> More than was fit for Subjects to receive,
> Ran to the same extreams; and one excess
> Made both, by striving to be greater, less.
> When a calm River rais'd with sudden rains,
> Or Snows dissolv'd, oreflows th'adjoyning Plains,
> The Husbandmen with high-rais'd banks secure
> Their greedy hopes, and this he can endure.
> But if with Bays and Dams they strive to force
> His channel to a new, or narrow course;
> No longer then within his banks he dwells,
> First to a Torrent, then a Deluge swells:
> Stronger, and fiercer by restraint he roars,
> And knows no bound, but makes his power his shores.

[l. 343]

Denham's dignified treatment of topical events preserves for the panegyric, through all the ferment and turbulence of the period to come, the level of high seriousness which Dryden was to renew and re-establish in due course. It is relevant to notice that both poets employ the "mask"—in both its modern and seventeenth century meanings—as a medium capable of conveying a complex sense. If the stag hung adum-

not have seen *himself* in the river's clear water (l. 214) because he would have known the appointed difference between ruler and subject. The "surly supercilious Lords" of 1642 who become the proud Mountain of 1655 suffer, in the storms of the upper air, the common fate of the high and great. The spacious plain—the undifferentiated mass of the common people—is embraced between river and mountain, is shaded and sheltered by the latter, the mighty of the land, but derives fundamental values, material and metaphysical, from the river: "the kind River Wealth and Beauty gives." The transition at the end of the poem, when the river at Runnymede becomes a similitude for political power, is perfectly consonant with this major sense.

brates—it would be too much to say "represents"—the trial and death of Strafford,[16] it does so by giving the naturalistic details of the chase as such their full value while nevertheless insistently imputing human motive to the hunted and suffering creature. A conductor is thus established between "eye" and "fancy" through which the current of arcane meaning flows when sparked by such explicit statements as "Then tries his friends, among the baser herd" or "Like a declining States-man, left forlorn." What is thus elaborately conveyed is at once apologetic for the King and compassion for the noble quarry, the one as firmly held as the other.

Denham proposed to himself no such complex task in the poem *On the Earl of Strafford's Tryal and Death*, in which he unequivocally expresses his sympathy for the Earl "crusht by Imaginary Treasons weight." That poem is directed against the legislative machinations and "publick hate" of Parliament,[17] whereas in *Cooper's Hill* he must defend the King's signature of the Bill of Attainder, and in the face of Strafford's steadfast royalist devotion. One cannot but be tempted to wonder how far such a poem may have influenced Marvell's *Horatian Ode*, despite the latter's scurrility at Denham's expense in the Clarendon poems of the Restoration period. The two poets, as "instructors" of painters, have had a curious literary relationship imposed upon them. It may well be that *Cooper's Hill* and the *Ode*, both written before the Restoration decline in manners and morals, represent their real poetic relationship. For though in the latter the King plays the part not of hunter but

[16] I am indebted to Wasserman (p. 72 ff.) for his conclusively argued interpretation of the stag as Strafford. A few of the details of the pursuit and flight of the stag and some of the imputed motives were added only in 1655, e.g.:

And now too late he wishes for the fight
That strength he wasted in ignoble flight [l. 293]

But the variations make no material difference to the principle of presentation.

[17] The earlier version (in Banks, p. 153) expresses more mixed feelings but no less sympathy for the "greate soule," the eloquence, composure, and dignity of whose conduct during the trial make him "our nations glory" as he has been "our nations hate."

[35]

of hunted, the two poems share a comprehensiveness of view, a felt gravity of the issues involved, and a sense of what is due to the heroic role played grandly in defeat. Moreover, just as Marvell's augury of the state's "happy fate" from the bleeding head at its initiation is acceptable only as intended in sober earnestness, so Denham's "more innocent and happy chase" [l. 323] can be other than outrageous, applied to the most tragic *cause célèbre* of Charles' reign, only if the comparison with the danger to liberty before Magna Carta is the fruit of a considered historical judgment. And this condition, indeed, for the poem's proper communication is an aspect of a further and final respect in which *Cooper's Hill* differs significantly from Waller's *Upon His Majesty's Repairing of St. Paul's*. It fixes the panegyric firmly in the setting of realistic historical interpretation rather than of eulogistic mythology. So also his lines on the destruction of the monasteries ponder the question of political motivation, or political good and evil, to which kings themselves are subordinate:

What crime could any Christian King incense
To such a rage? Was't Luxury, or Lust?
Was he so temperate, so chast, so just?
Were these their crimes? They were his own much more:
But wealth is Crime enough to him that's poor,
Who having spent the Treasures of his Crown,
Condemns their Luxury to feed his own.
And yet this Act, to varnish o're the shame
Of sacriledge, must bear devotions name.
No Crime so bold, but would be understood
A real, or at least a seeming good . . .
Who sees these dismal heaps, but would demand
What barbarous Invader sackt the Land?
But when he hears, no *Goth*, no *Turk* did bring
This desolation, but a Christian King;
When nothing, but the Name of Zeal, appears
'Twixt our best actions and the worst of theirs
What does he think our Sacriledge would spare,
When such th'effects of our Devotions are? [l. 118]

[36]

Cooper's Hill entered the annals of literary history as an original kind—the topographical poem.[18] More illuminating of its true nature, however, is the use of local description for purposes of panegyric. It is consciously related to the panegyric tradition, and its originality in that respect lies in its attempt to realize the aim of high seriousness through a philosophically rational treatment in an historical context, above the level of hero worship or propaganda or occasional compliment. Dryden was later to define the idea of the serious that is meant here in his analysis of the serious play. It is "Nature wrought up to an higher pitch; the plot, the characters, the wit, the passions, the descriptions, are all exalted above the level of common converse, as high as the imagination of the poet can carry them, with proportion to verisimility." [19]

Throughout the century and beyond, under the influence of Denham's most famous poem, serious writers of panegyric will seek, whether by means of topography, history, or allegory, to give a due generality to the treatment of contemporary political events in addition to that support of cause or King which came more and more to be the common *raison d'étre* of panegyric.

The tone, method, and conception of Cowley's *Poem on the Late Civil War* leaves the invincible impression that he was the first of Denham's followers in this new attempt, which must have appealed to his own skeptically rationalistic mind more than the ritualistic fervor of his own first attempt at panegyric. The far soberer and more mature treatment of *On His Majesties Return out of Scotland*, which he included in the collected works from which he omitted the Juvenilia, bears this out. Gratitude for peace is the main theme, rather than the greatness

---

[18] Johnson, *Lives of the Poets*, ed. Waugh, Vol. I, p. 90, records: "He seems to have been, at least among us, the author of a species of composition that may be denominated *local poetry*, of which the fundamental subject is some particular landscape, to be poetically described, with the addition of such embellishments as may be supplied by historical retrospection, or incidental meditation." Pope, it is worth noticing, considered the "reflections upon moral life or political institutions" to be the distinguishing excellence of *Cooper's Hill*. (*Works*, ed. Elwin and Courthope, Vol. I, p. 336.)

[19] *Essays*, ed. Ker, Vol. I, pp. 100–101.

of Charles, and the resemblance to the cast of Denham's mind
is to be perceived in passages like the following:

> The gain of *Civil Wars* will not allow
> *Bay* to the *Conquerors Brow.*
> At such a *Game* what fool would venture in,
> Where one must *lose,* yet neither side can *win?*
> How justly would our *Neighbours* smile
> At these mad quarrels of our Isle
> Sweld with proud hopes to snatch the whole away,
> Whilst we *Bet all,* and yet for *nothing Play?* [20]

But in the *Poem on the Late Civil War* [21] there is a highly
significant extension of Denham's mode of treatment. Cowley
has replaced the predominantly spatial perspective of the latter
by a completely temporal perspective. He is thus led to consider, not the condition of monarchy, which is Denham's
primary concern even where he interprets past events, but its
dynamic progress in time. In other words his approach is
essentially an historical one. The poem is a kind of grand
remonstrance given epic status by its projection in terms of
the national past. It sets before the reader the glorious history
of England's royal wars against a foreign enemy, in contra-

[20] *Poems,* ed. A. R. Waller (Cambridge, 1905), p. 23.
[21] This poem appeared in no collected edition of Cowley's works. It
may well have been the work referred to by Cowley in his 1656 preface
as the "Lawrels for the Conquered" which it would be ridiculous to
make. The reference to Hampden's death makes 1643 a likely date of
composition, as indeed does the whole tenor of the work. A fragment,
printed in 1679, remains; and it was included, apparently complete, in
Dryden's *Examen Poeticum* in 1693. Quotation here is from Tonson's
1716 edition of all six volumes of the miscellanies, where the inclusion
of the poem, and its ascription, is defended in the preface with this
judgment: "He [Cowley] could write nothing that was not worth the
preserving, being habitually a *Poet,* and always *Inspir'd.* In this *Piece*
the Judicious Reader will find the Turn of the Verse to be his; the same
warmth of Passion and Delicacy of Wit that sparkles in all his Writings"
(Vol. III, M2 v.). Since Cowley disclaimed *The Iron Age* (1648), which
had been ascribed to him, this poem must be that which he mentions as
"three Books of the Civil War it self, reaching as far as the first *Battel*
of *Newbury,* where the succeeding *misfortunes* of the *party* stopt the
work." (*The Preface,* Spingarn, Vol. II, p. 83.) The Battle of Newbury
was in September 1643.

distinction to her shameful civil wars. The heroic conception of the work keeps the diction consistently dignified and magnificent:

What Rage does England from it self divide,
More than the seas from all the World beside!
From every part the roaring Cannons play,
From every part Blood roars as loud as they.
What English Ground but still some Moisture bears,
Of young Mens Blood, and more of Mothers Tears! . . .
. . . Alas what Triumphs can this Victory show,
That dies us Red in Blood and Blushes too!
How can we wish that Conquest, which bestows
Cypress, not Bays, upon the Conquering Brows?
It was not so, when Henry's dreadful Name,
Not Sword, nor Cause, whole Nations overcame.
To farthest West did his swift Conquests run,
Nor did his glory set but with the sun . . .   [p. 229]

It was not so when Edward prov'd his Cause,
By a Sword stronger than the *Salique* Laws . . .
Where's now that Spirit with which at Cressy we,
And Poictiers forc'd from Fate a Victory?
Two Kings at once we brought sad Captives home,
A Triumph scarcely known to ancient *Rome*;
Two Foreign Kings! But now alas we strive,
Our own, our own good Sovereign to Captive! . . .
[p. 230]

It was not so, when that vast Fleet of *Spain*
Lay torn and scatter'd on the English main;
Through the proud World, a Virgin Terror struck,
The *Austrian* Crowns and *Romes* seven Hills she shook:
To her great *Neptune* Homag'd all his Streams,
And all the wide stretch'd Ocean was her *Thames*.   [p. 231]

The present war itself, shameful though it be, is also presented in terms of historically world-shaking and dire events through traditional "disorder" imagery fully charged with ominous suggestions of chaos:

Worster first saw't and trembled at the view, . . .
Here first the Rebel Winds began to roar,
Brake loose from the first fetters which they bore,
Here mutinous Waves above their Shore did swell,
And the first Storm of that Dire Winter fell.   [p. 234]

Thus where the other panegyrics discussed inhabit an ideal world of ethical or metaphysical definitions, or mythological eulogy, Denham and Cowley are the first to fix the panegyric firmly in the real world of historical events. It was Cowley's sense of the real movement of events in history which enabled him to achieve so fine a "character" as the portrait of Hampden, despite the presence in the same poem of a series of allegorical figures—Schism, Ignorance, Sedition, Loyalty, Justice, Learning, and so on—which take up their opposing stands upon the battlefield. Such allegorizing was a false trail for the times, already out of date in 1643, though it was to reappear sporadically during the Restoration. But the character of Hampden, in its fusion of the realistically satiric with the heroic mode, anticipates what is generally regarded as Dryden's unique contribution to political poetry:

. . . Where H...n both began and ended too
His curs'd Rebellion, where his Soul's repaid
With Separation, great as that he made.
H...n, whose Spirit moved o'er the mighty Frame
O'the'British Isle, and out this Chaos came.
H...n, the Man that taught Confusion's Art,
His Treasons restless, and yet noisless Heart,
His active Brain, like Aetna's Top appear'd,
Where Treason's forg'd, yet no Noise outward heard,
'Twas he contriv'd whate'er bold *Martyn* said,
And all the popular noise that *Pym* has made.
'Twas he that taught the *Zealous Rout* to rise,
And be his Slaves for some fain'd Liberties.
Him for this Black Design Hell thought most fit,
Ah! wretched Man, curs'd by too good a Wit.   [p. 239]

This kind of characterization found fit expression in the antithetical couplet which Denham's practice must have taught

Cowley, and which was a form particularly well adapted for serious witty criticism of contemporary realities. Cowley makes the fullest and most successful use of the antithetical stopped couplet in his *The Puritan and the Papist*,[22] which he must have been writing at about the same time as the *Poem on the Late Civil War*, very possibly as a satirical counterpart to the latter. But many such passages take their place in the *Poem on the Late Civil War* side by side with the heroically elevated style of the greater part of that poem:

> How could a War so sad and barb'rous please,
> But first by sland'ring those blest Days of Peace?
> Through all the Excrements of State they pry,
> Like Empricks, to find out a Malady;
> And then, with desperate Boldness, they endeavour
> Th' Ague to cure, by bringing in a Feaver. [p. 232]

> To what with Worship the fond Papist falls,
> That the fond Zealot a curs'd Idol calls.
> So, twixt their double Madness, here's the odds,
> One makes false Devils, t'other makes false Gods.
>
> [p. 231]
>
> Beggary and scorn into the Church they'd bring,
> And make God Glorious, as they made the King.
>
> [p. 239]

The general resemblance to, or pre-figuring of, Dryden's ultimate mastery of the mixed heroic-satiric style throws into relief the marked parallel, in their state verse, in the development of the art of the two poets. Each in his turn responded to the pressure of events as these arranged themselves in the two great revolutionary cycles of their respective generations. Each moved from panegyric, through reflection upon the nature of the heroic in life and in poetry, to satire, and thence to the expression of personal philosophy. Each had a strong tendency to skeptical fideism. And though the mature Dryden of the neo-classical point of view, and under the influence of Boileau, could reject Cowley's heroic style in the *Davideis* for its "points

[22] 1643. See Chapter 2.

of wit, and quirks of epigram" [23] as detracting from the "dignity and state of an heroic poem," [24] yet it will be remembered that he was "the darling of my youth" and, as late as 1669, "his authority (was) almost sacred to me."

THE PAPER WAR

If the aspiration to high seriousness in minds moderate and critical could produce panegyric of a lasting excellence in the form and with the perspective of historical reflection, the pressures of civic contention yielded panegyric of a very different kind. It was Cleveland who, upon the same occasion which had called forth Cowley's first panegyric, erupted onto the literary and political scene with a series of panegyrics which are neither ritual nor compliment nor moral nor historical interpretation, but frankly weapons in a political war. That they were regarded as effective weapons is sufficiently shown by the fact that there were over twenty editions of Cleveland's poems (many spurious) between 1651 and 1677.[25] They became indeed the chief paper artillery of the royalist militant.

Upon the King's Return from Scotland, 1641,[26] one of Cleveland's earliest attempts at political poetry, consists of a series of violent conceits, drawn from various "places of invention," to illustrate the idea of the inseparability of King and State. The first few lines carry an easy conviction because the analogy King-State, Soul-Body brings with it a great weight of traditional reference; but for the rest, the chop-logic of the metaphysical conceit has become a hyperbolic and wire-drawn rhetoric, heightened by consciousness that its assertions *are* assailable.

> Return'd, I'll ne'er believe't; first prove him hence;
> Kings travel by their beams and influence.

[23] "Discourse Concerning Satire," p. 320.
[24] "Of Heroic Plays," Preface to *The Conquest of Granada* (1669–1670), (printed 1672), Mermaid edn., Vol. I, pp. 31–32.
[25] J. M. Berdan, in the introduction to his edition of the poems (Yale, 1903), deals thoroughly with the problem of establishing a canon.
[26] *The Caroline Poets,* ed. G. Saintsbury (Oxford, 1921). Quotation is from this edition, pp. 15–94.

Who says the soul gives out her gests, or goes
A flitting progress 'twixt the head and toes?
She rules by omnipresence, and shall we
Deny a prince the same ubiquity?   [l. 1]

Here the panegyrist does not expatiate upon accepted, or even
hypothetical, moral or metaphysical propositions, but sets out
to defend a debated position with a barrage of ingenious image-
arguments.[27]

In the *Rupertismus*, 1642, which is three-quarters satire, the
function of political assertion is even clearer than in *The
King's Return* in proportion as the former is more vigorous
than the latter.

Go on, brave Prince, and make the world confess
Thou art the greater world and that the less.
Scatter th'accumulative king; untruss
That five-fold fiend, the State's Smectymnuus . . .
[l. 165]

The Prince's magnificent acts, his sterling value, his illustrious name, his courage and prudence are now counters in
a militant polemic. They are valued for the wonder and awe
they are asserted to inspire, and the fear they cast upon the
enemy, more than for their ethical or didactic value as attributes of absolute virtue.

Where providence and valour meet in one,
Courage so poised with circumspection
That he revives the quarrel once again
Of the soul's throne; whether in heart, or brain,
And leaves it a drawn match . . .   [l. 101]

As light itself when styled God's shadow is made thereby more
glorious:

So 'tis illustrious to be Rupert's foil
And a just trophy to be made his spoil . . .   [l. 93]

[27] In this he is realizing an accepted principle of Renaissance poetic, as
is indicated by Rosamund Tuve in Part II of her *Elizabethan and
Metaphysical Imagery* (Chicago, 1947).

Classical allusion, no longer decorative and epic, is also turned
to the purpose of ingenious hyperbole:

> Sure, Jove descended in a leaden shower
> To get this Perseus; hence the fatal power
> Of shot is strangled. Bullets thus allied
> Fear to commit an act of parricide.   [l. 161]

It is Cleveland's yoking of his panegyric to the needs of
political controversy [28] which has changed the tone of this
poem from an heroic decorum to a bold colloquiality which
can encompass the requirements of satiric denigration as well
as panegyric admiration.

> No wonder they'll confess no loss of men,
> For Rupert knowcks 'em till they gig again . . .
> [l. 119]

> In fine the name of Rupert thunders so,
> Kimbolton's but a rumbling wheelbarrow.   [l. 179]

Saintsbury has suggested that Cleveland caricatured, or near-
burlesqued, the metaphysical manner. But in the light of the
whole body of seventeenth century political verse, and his influence upon Butler,[29] it would be more appropriate to see in
the oddities of his style a first attempt to solve the central
problem of decorum which faced the partisan writer. He must
find, or invent, a style which will express both adulation and
animus. It is Cleveland's wit, his catachresis, his contorted conceit, which serves as a unifying medium between the two
poles. Already in his own day the dualism was noted and
praised. Anthony à Wood recounts: "At length upon the eruption of the Civil War, he was the first Champion that appeared
in verse for the King's Cause against the Presbyterians; . . .
Whereupon retiring to Oxon the King's head-quarter, lived
there for a time, and was much venerated and respected not

---

[28] It is interesting to note that Aubrey says of Cleveland that "he was
a fellow of St. John's College in Cambridge, where he was more taken
notice of for his being an eminent disputant, than a good Poet." (*Brief
Lives*, ed. Clark, 1898.)

[29] See Chapter 8.

only by the great Men of the Court, but by the then Wits remaining among the affrighted and distressed Muses for his high Panegyrics and smart Satyrs." [30]

But it is David Lloyd, writing of Cleveland in 1668, whose tortured syntax unwittingly reveals the exact nature of the difficulty involved in the performance of that dual function: ". . . his life at Oxford, where he managed his pen as the highest panegyrist, (witness his Rupertismus, his Elegy on my Lord of Canterbury, etc., on the one hand) on the one side to draw all good intentions to virtue; and the Scots' Apostasy, the Character of a London Diurnal, and a Committee Man, (blows that shaked triumphing Rebellion, reaching the soul of those not to be reached by Law or Power, striking each Traitor to a paleness beyond that of any Loyal Corpes that bled by them; the Poet killing at as much distance as some Philosophers, beat scars lasting as time, indelible as guilt-stabs beyond Death,) on the other, to shame the ill from vice. . . ." [31]

To draw all good intentions to virtue, on the one hand, and to shame ill from vice, on the other, was the dual purpose to which the partisan poets of the mid-seventeenth century bent their best endeavors. This was the shaping influence upon their choice of style; and this was the banner under which panegyric and satire entered the political lists. For the virtue and vice so incessantly invoked had begun to be identified (in diametrically opposed application, of course, according to partisan interests) with the great rival factions which clashed in civil war.

The King's Disguise, 1647, is a good example of Cleveland's panegyric method. As the "first Champion" to appear in verse for the King's cause, and as a disputant, he evidently needed a controversial theme upon which to whet his wit. Abuse is an essential motivation for his writing; and it is interesting to notice that the most vigorous part of the poem is that in which he chides the King for betraying his royal self to the "mouldy bread and clouted shoes" of his flight and disguise. He is of

[30] *Athenae Oxonienses* (1691).
[31] *Memoirs* . . . (London, 1668), p. 617.

course really chiding those who have put the King to such straits, but it is only in the first few lines that the fusion of compassion and reverence with the anger makes itself felt:

> And why a tenant to this vile disquise
> Which who but sees, blasphemes thee with his eyes?
> My twins of light within their penthouse shrink,
> And hold it their allegiance now to wink.
> O, for a state-distinction to arraign
> Charles of high treason 'gainst my Sovereign!   [l. 1]

The castigating motive breaks through in:

> His ruins prove him a religious house! . . .   [l. 10]

> Like to a martyred abbey's coarser doom,
> Devoutly altered to a pigeon-room;
> Or like a college by the changeling rabble,
> Manchester's elves, transformed into a stable;
> Or if there be a profanation higher;
> Such is the sacrilege of thine attire,
> By which thou'rt half deposed.—Thou look'st like one
> Whose looks are under sequestration;
> Whose renegade form at the first glance
> Shows like the Self-denying Ordinance.   [l. 29]

The King himself is put in an invidious light. One can hardly shame vice and laud virtue in one and the same figure—even in one and the same poem it proved itself difficult enough—and the poem recovers its precarious balance between zealous reverence and harsh ridicule only towards the end:

> But pardon, Sir, since I presume to be
> Clerk of this closet to your Majesty.
> Methinks in this your dark mysterious dress
> I see the Gospel couched in parables.
> At my next view my purblind fancy ripes
> And shows Religion in its dusky types;
> Such a text royal, so obscure a shade
> Was Solomon in Proverbs all arrayed.
> Come, all the brats of this expounding age

[46]

and subjects hearts their strings"

To whom the spirit is in pupilage,
You that damn more than ever Samson slew,
And with his engine, the same jaw-bone too!
Keys for this coffer you can never get;
None but St. Peter's opes this cabinet,
This cabinet, whose aspect would benight
Critic spectators with redundant light.
A Prince most seen is least. What Scriptures call
The Revelation, is most mystical. [l. 91]

It makes a triumphant debater's point. But it is also an indication that, for the moment at least, the felt need of "this
expounding age" was for "smart satyrs" rather than "high
panegyrics."

CHAPTER TWO

The "Disfiguring of Sin"

"INDIGNATION VISAG'D LIKE A LION"

In 1656, in his "recantation" preface, Cowley wrote: ". . . I have cast away all such pieces as I wrote during the time of the late troubles, with any relation to the differences that caused them, . . . for it is so uncustomary as to become almost *ridiculous*, to make *Lawrels* for the *Conquered*. Now, though in all *Civil Dissentions*, when they break into open hostilities, the *War* of the *Pen* is allowed to accompany that of the *Sword*, and every one is in a maner obliged with his *Tongue* as well as *Hand* to serve and assist the side which he engages in; yet when the event of battel and the unaccountable *Will* of *God* has determined the controversie, and that we have submitted to the conditions of the *Conqueror*, we must lay down our *Pens* as well as *Arms*, we must *march* out of our *Cause* it self, and *dismantle* that, as well as our *Towns* and *Castles*, of all the *Works* and *Fortifications* of *Wit* and *Reason* by which we defended it." [1]

Except for the *Rupertismus* and *Cooper's Hill* and a tribute to Rupert in *A Poem on the Late Civil War*, laurels had indeed ceased to be made by the 1640's. The works and fortifications of Wit and Reason which defended the opposing causes were by then taking the form of satire and polemic, and the satirists were encountering, as had the panegyrists when they turned from a select to a wider audience, a central problem in literary craftsmanship. Which was more effective a method for polemic in verse, the high style or the low? Invective or ridicule? Grandiloquent vituperation or the grotesquerie of burlesque?

In Milton's mind there was no doubt about the answer. His fierce and ardent conviction found the way to combine soar-

[1] Preface to *Poems* (1656). In Spingarn, Vol. ii, pp. 83–84.

ing moral indignation with the telling home-thrusts of a scorn-
ful abuse. His *On the New Forcers of Conscience,* 1646,[2]
turns an accomplished rhetoric of vigorously colloquial scorn
upon the Presbyterians; the two sonnets on *Tetrachordon*[3]
modulate between the direct abuse of "But this is got by
casting Pearl to Hoggs," and the moving invocation:

> Thy age, like ours, O Soul of Sir *John Cheek,*
> Hated not Learning wors then Toad or Asp;
> When thou taught'st *Cambridge,* and King *Edward* Greek.

The clue to this tone, or modulation of tones, unique among
satirists of the time, would seem to lie in Milton's dedicated
sense of identification with, or responsibility for, the people he
castigates so unremittingly. This it is that gives him the moral
freedom so sternly to lash. "I did but prompt the age to quit
their cloggs. . . ."—this is the prophetic note in his satire of
which he himself was fully aware. An *Apology against a Pamphlet,* 1642,[4] offers a theory of satire, and contains in effect a
zealous republican polemicist's manifesto. He inveighs against
the Modest Confuter's levity, his "frumps and curtal gibes,"
and advises him to remember what it is "to turn the sinnes of
Christendome into a mimicall mockery, to rip up the saddest
vices with a laughing countenance" [p. 295, l. 13]. He calls
him "a cursing Shimei, a hurler of stones, as well as a rayler"

[2] Though so well-known, it is perhaps worth recalling the poem here
in the context of other political satires of the time:
> Men whose Life, Learning, Faith and pure intent
> Would have been held in high esteem with *Paul*
> Must now be nam'd and printed Hereticks
> By shallow *Edwards* and Scotch what d'ye call:
> But we do hope to find out all your tricks,
> Your plots and packing wors then those of *Trent,*
> > That so the Parliament
> May with their wholsom and preventive Shears
> Clip your Phylacteries, though bauk your Ears,
> > And succour our just Fears
> When they shall read this clearly in your charge
> *New Presbyter* is but *Old Priest* writ large.

[3] All three poems are given in *The Works of John Milton,* ed. F. A.
Patterson (New York, 1931–1938), Vol. I, part I, pp. 62, 71.
[4] *Ibid.,* Vol. III, part I, p. 282.

[p. 309, l. 19] while defending his own "plain . . . home-speaking vehemence" with the authority of Christ himself, who "scruples not to name the dunghill and the jakes" [p. 308, l. 25] and teaches "the highest things by the similitude of old bottles and patcht cloaths" [p. 311, l. 26]. ". . . Thus I take it to be manifest," he says, "that indignation against men and their actions notoriously bad, hath leave and authority oft times to utter such words and phrases, as in common talke were not so mannerly to use. . . ." [p. 316, l. 26]

On the other hand he will have no truck with the "drawling," "wretched," "mawkin" verse of the academic classicizing author of the *Virgidemiarum*, for "a satyr as it was born out of a Tragedy, so ought to resemble his parentage, to strike high, and adventure dangerously at the most eminent vices among the greatest persons, and not to creepe into every blinde tap-house that fears a constable more than a satyr." [p. 329, l. 12]

With regard to the question of emotion in moral reprehension, the question which was to be re-opened after the Restoration and to provide matter for most of the critical discussion of satire, he is unequivocal: "If therefore the question were in oratory, whether a vehement vein throwing out indignation, or scorn upon an object that merits it, were among the aptest *ideas* of speech to be allow'd, it were my work, and that an easie one, to make it cleare . . . (that) staid moderation and soundnesse of argument, to teach and convince the rationall and sober-minded . . . (is) not . . . to be thought the only expedient course of teaching, for in times of opposition, when either against new heresies arising, or old corruptions to be reform'd, this coole unpassionate mildnesse of positive wisdome is not anough to damp and astonish the proud resistance of carnall and false Doctors, then (that I may have leave to soare a while as the Poets use) Zeal . . . ascends his fiery Chariot, drawn with two blazing Meteors, figur'd like beasts, . . . the one visag'd like a lion, to expresse power, high autority, and indignation, the other of count'nance like a man to cast derision and scorne upon perverse and fraudulent seducers . . ." [p. 312, l. 13 et seq.]

"Thus," Milton concludes, "did the true prophet of old

combat with the false." For Milton the question of the "confounding of jest and earnest" is settled, first no doubt, for reasons of temperament, but also because of his ardour for the high heroic republican cause which it was satire's duty, as he conceived it, prophetically to serve. He has therefore a definitive ethical and political criterion with which to distinguish between "tankard drollery," mere buffoonery, which reduces "grave controversies" to the level of the idle and the paltry, and that righteous and sublime scorn, Juvenal's *Saevo indignatio*, which alone can teach the fool his folly. It is his heroic revolutionary zeal which finds in the shafts of martyrs and prophets the proper prototype of a satire: ". . . many of the martyrs in the midst of their troubles, were not sparing to deride and scoffe their superstitious persecutors . . . was it to shew his wit, or to fulfil his humour (that) Eliah mocked the false Prophets? . . . Doubtlesse we cannot imagine that great servant of God had any other end in all which he there did, but to teach and instruct the poore misledde people." [p. 317, l. 16 et seq.]

It was not until Milton's own secretary engaged in later controversy with another pamphleteering divine that the question of "laughter and reprehension," of "railing" and "raillery" in satire was re-opened; a "rational and sober-minded moderation" produced a very different manifesto in *The Rehearsal Transpros'd*. In the meantime, however, though Milton undoubtedly voiced the preference of the age as a whole for a "vehement vein," his own particular blend of virulent meiosis and passionate indignation, his own extraordinary range of vocabulary from the vivid colloquial to the stately and sonorous, was inimitable. It sprang directly from his epic feeling for the cause of "a noble and puissant nation" whose mission was to realize and reveal the purpose of God in a people's history. His is the first and most distinguished of the many voices which will sound the note of Puritan zeal in satire during the course of the century. His immediate followers could often sustain no more than a fumbling, if spirited, righteousness: *A Satyre against the Cavaliers*,[5] written in reply to the much more ac-

5 London (1643).

complished *Satyre against Separatists* [6] is only very faintly "visag'd like a lion, to express power, high authority, and indignation" or "of count'nance like a man, to cast derision and scorne upon perverse and fraudulent seducers." Such an aim is clearly present, but the accomplishment of a rhetoric, either of witty homeliness or of soaring invective, is sadly lacking:

> Plots and devices! Take them to yourselves
> True sonnes of mischief, and your popish Elves
> That with your loyall treasons hug our King
> Unto his owne, and Kingdomes ruining . . .
> Such Lords, whose vanities teach them no more
> Than art to please in Court, to dice and whore,
> Are now the sticklers for the Cavall'rie,
> With the blind Howlets of Philosophy . . .

> But know, there is above a power Divine
> Will give's us a Tully, for each Catiline.

RIDICULE AND INVECTIVE

Milton's contemporaries on the Cavalier side were motivated not by the righteous zeal of reform but by the self-confident mockery of a conservative class-consciousness. They, too, were to make a variety of attempts to solve the complex problem of articulating within the discipline of verse the anger, hostility, or contempt they felt—and wished others to feel—for their adversaries.

Cleveland, though not to be accused of cool, unpassionate mildness, yet begins his satirist's career more in jest than in earnest. His first sally takes unconditionally the direction of sarcastic ridicule. The two Puritans conferring over the Oath in *A Dialogue between two Zealots*, 1640, are comic figures whose suspicions and whose style in general is burlesqued from the standpoint of social and intellectual superiority:

> . . . this same clergy-elf,
> Encountering with a brother of the cloth,
> Fell presently to cudgels with the Oath.

[6] See p. 64 ff., below.

The quarrel was a strange misshapen monster,
&c., (God bless us) which they conster
The brand upon the buttock of the Beast,
The Dragon's tail tied on a knot, a nest
Of young Apocryphas, the fashion
Of a new mental Reservation. . . .

While Roger thus divides the text, the other
Winks and expounds, saying, 'My pious brother,
Hearken with reverence, for the point is nice.
I never read on 't, but I fasted twice,
And so by revelation know it better
Than all the learn'd, idolaters o'th'letter.'
With that he swelled, and fell upon the theme
Like great Goliath with his weaver's beam.
'I say to thee, &c., thou li'st!
Thou art the curled lock of Antichrist;
Rubbish of Babel: for who will not say
Tongues were confounded in &c.?
Who swears &c., swears more oaths at once
Than Cerberus out of his triple sconce.
Who views it well, with the same eye beholds
The old half Serpent in his numerous folds . . . [l. 8] [7]

In *Smectymnuus, or the Club-Divines,* 1641, Cleveland lav-
ishes his wit in similar tone upon the notion of five-in-one,
with the clear and sole intention of deflating any pretensions
to serious consideration which the reverend brotherhood might
be conceived to have had. The obliquity is instructive. There is
no attempt to deal with content or an actual issue. Fastening
upon the oddity of the name implies that no other attribute of
the Club-Divines is worthy of a moment's consideration:

Smectymnuus! The goblin makes me start!
I 'th'name of Rabbi Abraham, what art?

[7] The "oath" was formulated in 1640 by Convocation. It was to be
taken by all the clergy; it approved the doctrine, discipline, and government of the Church, and disclaimed Popish doctrine. But unfortunately
it referred to the government of the Church as being by "archbishops,
bishops, deans, and archdeacons, etc.," which alarmed the Puritans.

Syriac? or Arabic? or Welsh? what skill't? . . .
But do the brotherhood then play their prizes
Like mummers in religion with disguises,
Out-brave us with a name in rank and file?
A name, which, if 'twere trained, would spread a mile!

[l. 1]

I think Pythagoras' soul is rambled hither
With all the change of raiment on together.
Smec is her general wardrobe; . . .
The Sadducees would raise a question
Who must be Smec at th' Resurrection.
Who cooped them up together were to blame.
Had they but wire-drawn and spun out their name,
'Twould make another Prentices' Petition
Against the bishops and their superstition.   [l. 35]

Ridicule and sheer high spirits issues in the ingenious indecency
of the passage which speculates upon the betrothal of Smectymnuus to Et Caetera:

See what an offspring every one expects,
What strange pluralities of men and sects! . . .
But their cross fortunes interdict their trade;
The groom is rampant but the bride displayed.   [l. 81] [8]

The Character of a London Diurnall, 1647, Cleveland's most
famous prose philippic and the first of the "characters" to be
adapted to political purposes [9] is instructive in showing the
direction Cleveland's satire was to take as he was gradually
forced to take his opponents more seriously. Characteristic at
first is the derision of: "The next *Ingredient* of a *Diurnall* is
plots, horrible plots; which with wonderfull sagacity it hunts
drie-foot, while they are yet in their causes, before *Materia
prima* can put on her smock. How many such fits of the Mother
have troubled the Kingdoms, and (for all Sir Walter Erle looks

---

[8] Saintsbury notes that the 1677 edition has "is spade," i.e., "spayed,"
which makes better sense in the context, though at the expense of
heraldry.

[9] It was followed by *The Character of a County Committee Man,*
1647, and by Sir John Birkenhead's *The Assembly Man,* also in 1647.

like a Man-Midwife) not yet delivered of so much as a cushion!" [10] But in the passage on Cromwell a new note can be detected:

". . . now begins a *Hosanna* to *Cromwel,* one that hath beat up his Drums clean through the Old Testament: you may learn the Genealogy of our Saviour, by the names in his Regiment . . . with what face can they object to the King in bringing in of Forrainers, when themselves entertain such an army of *Hebrews?* This *Cromwel* is never so valorous, as when he is making speeches for the Association, which nevertheless he doth somewhat ominously, with his neck awry, holding up his ear, as if he expected *Mahomets'* Pigeon to come and prompt him. He should be a bird of Prey too, by his bloody beak: his Nose is able to try a young Eagle, whether she be lawfully begot . . . what we wonder at in the rest of them is naturall to him, to kill without bloodshed: for, most of his Trophees are in a Church-window, when a looking-glasse would shew him more superstition. He is so perfect a hater of Images, that he hath defaced God's in his own *countenance.* If he deale with men tis when he takes them napping in an old *Monument:* then down goes *dust and ashes:* and the stoutest Cavalier is no better. *O brave Oliver! Times Voider, Sub-sizer to the Worms:* in whom Death, that formerly devour'd our Ancestors, now chews the cud." [pp. 5–6]

In such a passage the strife between two opposing impulses is clearly felt. The desire to express contempt in burlesque or farcical images clashes with the need to present the enemy in terms larger than life. Instead of comic exaggeration, designed to deflate the importance of the satire's object, Cleveland verges towards the exaggeration of invective which raises the object to heroic proportions, though of a monstrous, not virtuous, kind. Thus the defacer of the image of God in his own countenance sorts ill with the orator holding up his ear to catch the prompting of Mahomet's pigeon; and equally incongruous is the vision of Death chewing the cud. The dual impulse towards ridicule and invective is one which is not brought into focus or unified easily. It is indeed the rock upon which the waves of satire broke constantly throughout the period of the

[10] 1651 edn., p. 2.

Commonwealth and Restoration. Davenant had taken note of the problem when he assured Hobbes that ". . . I never meant to prostitute Wickednesse in the Images of low and contemptible people, as if I expected the meanest of the multitude for my Readers, since only the Rabble is seen at common executions, nor intended to raise iniquity to that height of horrour, till it might seem the fury of something worse than a beast." [11] And he points out that the Spartans "to deter their children from Drunkennesse, accustom'd their Slaves to vomit before them, (but) did . . . rather teach them to disdain the Slaves than to loath Wine, for Men seldom take notice of the vice in abject persons. . . ." [p. 11]

Milton's belittling of the object of his anger did not lower the tone to mere disdain, nor detract from the high seriousness of the theme, because of his prophetic conviction of a divine cause at stake, and his prophet's pain at the spectacle of the iniquities of backsliders. Cleveland, on the other hand, fails through ambivalence. He speaks not from hard-won conviction but from a taken-for-granted assumption of automatic superiority normally unexamined, but shaken into an uncertain aggression when felt to be endangered.

The theme of *The Mixed Assembly* is the incongruous composition—peers and commoners, divines and laymen—of the Westminster Assembly which met in 1643. There are lines of purely comic invention:

> So mixed they are, one knows not whether's thicker,
> A layer of burgess, or a layer of vicar. [l. 21]

but also lines which are castigation rather than burlesque:

> Such may their stript-stuff-hangings seem to be,
> Sacrilege matched with codpiece simony.
> Be sick and dream a little, you may then
> Fancy these linsey-woolsey vestry-men. [l. 49]

The "jig" which ends the poem is farce more abusively grotesque, less refined by the inventions and conceits or wit than

---

[11] "Preface to Gondibert," in Spingarn, Vol. II, pp. 16–17.

in any previous piece of Cleveland's (if we except the shaft
against Pym and Madam Smec): [12]

> Then Saye and Sele must his old hamstrings supple,
> And he and rumpled Palmer make a couple.
> Palmer's a fruitful girl if he'll unfold her;
> The midwife may find work about her shoulder.   [l. 71]

Thus *The Mixed Assembly*, except for one or two seriously
satiric lines, is still in burlesque mood, whether the burlesque
take the form of grotesque farce or of insulting insinuation.
It is in *The Rebel Scot*, 1644, that Cleveland realizes fully for
the first time the possibilities of fierce invective. It is very
likely that the transposition of the hated object from a socio-
political to a national plane liberated him from that convention
of low-comic ridicule for his socially inferior opponents which
was the Cavalier's social and stylistic inheritance.

> What? shall our nation be in bondage thus
> Unto a land that truckles under us?
> Ring the bells backward: I am all on fire.
> Not all the buckets in a country quire
> Shall quench my rage. A poet should be feared,
> When angry, like a comet's flaming beard.
> And where's the stoic can his wrath appease,
> To see his country sick of Pym's disease?   [l. 3]

> Come, keen iambics, with your badger's feet
> And badger-like bite till your teeth do meet.
> Help, ye tart satirists, to imp my rage
> With all the scorpions that should whip this age.
> Scots are like witches; do but whet your pen,
> Scratch till the blood come, they'll not hurt you then.
> Now, as the martyrs were enforced to take
> The shapes of beasts, like hypocrites, at stake,
> I'll bait my Scot so, yet not cheat your eyes;
> A Scot within a beast is no disguise.   [l. 27]

[12]   "If they two truck together, 'till not be
         A child-birth, but a gaol-delivery . . ."   [l. 85]

The keen iambics bite with a new energy of scorn, direct and scathing:

> They are the Gospel's life-guard; but for them,
> The garrison of New Jerusalem,
> What would the brethren do? The Cause! The Cause!
> Sack-possets and the fundamental laws!
> Lord! what a godly thing is want of shirts!
> How a Scotch stomach and no meat converts!
> They wanted food and raiment, so they took
> Religion for their seamstress and their cook . . .
> Hence then, you proud impostors; get you gone,
> You Picts in gentry and devotion;
> You scandal to the stock of verse, a race
> Able to bring the gibbet in disgrace. [l. 97]

The *Rebel Scot* was the best known and most popular of Cleveland's poems and is the only one which is found in every edition. In 1646 *The Scots' Apostasy* continues in similar vein, assimilated to the formal curse:

> The infamy this super-treason brings
> Blasts more than murders of your sixty kings; . . .
> Kings only suffered then; in this doth lie
> Th'assassination of Monarchy.
> Beyond this sin no one step can be trod,
> If not t'attempt deposing of your God.
> Oh, were you so engaged that we might see
> Heaven's angry lightning 'bout your ears to flee
> Till you were shrivelled to dust, and your cold Land
> Parched to a drought beyond the Lybian sand! [l. 19]

> . . . may your scabby Land be all
> Translated to a general hospital:
> Let not the sun afford one gentle ray
> To give you comfort of a summer's day;
> But, as a guerdon for your traitorous war,
> Live cherished only by the Northern Star:
> No stranger deign to visit your rude coast,
> And be to all but banished men as lost: . . .

To sum up all—let your religion be,
As your allegiance, masked hypocrisy,
Until, when Charles shall be composed in dust,
Perfumed with epithets of good and just,
He saved, incensed Heaven may have forgot
T'afford one act of mercy to a Scot . . .   [l. 45]

On only two occasions did Cleveland's political verse depart from either boisterous ridicule or hectic vituperation. On those two occasions he achieves a tragic distance and generality which remind one that Cleveland, though so fierce a partisan, nevertheless still inhabited the world of the Jacobean dramatists or, rather, that the rhythms and intuitions of that world had not yet entirely disappeared. The *Epitaph on the Earl of Strafford*, 1641, is the first of these two instances, unusually moving in its grave paradox:

> Here lies wise and valiant dust
> Huddled up 'twixt fit and just;
> Strafford, who was hurried hence
> 'Twixt treason and convenience.
> He spent his time here in a mist;
> A Papist, yet a Calvinist; [13]
> His Prince's nearest joy and grief;
> He had, yet wanted all relief;
> The prop and ruin of the State;
> The People's violent love and hate;
> One in extremes loved and abhorred.
> Riddles lie here, or in a word,
> Here lies blood: and let it lie
> Speechless still and never cry.

The General Eclipse, 1645, which appears in the 1677 edition but not in the 1653, is as fine as Lovelace's best songs in its lyric expression of deeply held Cavalier attitudes:

[13] C. V. Wedgewood explains this odd line in an article in *The Listener*, May 8 (1958), p. 770. Strafford, as strong supporter of King and Archbishop, would no doubt have been called "Papist" by the Puritans. His private religion was in fact, however, close to Calvinism. This would have been known at least at St. John's College, Cambridge, where Cleveland was a Fellow.

The "Disfiguring of Sin"

Ladies that gild the glittering noon,
And by reflection mend his ray,
Whose beauty makes the sprightly sun
To dance as upon Easter-day,
  What are you now the Queen's away?

Courageous Eagles, who have whet
Your eyes upon majestic light,
And thence derived such martial heat
That still your looks maintain the fight,
  What are you since the King's good-night?

Cavalier-buds, whom Nature teems
As a reserve for England's throne,
Spirits whose double edge redeems
The last Age and adorns your own,
  What are you now the Prince is gone?

As an obstructed fountain's head
Cuts the entail off from the streams,
And brooks are disinherited,
Honour and Beauty are mere dreams
  Since Charles and Mary lost their beams!

Criminal Valours, who commit
Your gallantry, whose paean brings
A psalm of mercy after it,
In this sad solstice of the King's,
  Your victory hath mewed her wings!

See, how your soldier wears his cage
Of iron like the captive Turk,
And as the guerdon of his rage!
See, how your glimmering Peers do lurk
  Or at the best, work journey-work!

Thus 'tis a general eclipse,
And the whole world is al-a-mort;
Only the House of Commons trips
The stage in a triumphant sort.
  Now e'en John Lilburn take 'em for't!

The "Disfiguring of Sin"

The central image of the "eclipse of the sun" has deep roots in world order. The poem is an epitaph upon an entire period, a total outlook. Roi-Soleil returns with the Restoration, but never again has this innate conviction nor this vital relation to the dream of honor and beauty.

It would seem that Cleveland had exhausted his capacity with *The General Eclipse*, for *The Hue and Cry after Sir John Presbyter*, 1645, not only is his most obscure poem, but has neither the fire nor the fun of his previous work. It is simply scurrilous, and hovers uncertainly between burlesque and diatribe. It is probably a fair index to the uncertainty of attack in royalist ranks at that date:

> . . . Those New Exchange men of religion?
> Sure, they're the antick heads, which placed without
> The church, do gape and disembogue a spout.
> Like them above the Commons' House, have been
> So long without; now both are gotten in.   [l. 34]

> Episcopacy minced, reforming Tweed
> Hath sent us runts even of her Church's breed,
> Lay-interlining clergy, a device
> That's nickname to the stuff called lops and lice.   [l. 23]

But he has already produced enough satire of pungency, vigor, and variety to prove a mine to his colleagues as well as his successors in the future.

"A plague o'both your houses"

If Cleveland was a fierce and wholehearted partisan, Cowley, an active royalist, save for a short republican phase, was a man of moderate temper and increasingly skeptical detachment. His *The Puritan and the Papist*, 1643,[14] raises the familiar allegations against the Puritans to a level of criticism capable of enunciating general principles. The wit of the poem is braced, balanced, and given antithetical point by the "a plague o'both your houses" comparison which is the theme of the poem. Where Denham,

---

[14] In *Wit and Loyalty Reviv'd* (1682), ed. W. Scott, Somers Collection of Tracts, Vol. v (London, 1811), p. 480.

a similarly moderate and discursive mind, had treated such a idea from the generally philosophical standpoint of a theory of knowledge, Cowley, as satirist, very properly modifies his analysis in the direction of condemnatory exposure. The stopped couplet in both cases admirably serves the purpose of the double criticism:

> They keep the people ignorant, and you
> Keep both the people and yourselves so too.
> They blind obedience, and blind duty teach;
> You blind rebellion and blind faction preach.
> So two rude waves, by storms together thrown,
> Roar at each other, fight and then grow one.
> Religion is a circle, men contend,
> And run the round with dispute without end,
> Now in a circle who go contrary,
> Must, at the last, meet of necessity.
> The Roman cath'lique, to advance the cause,
> Allows a lye, and calls it *pia fraus*.
> The Puritan approves, and does the same,
> Dislikes nought in it but the Latin name. [p. 481]

> They, in a forraign and unknown tongue pray,
> You in an unknown sence your prayers say;
> So that this difference 'twixt ye does ensue,
> Fools understand not them, nor wise men you. [p. 482]

Where Cleveland's wit took the form of a pyrotechnic display of conceit, Cowley's projects itself with the clarity of the rational proposition. It is perhaps this solid grounding of Cowley's criticism which accounts for the tonal range he can command. With no sense of jarring incongruity such as Cleveland's brutal meiosis introduces at times into the *Rebel Scot*, for instance, or, for that matter, into the *Rupertismus*, Cowley can modulate in one passage between witty colloquial repartee to a vehemently serious, heroically pitched denunciation:

> They dare kill kings; and twixt ye here's the strife,
> That you dare shoot at kings, to save their life,

And what's the difference, pray, whether he fall
By the Pope's bull, or your Oxe General?   [p. 484]

Ye boundless tyrants, how do you outvy
Th'Athenian thirty, Rome's decemviry?
In rage, injustice, cruelty as far
Above these men as you in numbers are.
What mistr'ies of iniquity doe we see?
New prisons made to defend libertie:
Our goods forc'd from us for propriti's sake
And all the real nonscence which you make . . .
The high Commission you call'd tyranny,
Ye did; good God! what is the high Committy?   [p. 484]

This level of style, rationally based, seriously intended, and
salted with the neat couplet wit, will not be attained again
until the Restoration, when satirists and polemicists lay down
its principles and pursue it with conscious insight. Its seriousness derives not from the prophetic enthusiasm of a Milton,
but from a seriously held rationalism. Thus even the familiar
jibes and jeers against Puritan mores have greater conciseness,
stronger logic, than those which spring from too automatic a
sense of a taken-for-granted order:

Nay though you keep no eves, Fridays nor Lent,
Not to dress meat on Sundays you're content;
Then you repeat, repeat, and pray, and pray;
Your teeth keep Sabbath, and tongues working day.
They love church-musick; it offends your sence,
And therefore ye have sung it out from thence,
Which shews, if right your minds be understood,
You hate it not as musick but as good;   [p. 483]

Witty denigration characterizes also the invidious personalities
with which the poem is enlivened. Acidly drawn thumbnail
sketches of this kind were to become a staple method of political satire during the Restoration:

Nay Lowry, who does new church-government wish,
And prophesies, like Jonas, 'midst the fish,

Who can such various business wisely sway,
Handling both herrings and bishops in one day.   [p. 484]

"A STAKE AMONGST THE RABBLE" [15]

A year before *The Puritan and the Papist* appeared *A Satyre against Seperatists,* by one A. C. Generosus,[16] at one time supposed to have been Cowley himself, though the supposition is unlikely on internal evidence. The approach, if not the poetic method, recalls Cleveland's in his *Dialogue between Two Zealots*—ridicule by caricature and parody with the addition of a good deal of scurrilous innuendo. Of the Brownist's women, for instance, he says:

The signe of the Crosse the forehead must not beare
Twas only they were borne to plant signes there.
No Font to wash native concupiscence in,
You like that itch still of originall sin,
No organ Idoll with pure Eares agree, . . .
Theres new Church musique found instead of those,
The womens sighs tun'd to the teachers nose.   [p. 7]

The poem recounts a visit to the Brownist's church, where the author's suffering during the age-long sermon owes something to Donne's humorously anguished martyrization in Satire IV:

. . . to Heaven at first hee speakes it, there
He hummes, then whispers strait, and next does roare,
Now drawes his long words, and now leaps them ore,
So various tones, that I admir'd and said
Sure all the Congregation in him praid . . .
No feaver a mans eyes could open keepe,
All Argus body hee'd have preach'd asleepe
In half an hour. . . .   [p. 2]

[15] Dryden's phrase in the Preface to *Religio Laici* (*Poetical Works,* ed. Noyes, p. 161), where he complains of those "Presbyterian scribbler(s) who sanctified libels and scurrility to the use of the Good Old Cause . . . that they might compass by railing what they had lost by reasoning; and when their cause was sunk in Court and parliament, they might at least hedge in a stake amongst the rabble."

[16] London (1642).

The "Disfiguring of Sin"

And now the Christian Bajaset begins;
The suffering Pulpit groanes for Israel's sinnes.
Down, down as low as earth must all things goe
There was some hope the Pulpit would downe too . . .
Next he cuts out set Prayer, even the Lords,
And binds the spirit he sayes as 'twere with cords,
Yea with whip cords; Next must authority goe,
Authoritie's a kind of binder too.
First then he intends to breath himself upon
Church Government: have at the King anon.
The thing's don straight, in poor six minutes space
Titus, and *Timothy* have lost their place;
Nay with th'Apostles too it eene went hard,
All their authority two thumps more had mard,
Paul and St. Peter might expect their doome
Knew but this frantick foole they'd bin at Rome.

Plots, plots he cries, ther's jealousies, and feares,
The politick Saints shake their misterious eares,
Till time (long time which doth consume and wast
All things) t'an end his Sermon brought at last.   [pp. 4–5]

Hypocrisy, fruitful topic, produces some of the author's best
sallies:

Oh how the Saints enjoyed the creatures there!
Three Pasties in the minute of an houre,
Large, and well wrought, they roote and branch devour.
[p. 4]

Ironic distance, however, is not maintained under the increasing pressures of war and defeat. In John Quarles' *A Dreame*,[17]
parody reaches beyond the limits of ridicule and transforms
itself naturally into what was to prove a popular convention—the mock confession, whose heavy sarcasm lies in the
absence of the author's comment upon the candor and the glee
with which the "accused" states his dreadful doctrines or reveals his ulterior motives.

[17] London (1649).

Had I the crowne . . .
I'd make my subjects die at my command;
I'd lop the great ones off, and make the low
Subordinate to me, I'd make them know
The reines were mine; but at the first I'd steale
Into their hearts, and fool them with my zeal,
I would declare unto the world, and take
An Oath, I acted for Religion's sake: . . .

Sister, thou know'st tis no disgracing stealth
To make Religion rob the Commonwealth.   [pp. 10–11]

These poems of Machiavellian or Jesuitical imputation enjoyed a long life. They were usually written at an informally popular or familiar level of diction until Oldham adopted the method for his *Satires upon the Jesuits* in 1678, and endowed his Jesuits with the epic quality of archetypal villainy.

Cavalier satire reaches an apex of venomous wrath in John Phillips' *Satyr against Hypocrites*.[18] The poem follows the structure and the themes of the earlier *Satyre against Seperatists*, but thirteen years of strife and the victory of the Saints have darkened irony to abuse, and mockery to vilification. Puttenham's "Disabler," meiosis, as gross and physically grotesque as possible, is the main element in Phillips' satire. Relevance and point are freely sacrificed to derisive images of repulsion, though a certain crude vigor is often attained:

While these cough up their morning phlegme, and those
Doe trumpet forth the snivel of their nose;
Straight then the Clerk began with potsheard voice
To grope a tune, singing with wofull noise, . . .
Discords and Concords O how thick they jumble!
Like untam'd horses tearing with their throats
One wretched stave into an hundred notes.

. . . then mark when he pray'd . . .
In a most doleful *recitative style*,
His buttocks keeping crotchet time the while.

[18] London (1655).

[66]

And shewing his broad teeth, and grinning wide,
Aloud, *Free grace, free grace, free grace,* he cry'd.
Another mounts his chin, East, West, North, South,
Gaping to catch a blessing in his mouth. [pp. 5–7]

The preacher's division of the text is parodied as usual:

Here *Daniel* is the Church, the *World's* the Den
By Lyons are meant Monarchs, Kings of Nations,
Those worse than heathenish abominations. . . .
Be sure to feed young Daniel, thats to say,
Feed all your Ministers that Preach and pray.
First of all cause 'tis good. I speak that know so.
Fourthly, cause 'tis no evill for to do so.
Thirdly, because 'tis very good, and twelfthly
Cause there's nought better, unless myself lye. [pp. 13–14]

The "Puritan" attitude to creature comforts at dinner is roughly
treated:

Now then like Scanderbeg he falls to work,
And hews the Pudding as he hew'd the Turk,
Upon the Pasty though he fell anon,
As if't had been the walls of *Babylon.* [p. 16]

The women provide coarse comedy of low manners:

And now the silk'n Dames throng in, good store,
And casting up their noses, to th'pew dore . . .
Straight that she sits not uppermost distast
One takes; 'Tis fine that I must be displac't
By you, she cries then, Good Mistris Gill Flurt;
Gill Flurt, enrag'd cries t'other, Why ye dirt-
ie piece of Impudence, ye ill-bred Thief . . .
I scorn your terms, good Mistris Thimble-mans wife . . .
At which the other mad beyond all law,
Unsheaths her talons, and prepares to claw . . . [pp. 2–4]

or of lower morals:

There sits a Chamber-maid upon a Hassock,
Whom th'Chaplain oft instructs without his Cassock . . .

[p. 4]

[67]

In fine, the Spirit provokes a fastidious distaste for the vulgar and illiterate in whom it chooses to abide:

> Then comes old Robin too,
> Who although write or reade he neither doe,
> Yet hath his Testament chain'd to his waste,
> And his blind zeale feels out the proofs as fast,
> And makes as greasie Dogs-ears as the best.   [p. 1]

The satire begins with a quotation from Juvenal and rises at the end to a solemn protest:

> Oh what will men not dare, if thus they dare,
> Be impudent to Heaven, and play with Prayer!
> Play with that feare, with that religious awe
> Which keeps men free, and yet is mans great law . . .
> Are these the men that would the Age reforme,
> That down with superstition cry, and swarme
> This painted Glass, that Sculpture to deface,
> But worship pride, and avarice in their place.
> Religion they bawle out; yet know not what
> Religion is, unless it be to prate.
> And angry, will not have Our Father said,
> 'Cause it prayes not enough for daily bread . . .
> Vaine foolish people, how are ye deceiv'd?
> How many severall sorts have ye receiv'd
> Of things call'd truths, upon your backs lay'd on
> Like saddles for themselves to ride upon.   [pp. 20–21]

But even in the peroration high remonstrance sorts uneasily with, and is vitiated by, low ridicule. The motivating factor is hardly religious or political principle, which could give rise to serious satirical attack on doctrine, so much as aristocratic outrage at the presumption of "this wilde monster, the People" [19] to hold opinions and the reins of government at all. The difficulty of literary performance is linked with the question of political or social outlook. For the Cavaliers had received the stylistic inheritance of the ancient world which strictly

---

[19] Davenant, in Spingarn, p. 35.

separated the modes and tones suitable for portraying noble
and menial ranks in society. At the same time, the more the
Cavalier was thrown on the defensive, the more incapable he
became of any patrician coolness in the treatment of his low-
comic material, the more emotionally vituperative he became
in his effort to put his inferiors in their place, and consequently
the more his verse became assimilated to the lampoon level of
tone and matter of the street ballad. This satire is not "polite"
—in any modern or previous sense. For the urbanity or artistry
implied by the word, satire would have to wait for the late
Restoration, with its rationalistic skepticism and the fine gentleman's raillery of its Truewits.

The *Satyr against Hypocrites* was highly successful in its
day.

AN EARLY MIXED STYLE

If the *Satyr against Hypocrites* owes little to Cleveland's
technique, having in common with the latter only a thematic
family resemblance—the Cavalier contempt for the vulgar upstart which underlies the attack on hypocrisy—the same is not
true of the Marvell of 1653. At that date Marvell was still sufficiently, automatically, Cavalier in his outlook to adopt a similarly aristocratic attitude to Holland, particularly since the
chauvinism of national sentiment, unleavened as yet by dreams
of universal republican reform, is present to encourage a generalized contempt. Though Marvell's view of the "unfashion'd
Sons" of the new age is far more penetrating and comprehensive than that of his royalist contemporaries, the common point
of departure is clearly to be detected in, for instance, the disdainful:

> Nor can Civility there want for Tillage,
> Where wisely for their Court they chose a Village.[20]

[20] *The Character of Holland* (1653), l. 77. References in the satire
are to 1653. A conclusion, ll. 100–152, was added in 1665, with reference
to the Dutch war of 1665–1667. The poem appeared complete for the
first time in print in the folio of 1681. See *Poems*, ed. Margoliouth
(Oxford, 1927), p. 243. Citation of Marvell is from this edition throughout.

The burlesque conceit and the pun serve Marvell in his attack upon Holland as they served Cleveland in his attack upon the Puritans and the Scots:

> Yet still his claim the Injur'd Ocean laid,
> And oft at Leap-frog ore their Steeples plaid: . . .
> The Fish oft-times the Burger dispossesst,
> And sat not as a Meat but as a Guest;
> And oft the *Tritons* and the *Sea-Nymphs* saw
> Whole sholes of *Dutch serv'd up for Cabillau.*   [l. 23]

> To make a *Bank* was a great *Plot of State;*
> Invent a *Shov'l* and be a *Magistrate.*
> Hence some small *Dyke-grave* unperceiv'd invades
> The *Pow'r*, and grows as 'twere a *King of Spades.*   [l. 47]

The poem opens upon a note of harsher scorn than is conveyed by the hyperbolic comedy of those lines, but the method is still Cleveland's: the contempt is canalized, as it were, through an elaborate conceit, or series of conceits, though these are more carefully articulated than Cleveland's. The effect of wit lies partly in the clash between the diminishing "tenor" of the metaphor, and its highly wrought "vehicle." The result is a distancing and a holding in poise of contempt which never overbalances into vituperation:

> *Holland,* that scarce deserves the name of *Land,*
> As but the Off-scouring of the *Brittish Sand;*
> And so much Earth as was contributed
> By *English Pilots* when they heav'd the Lead;
> Or what by th'Oceans slow alluvion fell,
> Of shipwrackt Cockle and the Muscle-shell;
> This indigested vomit of the Sea
> Fell to the *Dutch* by just Propriety.
> Glad then, as Miners that have found the Oar,
> They with mad labor fish'd the *Land* to *Shoar;*
> And div'd as desperately for each piece
> Of Earth, as if't had been of *Ambergreece;*
> Collecting anxiously small loads of Clay,
> Less than what building Swallows bear away;
> Or then those Pills which sordid Beetles roul,

Transfusing into them their Dunghill Soul.
How did they rivet, with Gigantick Piles,
Thorough the Center their new-catched Miles;
And to the stake a strugling Country bound,
Where barking Waves still bait the forced Ground;
Building their *watry Babel* far more high
To reach the *Sea*, then those to scale the *Sky*. [l. 1]

The finer logic of Marvell's conceits makes possible also a
higher degree of rationalistic irony than was usual with Cleveland. And the influence of the judicious end-stopped antithetical
couplet of Denham and Cowley makes itself felt in the distinction between "Our sore new circumcised *Commonwealth* . . .
Darling of Heaven, and of Men the Care" and the "Staple of
Sects and Mint of Schisme" which he finds to be the religion
of the Netherlands:

Sure when *Religion* did it self imbark,
And from the *East* would *Westward* steer its Ark,
It struck, and splitting on this unknown ground,
Each one thence pillag'd the first piece he found:
Hence *Amsterdam, Turk-Christian-Pagan-Jew,*
Staple of Sects and Mint of Schisme grew;
That *Bank of Conscience,* where not one so strange
Opinion, but finds Credit, and Exchange.
In vain for Catholicks our selves we bear;
The *universal Church* is onely there. [l. 67]

Nevertheless, it is distinctly in Clevelandesque fashion that
farcical invention, verbal wit, and colloquial meiosis combine
in the description of the quarreling Dutchmen:

Or what a Spectacle the *Skipper gross,*
A *Water-Hercules Butter-Coloss,*
Tunn'd up with all their sev'ral *Towns of Beer;*
When Stagg'ring upon some Land, *Snick and Sneer,*
Then try, like Statuaries, if they can,
Cut out each others *Athos* to a Man:
And carve in their large Bodies, where they please,
The Armes of the *United Provinces.* [l. 93]

Cleveland's ridiculing burlesque and the conceit, tending to run on, and pulling against the couplet, form the basis of *The Character of Holland;* throughout, however, these bear the stamp of Marvell's fine-grained imagination and of his droll learnedness. These, in one remarkable passage, create by a kind of spontaneous combustion what is in fact an early essay in mock-heroic, twenty-one years before the translation of Boileau's *Le Lutrin* into English, and at a time when the requisite "aesthetic distance" for mock-heroic is hardly to be found in England. Of the stoves which are taken to church in Holland Marvell writes:

> A vestal Turf enshrin'd in Earthen Ware
> Fumes through the loop-holes of a wooden Square.
> Each to the *Temple* with these *Altars* tend,
> But still does place it at her *Western End:*
> While the fat steam of *Female Sacrifice*
> Fills the *Priests Nostrils* and puts out his *Eyes.*   [l. 87]

In *The Character of Holland* disdainful mockery, urbane artistry, ingenious burlesque, and rationalistic irony fuse into one of the least characteristic and most distinguished philippics of the period. The peroration has even more than a touch of that "majesty" so valued by Dryden:

> For now of nothing may our *State* despair,
> Darling of Heaven, and of Men the Care;
> Provided that they be what they have been,
> Watchful abroad, and honest still within.
> For while our *Neptune* doth a *Trident* shake,
> Steel'd with those piercing Heads, *Dean, Monck* and *Blake,*
> And while *Jove* governs in the highest Sphere,
> Vainly in *Hell* let *Pluto* domineer.   [l. 145]

Before Dryden, at all events, only Marvell and Cowley were possessed of sufficient detachment to be capable of synthesizing in some sort the literary and popular modes of satire of the time; or of mixing the grave and serious with the grotesque and incongruous in such a way as to achieve a new mutation of style.

It is a pity, one feels, that Dryden has left no further record of his reading of Marvell's satires than the contemptuous dismissal in the preface to *Religio Laici*, where he refers to the Elizabethan Martin Mar-prelate as "the Marvell of those times . . . the first Presbyterian scribbler who sanctified libels and scurrility to the use of the Good Old Cause." [21] He evidently has in mind here Marvell's anti-Clarendon pieces written in the distressed period of recession and disillusion which followed Charles II's triumphant return. They were undoubtedly irksome to the author of a fervent panegyric to the Lord Chancellor; and there is no doubt that they mark a surrender, on Marvell's part, to the scurrilous lampoon level, the "Billingsgate," of the popular broadside. Moreover, Dryden's insistent and consistent neo-classical pursuit of "sublimity of the expression," "beautiful turns of words & thoughts" [22] led him to discountenance "points of wit, and quirks of epigram" [23] or the "jingle of a more poor *paronomasia*" [24] such as characterize the satire of Cleveland, or the early Marvell. Nevertheless, when Marvell recovered his emotional balance after the collapse of his republican enthusiasm, and encountered again an issue—toleration—important enough for him to deploy his most fanciful wit and his most serious irony in its service, the resulting polemic played an important part in the development of the Restoration's "sharp, well-manner'd way of laughing a folly out of countenance" which Dryden granted to be the "best and finest manner of satire." [25]

Certainly nowhere in the satire of the civil war and Commonwealth period, the period when Dryden concluded his studies at Cambridge and went to London to "set up for a poet," could he have found what he demanded: "the majesty of the heroic, finely mix'd with the venom of the other" [26] except in Milton (across the great gulf separating their temperaments, their aims and their views), in Cowley, and in Marvell.

[21] *Poetical Works*, ed. Noyes, p. 161.
[22] *Ibid.*, p. 319. ("Discourse Concerning Satire").
[23] *Ibid.*, p. 320.
[24] *Ibid.*, p. 25 (Preface to *Annus Mirabilis*).
[25] *Ibid.*, p. 318 ("Discourse Concerning Satire").
[26] *Ibid.*, p. 319.

CHAPTER THREE

"Crownes are for Hero's"

THE PROBLEM OF CROMWELL

THE PERIOD under consideration in these pages falls naturally into four divisions: the reign of the first Stuarts, the civil wars, the Commonwealth, and the Restoration. Each decade expresses itself characteristically in its state verse, which is, for the most part, formal, official, and declarative. While satire was the dominant mode of political verse during the civil war period, the writers of both the Commonwealth and the Restoration, as those of the Stuart regime preceding them, cast their public expressions of allegiance into the form of the panegyric. Or (it would perhaps be truer to say), in each case the party in power enlisted the panegyric in the campaign to mould public opinion, while the opposition had recourse to ballad and broadside [1] to carry on the guerrilla warfare, as it were, of the street; these were in popular lyric measures as opposed to the formal couplet.

Where, however, the task of the Caroline panegyrists had been, ideologically, relatively simple, the issues facing the panegyrist of the Commonwealth were considerably more complex and problematic. The former, whether he had adopted an approach which was ritualistic, or philosophical, or defensively polemical, could always assume his prince's status and virtues to be part of a divinely ordained order of nature and society. The latter had to face the problem created by the fact that his hero, Cromwell, was an overthrower of that order; and the public to whom he addressed himself, bred in a long tradition of horror at usurpation, was still nourished by

[1] Two good collections are W. W. Wilkins, *Political Ballads of the 17th and 18th Centuries* (1860), and C. Mackay, *The Cavalier Songs and Ballads of England from 1642–1684* (1863).

the unanimously monarchical verdict of the Jacobean drama concerning its ambitious villain politicians. Thus, when regarded as an usurper, the killer of the King, Cromwell's qualities of greatness, his "admirable circumspection and sagacity, . . . (his) most magnanimous resolution," as even Clarendon described them,[2] could not be taken for granted as natural attributes of the perfect Prince. History and world-order had to be re-interpreted in order to include Cromwell among its saints. The record of that emerging re-interpretation, one of the seventeenth century major shifts of public opinion and sentiment, can be read in the republican panegyric of the 1650's.

As the tide turned against the King, royalist panegyric took the form of elegy. But whether elegy or panegyric, the appeal was always to Divine Right and Charles' personal virtue. The republicans, the revolutionary party climbing to power, set against these, in Cromwell's defence, Divine Providence and success. To justify one's hero on the grounds of successful conquest, however, comes close to Machiavellianism as this was traditionally understood, and this charge could be circumvented only by insisting upon the supremacy of the divine plan in history over the accidents and rewards of mere fortune. The ideological problem centered therefore upon four key terms: the Prince, governor of the state and moulder of its destiny; Fortune or Chance, mutability in the nature of things; Virtue, the good and noble qualities by which the Prince's rule is justified; and *Virtu*, the innate power and capacity of a Prince to achieve and establish his rule. It had been for centuries observed that Fortune was often strangely inimical to virtuous princes, causing them inexplicably to fall; while conversely, the possessors of *virtu*, rising to power, often exhibited qualities diametrically opposed to the accepted ethical notions of virtue. Occasionally, happily, Providence had been known to enlist capricious Fortune in the task of punishing overweening *virtu* in a Prince. But could that same Providence, defender and supporter of virtue, be enlisted on the side of a would-be Prince bearing the unmistakable stigmata of an almost excessive, an "overreacher's" *virtu?*

[2] *Selections from Clarendon*, ed. G. Huehns (Oxford, 1955), p. 356.

The question at issue between Cavalier and Roundhead, then, was whether Cromwell was to be regarded as a figure of *virtu* ruthlessly climbing to power and favored by accidental collocations of events, or whether he was the epitome of a greater virtue than that possessed by the hereditary Prince, who held power by an accident of genetics. The royalist saw Charles, armed with Divine Right and dutiful virtue, facing in Cromwell an archetypal Machiavellian fortune-hunter; while the republican author of *Anglia Rediviva*,[3] for instance, categorically affirmed the moral primacy of the right of conquest over *jus divinus:*

> 'Tis *Fortune* to be Kings as others be,
> But onley *Virtue* to be one like thee.

Confirmation for either position could be sought only in a theory of history. History could be seen as cyclic and repetitive; perpetually lapsing, in this sublunary world, from ideal world order in which divinely established monarchy and divinely established virtue were one. Fortune's wheel, under Providence, is the medieval image for this theory of history. On the other hand, history can be seen as in some sense evolutionary, with Providence working through the unshaped dough of events like a yeast, upon the upsurge of which rides God's chosen paradigm, or agent. It will be clear that *virtu* can be vice (overweening ambition, resolution, prowess, etc.) in the first view, but may easily, issuing in successful achievement, be the very sign of the elect in the second.

It could have been at best only vaguely realized that the conflict outlined here is yet another aspect of the collision in European culture between the classical Greek and the Biblical Hebrew view of history. Yet it was of course the Old Testament reading Puritans who interpreted their history as the unfolding revelation of God's plan and purpose; and the classically educated Cavaliers who, as their sun sets, and even when it rises again, adopt the attitudes of a Stoic detachment or the varieties of Epicurean fatalism.

The panegyrics to be discussed in the following chapters

[3] See p. 84 ff. below.

illustrate the stresses and dilemmas of the time, and the range of positions taken up with regard to the Great Man of the age and his role in history. There was the more or less naïve extremist position of the totally committed on either side as well as the more or less sophisticated eclecticism of those who became aware of anomalies. While few at the time were capable of secularizing the idea of Providence into a formulated theory of historical or social forces determining the rise of men and the outcome of events, there is, in Marvell, at least, the beginning of a dialectical determinism which, through a new analysis of the nature and function of the republican leader, of authority vested not alone in personal power but in a collective public body, can reconcile the hero's personal significance and value with his historical instrumentality.

Providence and the Personal Heresy

For the confirmed royalist there was no ideological problem. Clarendon's "bad brave man" is the classical Cavalier verdict of the period upon Cromwell: "He was one of those men, *quos vituperare ne inimici quidem possunt, nisi ut simul laudent;* for he could never have done half that mischief without great parts of courage, industry and judgement. He must have had a wonderful understanding in the natures and humours of men, and as great a dexterity in applying them; who, from a private and obscure birth, (though of a good family,) without interest or estate, alliance or friendship, could raise himself to such a height, and compound and knead such opposite and contradictory tempers, humours, and interests into a consistence, that contributed to his designs, and to their own destruction; whilst himself grew insensibly powerful enough to cut off those by whom he had climbed. . . . Without doubt, no man with more wickedness ever attempted any thing, or brought to pass what he desired more wickedly, more in the face and contempt of religion, and moral honesty; Yet wickedness as great as his could never have accomplished those trophies, without the assistance of a great spirit. . . ." [4]

The vituperation is often far greater than the praise. Richard

[4] *Selections,* ed. Huehns, pp. 355–356.

III, Catiline, Satan himself are frequently enough coupled with his name. But generous or vituperative, the assessment is always, for the Cavalier, in the realm of morality and personality. That is to say, the great men of history, in this view, are genuine creators of events, innovators whose effect upon history cannot be derived, whether as symbol, expression, instrument, or consequence, from historical laws or the constellations of social forces in their day. And the Cavalier, even if uncensored, consequently tended to fall silent as he perceived the incompatibility between his derisive portrait of Red-Nosed Noll in the street ballads, and the all-too-powerful villain he conceived the protagonist of the times to be. To find the causes of events, under God, in the "natural" wickedness, ambition, pride and craft, or folly and levity, of the leading figures in those events, with the rabble behind them, was a view of history as normal to the traditionalist classically trained scholar or thinker of the Renaissance as it has been perhaps to the "common man" of any age, or to the propagandists of the party in violent opposition in any age, as they appeal to the sentiments of the "common man" for support.

On the other hand, it is equally natural to find the idea of divinely inspired and ordained mission fulfilling itself through the activities of an elect leader invoked by the revolutionary party as it rises to power. Thus the author of the tract *God's Unchangeableness*, 1655,[5] undertakes to "clearly demonstrate and prove, that Oliver Cromwell is by the Providence of God, Lord Protector of England, Scotland, Ireland, etc.": ". . . every mercy and every judgement is from God, ordered by him, and is not from men, whatsoever their designs are, or whatsoever they intend or aim at as their end, for all men good and bad are but Instruments in Gods hand, secondary causes, and can do nothing but what God by Providence leads them to do, or permits to be done to effect his own purpose and secret decree . . . not oppressing men, Nimrods of the earth, nor Satan himself can punish or afflict, till God will have them afflict, nor can continue the affliction either to a Nation or to a man, a day longer then the time God hath set. . . . This is

[5] G. Smith, *God's Unchangeableness* (London, 1655).

[78]

the man whom God by his secret Providence hath made the
instrument of our deliverance. . . . Whatsoever shall be are
not by accident, nor by the subtle contrivement or counsel of
men, but as all is ordered by Providence to effect God's will,
for man is not able of himself to bring any enterprise to
passe. . . ." [pp. 24, 29]

It will be noticed that these two extreme positions with regard to the responsibility for events are voiced by historians
—theoreticians, that is to say, whose concern for public opinion is, at the time of writing, remote. While the royalist view
of Cromwell as the wicked destroyer of his country need
undergo no modification as it passes from the privacy of manuscript to the publicity of broadsheet, the matter was far otherwise in the case of the republican apologist. God's providential
determinism seemed somewhat dry and abstract by comparison
with the theme of the gigantically wicked tyrant (counterpointed, as it were, at the level of the lampoon, by the ludicrous
Red-Nosed Brewer Noll), combined with the suffering martyred figure of Charles. The republican panegyrist must offer
an object to which sentiment might adhere, a person to be re-
vered and loyally followed. In *The Unparalleled Monarch, or,
the Portraiture of a Matchless Prince*, 1656, the outline of providential determinism is plain to be seen, but it is blended with the
desire to present for universal admiration an all-powerful hero.

"Every one of his actions have been ever full of miracle and
astonishment; every circumstance hath something in it of a
wonder and greatness; could they have been imagin'd and set
down in their colours before they became real, they would not
have seemed anything more than a meer illusion and fable, than
a Romance, and chimaera. . . .

". . . his very looks and countenance would command our
Allegiance, the very cast of his eye would sufficiently persuade
you, that his Authority is just and deserved, that it is a suitable
power, that it is the mind and very meaning of Providence, that
it is nothing more then God and nature intended, that he was
designed and cut out for our diadem. . . .

"The Idea and platform of all Royal performance cannot
better be drawn then by describing Him in his great Action

and Address. *Nature* hath done well for him, and Fortune (which is otherwise for the most part either counterfeit or foolish) in adopting Him her darling (if we may honour her to say it) hath now given a very strange president that she is both just and discreet." [6]

The author's ambiguous attitude to the idea of Fortune here is noteworthy. Capricious Fortune, the traditional enemy and snare of Virtue, whether Stoic or Christian, has shown herself, for once, on the side of the angels. Fortune *can* come under the aegis of Virtue, but only insofar as Virtue hesitates between its meaning as moral obedience to the will of God and its meaning as the Italian *virtu,* revived during the Renaissance, particularly in the drama, as the powerful and successful drive towards sovereign self-realization.

Machiavelli's own position, though cautious, is unmistakably towards a confirmation of the decisive role of heroic *virtu* in history. His letter to Soderini, *On Fortune and the Times,* attacks the doctrine, based on material familiar in medieval compilations on the Fall of Princes, that "the affairs of the world are so controlled by Fortune and the Divine Power that human wisdom and foresight cannot modify them." It is true, Machiavelli grants, that the hero, to be successful, must conform to the "spirit of the times"—a notion which he introduces as a mediating term between Fortune and the prince. There is no man so sagacious that he will *always* know how to do so, nor are there many men who readily deviate from the course to which their nature inclines them, or in which they have been previously successful. Nevertheless, given the requisite adaptability, a man may hope to master Fortune: ". . . and therefore, the cautious man, when it is time to turn adventurous, does not know how to do it, hence he is ruined; but had he changed his conduct with the times fortune would not have changed. I conclude therefore, that, fortune being changeful and mankind steadfast in their ways, so long as the two are in agreement men are successful, but unsuccessful when they fall out. For my part I consider that it is better to be adven-

[6] Anon, *The Unparalleled Monarch* (London, 1656), the Preface.

turous than cautious, because fortune is a woman, and if you wish to keep her under it is necessary to beat and ill-use her; and it is seen that she allows herself to be mastered by the adventurous rather than by those who go to work more coldly." [7] Thus Machiavelli, while making no overriding Carlylean claims for the effect of the Great Man upon history, sees Fortune—the concatenation of circumstances which the prince faces—as a woman, who *can* be mastered by *virtu* properly understood and practiced.

For Cromwell's panegyrists the question whether more credit for his greatness was due to Virtue or Fortune was a major crux. If Fortune is completely incorporated into the idea of Providence, as it is for the author of *God's Unchangeableness*, then no credit can be given to the hero's personal powers; and this is cold comfort for a hero-hungry populace. On the other hand, the more credit is given to personal prowess the more autonomous he becomes, the more a master of *virtu* (albeit, it is insisted, a "virtuous" *virtu*) dominating history. The panegyric appended to *The Unparalleled Monarch* makes the argument from Providence definitely secondary to the argument from heroic quality:

> Amidst the waves and raging billows tost
> Our broken ship was almost bulgd and lost
> But streight the trident held up in your hand
> The winds and seas obey your great Command . . .
> You save from judgments, save us from our crimes,
> The best of Princes in the worst of Times . . .
> Crownes are for Hero's, and the wise alone
> In factious states do best become the Throne . . .
> Such was your skill to solder and to heal
> A broken scepter and a broken weal.
> . . . the hand's the same and one
> That fixt the sun, and plact you in our throne.
> The Princely art and skill which you have shewn
> Is great enough to put the world in tune . . .

[7] Machiavelli, *The Prince*, Chap. xxv.

and it is not by chance that this eulogiser of "Princely art and skill" quotes Machiavelli as well as the hand that fixed the sun: "There is nothing (saith *Machiavel*) gives a *Prince* such repute as great exploits and rare trials of himself in heroick Actions. And tell me who can, did ever any man beat the paths of *Honour* and *Dignity* with more danger and hazard? who ever enjoyed the *Seat* of *Authority* with less ease and pomp?" [no sig.]

The republican, however, in principle was of course far from machiavellian; he was loth indeed to offer up on the altar of *virtu* the guiding hand of God. Just how difficult it was to reconcile the military valor and overmastering zeal of a hero who "holds the Fates fast bound in iron chains" with a Providence which orders all to the will of God, can be seen in the work of Thomas Manley. In the epistle dedicatory of *Veni; Vidi; Vici; The Triumphs of the Most Excellent and Illustrious, Oliver Cromwell . . . 1652,*[8] we are asked to consider how ". . . with more than *Herculean* strength he strook off the Head of the *Hydraes* of superstition with his Conquering Sword! How many *Centaures* breathing forth naught but slavery hath he tamed! How many Troopes of enraged enemies hath he overthrown, and offered them so humbled as so many satisfactory victims to the publike liberty;" [B 3v] as well as the proposition that "God alone is King of Kings, and Lord of Lords, . . . he *puts down Princes* from their Thrones, and disposes of the powers of the world after his own pleasure." [B 4v]

The panegyric which follows *Veni; Vidi; Vici*, however, records events with a different accent:

Thus happy *Cromwell*, daring greatest things,
Adds wounds to wounds, slaughters to slaughters brings;
Leaving the road, his *Sword* new wayes did hew
Through the base people, till a *conquest grew.* [p. 25]

A variety of famous classical conquering heroes are mentioned in order that the enthusiastic assertion of Cromwell's superiority over them all may be made:

[8] T. Manley, *Veni; Vidi; Vici;* (London, 1652).

"Crownes are for Hero's"

But you Great Sir, Greater than Caesar are,
The Empire of your Vertues reacheth far,
And keeping Passion, dost restrain
Its insolencies with the strongest rain . . .   [p. 72]

The poem would appear to have justified its invocation, and the ways of Cromwell to man:

Blest Hero, whose uprightness all commands,
Whose Joy in vertue more than Triumph stands, . . .
Thus doest thou valiant leader overthrow
Thine enemies, thy self thus conquer too.
Thy Countrey ownes thee as her Dearest *Son*,
Yet doth to thee as to a Father run.   [p. 11]

Manley indeed is unable to offer any reconciliation between the claims of providential determinism and the claims of an all-powerful prince, save an extreme eclecticism which in fact makes of the providential vocabulary he uses little more than a mask. In *To the Most Excellent, The Lord Generall of Great Brittayne, O.C.* printed in the same volume as *Veni; Vidi; Vici;* he says:

Tis not blind Fortune that attends
Vicissitudes of men, and things:
But heaven itself such changes brings;
Who gives and takes
Esteem from things, and makes
The smallest things grow great, and can
Change the renown of any man;
Though on a Throne today he sit on high,
Making his height upon the ground to lye.
Thou dost with meekness happy Guide,
The greatness of thy chance abide,
When formerly the war did grow,
By doubtful causes, hindred, slow,
Then there was need of you, great Sir, to lead.
In dangers by your humble prayer,

You move the Deity to hear,
Beloved Guardian sent us from on high,
Thus dost thou conquer even necessity.   [no sig.]

Heaven or the hero? It is truly difficult to decide which Manley meant. Despite appearances to the contrary, the moving power seems, after all, to be in the hero; for the gaining of heaven's alliance in the last four lines is really no more than the ultimate heroic attribute, if the humbling of the great by heaven is reserved, as it evidently is, for this great man's enemies alone.

The perplexity of the republican panegyrist is thus revealed, and matches that of the Cavalier satirist who wonders whether to aggrandize or deride the object of his attack. The republican's need for a saint is as great as his opponent's for a scapegoat; and he thus tends to fall into the personalist patterns of thinking of the monarchists themselves. Yet he does not wish to make the choice between usurper and king merely the choice of the greater over the lesser hero, for he is after all imbued with the sense of a Puritan mission which tells him that he is watching the revelation of God's purpose in the revolutionary historical events of his time. Accordingly, he finds that he must either extol the triumphant operations of Providence, working through Fortune, at the expense of his hero's personal powers; or Providence must become the mere footstool for a hero mightily endowed with *virtu*. If, moreover, he takes the latter course, he finds himself in an uncomfortably defensive position with regard to monarchical legitimacy. And it is this which accounts for the growing desire to prove Cromwell an eminently suitable *monarch* on the grounds that "Crownes are for hero's."

In *Anglia Rediviva . . . An Heroick Poem*, 1658,[9] the author's thesis, supported with traditional images from world order and the chain of being, is that monarchy is after all the proper form of government, and Cromwell the proper monarch. Reflection upon his career induces amazement and wonder:

[9] Anon, *Anglia Rediviva* (London, 1658).

[84]

"Crownes are for Hero's"

Never was greater resolution shown
(Cesars was Cesars but his own's his own)
With such celerity following victory
Such Vigor, such Impetuosity, . . .
Like Thunder or a threatning Ruine just
Falling o'th'foe, and crushing them to dust.

How one mans valor could alone suffice,
T'have gain'd so many mighty victories;
Or one mans wisdome could suffice alone,
So many mighty Affairs to have undergone . . . [p. 35]

He comes to the conclusion that

Whilst ours like an Intelligence in his sphere
Or orbe, doth everything, is everywhere,
Actuates, puts life in businesse, commands,
In Councell, is all head, in Act, all hands,
Perpetuall fast, perpetuall vigil keeps;
And when affaires exact, scarce eats or sleeps.
Tis Fortune to be Kings as other be,
But onely Virtue to be one like thee . . . [p. 20]
Never was any worthier th'esteem
Of being made for th'Crown, and th'Crown for him.
[p. 11]

This supreme virtue becomes itself an aspect of immutable natural order as had, once, the "good fortune" of primogeniture.

So having well resolved what to do,
As resolutely going through with't too,
He his conspicuous courses still holds on
Just as at midnight, the Celestial Moon,
Her constant motion ne're does intermit,
For all the midnight doggs that bark at it. [p. 43]

But if "crownes are for hero's," then the issue does after all become the choice of the greater over the lesser hero; and the result is an interesting seventeenth century version of the pattern of "personal heresy" made familiar through the recent history of Stalinism. The hero becomes the object of extravagant idolization, and the historic forces he once had been seen as representing and realizing disappear from view. Thus H. Dawbeny, in 1659, after the Protector's death, writes: "He was so much above the present pitch of men, that nothing but *Romance* can reach his Actions; and he as far surpassed all other princes of this later Age as any of those princes have outstript private persons. What panegyrick then can be too great for such a prince? What humane praise can ever amount to flattery? . . . he who shall take presumptuous pen in hand, or dare any other way undertake to give the World an exact Survey, of all the particular great dispensations, and Divine indulgences, vouchsafed to this high Favorite of Heaven, will quickly find himself overset in a Sea of Blisse . . . it being no lesse than impossible, as the curious in that Art inform us, to polish so much as the nailes of pieces of so great a Perfection." [10]

Providence here has dwindled to a kind of patron whose sole function is to dispense favors to her favorite. "Favour of Heaven" indeed, and "Good Fortune" are actually listed among the Thirty Degrees of princely perfection which constituted Cromwell's virtue and raised him to the height of honor; where "our second *Moses*, being mounted, as he was, to the highest pitch of Heroick Vertue, dispelled all opposition. Malice itself could neither find Bow nor Arrow to reach him; . . . so did all calumny crack itself before the truth of his vertue, which darted resplendent flashes into all eyes." [p. 79]

It is illuminating to list the moral qualities most often attributed by these later panegyrists to Cromwell. Though piety, or sanctity, or pious zeal are mentioned, for the most part the qualities which are dwelt upon—gallantry, magnificence, generalship, vigor, courage, vigilance, resolution, fortitude, quickness of mind, dexterity, prudence, and wisdom—constitute as standard an anatomy of *virtu*, classical or machiavellian, as one could find. The wheel has come full circle: virtue has become

[10] H. Dawbeny, Preface to *Historie and Policie Re-Viewed* (London, 1659).

virtu; might, right; and the prince, creator of his own circumstances, more powerful than history.

It is this view of Cromwell and his relation to events that Cowley sets out to refute in the *Vision* [11] with a deterministic theory of history of his own—deriving not, indeed, from republican convictions, but from a skepticism which had been growing steadily upon him since the writing of the Brutus ode.[12] The ironic encomium on *virtu* which he puts into the mouth of the "Protector" in the *Vision* is a clear and concise statement of the ethical issue as it was felt by an alert contemporary mind. The apparition of Cromwell, in the course of his debate with his interlocutor, Cowley, says:

"You seem to pretend extremely to the old obsolete rules of Virtue and Conscience, which makes me doubt very much whether from this vast prospect of three Kingdoms you can show me any acres of your own. . . . For this I perceive which you call Virtue, is nothing else but either the Frowardness of a Cynick, or the Laziness of an *Epicurean.* I am glad you allow me at least Artfull Dissimulation, and unwearied Diligence in my *Hero,* and I assure you that he whose Life is constantly drawn by these two, shall never be misled out of the way of Greatness. But I see you are a Pedant, and Platonical Statesman, a Theoretical Common-Wealth-Man, an Utopian Dreamer. Was ever Riches gotten by your Golden Mediocrities? or the Supreme place attained to by Virtues that must not stir out of the middle? Do you study *Aristotles* Politiques and write, if you please, Comments upon them, and let another but practise *Machiavil,* and let us see then which of you two will come to the greatest preferments. If the desire of rule and superiority be a Virtue (as sure I am it is more imprinted in human Nature than any of your Lethargical Morals; and what is the Virtue of any Creature, but the Exercise of those powers and Inclinations which God has infused into it?). . . ." [13]

[11] *A Discourse by Way of Vision,* Concerning the Government of Oliver Cromwell. Published anonymously in 1661, but written in part probably before.

[12] See Chapter 5 below, where Cowley's political writings and the development of his thought are treated in detail.

[13] In *Essays and Plays,* ed. A. R. Waller, pp. 372-373.

MILTON'S "DEFENSE
OF THE PEOPLE OF ENGLAND"

Of all Cromwell's panegyrists, few but Milton truly succeeded in treading the slippery path between emperor-worship
on the one hand and Calvinistic providentialism on the other.
Milton's view of Cromwell is unequivocally heroic, but distinguished from the pattern of apologetic in terms of heroic
virtu by his keen Puritan sense of providential purpose. Cromwell's career seen as proof of predetermined election to the
divine reforming mission combines with Milton's humanistic
preoccupation with the nature of the heroic spirit itself to produce a clearly formulated conception, not of heroic *virtu*,
but of heroic virtue, in which the whole people as well as its
great leader participate.

In the *Defensio Secunda* Cromwell is hailed as "the leader
of our councils, the general of our armies," and the saviour and
father of his country: ". . . this title do all good men hail you
with spontaneous voice sent forth from the heart. Other titles,
though merited by you, your actions know not, endure not;
. . . But though it can add nothing to dignity, yet as it is
expedient, for virtues even the most exalted to be finished and
terminated by a sort of human summit, which is counted
honour, you thought it right, and suffered yourself, for the
public benefit, to assume something like a title, resembling
most that of *pater patriae*, the father of your country; you
suffered yourself not to be raised indeed, but to descend so
many degrees from on high, and to be forced as it were into
the ranks; despising the name of king for majesty far more
majestic." [14] At the same time, the argument justifying power
by desert is given its maximum weight: "Cromwell, we are
deserted; you alone remain; the sovereign authority of the state
is returned into your hands, and subsists only in you. To your
invincible virtue we all give place . . . nothing in human society is more pleasing to God, or more agreeable to reason;
. . . there is nothing more just in a state, nothing more useful,

[14] "The Second Defense of the People of England," *The Works of
John Milton*, Vol. 8, ed. F. A. Patterson (New York, 1931), pp. 223, 225.

than that the most worthy should possess the sovereign power."
[p. 223]

If there is here a suspicion of polemical tight-rope walking
it may be accounted for perhaps by the heat of the debate, or
by the humanistic element in his thought which did not always coincide with his professed theology.[15] It is at all events
no more than a shadow of eclecticism upon a long and consistent defense of the *People* of England, the people whom
"of all governments a commonwealth aims most to make . . .
flourishing, virtuous, noble, and high-spirited . . . ," whom
monarchs would make "wealthy indeed perhaps, and well
fleeced, for their own shearing, and the supply of regal prodi-
gality; but otherwise softest, basest, viciousest, servilest, easiest
to be kept under. And not only in fleece, but in mind also
sheepishest. . . ."[16]

The republican vision is never lost in the enthusiasm for the
incomparable man. In the sonnet to Cromwell the balance between the great mission and the great missionary is kept true:

> Cromwell our chief of men, who through a cloud
> Not of warr onely, but detractions rude,
> Guided by faith & matchless Fortitude
> To peace & truth thy glorious way hast plough'd,
> And on the neck of crowned Fortune proud
> Hast reard Gods Trophies, & his work pursu'd. . . .[17]

If "faith" can be said to belong to virtue, and "fortitude" to
virtu, the syntax of the line subordinates the morally neutral
quality of fortitude to faith; while in the last two lines, with
their magnificent image of King Fortune cowed before God's
Trophies, the panegyric is purged, as it were, of the least dross
of worship accorded to the creature rather than the Creator.

It is significant that Milton reiterates the dialectical opposition between crowned Fortune and God's own Commonwealth

---

[15] Zvi Werblowsky, *Lucifer and Prometheus* (London, 1952), has revealed a similar pattern of conflict between the "Hellenic" and the
"Hebraic" attitudes in *Paradise Lost.*

[16] "The Ready and Easy Way to Establish a Free Commonwealth,"
1659, *The Works of John Milton*, Vol. 6, p. 111.

[17] *Ibid.*, Vol. 1, part 1, p. 65.

in the *Ready and Easy Way*, in the unexpected context of a rejection of partial rotation of members of Parliament: "But I could wish that this wheel or partial wheel in State, if it be possible, might be avoided, as having too much affinitie with the wheel of fortune . . . what can be expected firm or stedfast from a floating foundation? . . . Kingship it self is therefore counted the more safe and durable because the king and, for the most part, his council, is not changed during life: but a Commonwealth is held immortal, and therein firmest, safest and most above fortune: for the death of a king, causeth ofttimes many dangerous alterations; but the death now and then of a Senator is not felt; . . . I denie not but that ther may be such a king, who may regard the common good before his own, may have no vitious favourite, may hearken only to the wisest and incorruptest of his Parliament: but this rarely happens in a monarchie not elective; and it behoves not a wise nation to committ the summ of their well-being, the whole state of thir safetie to fortune." [Vol. 6, pp. 127, 135.]

The nature of the Creator's work which is to be pursued is given its clearest and most fervent delineation in the long peroration to the *Second Defense:* "And as for you, citizens, it is of no small concern, what manner of men ye are, whether to acquire, or to keep possession of your liberty. . . . Unless you banish avarice, ambition, luxury from your thoughts, and all excess even from your families, the tyrant, whom you imagined was to be sought abroad, and in the field, you will find at home, you will find within, and that a more inexorable one; yea, tyrants without number will be daily engendered in your own breasts . . . if it be against the grain, to be slaves, learn to obey right reason, to be masters of yourselves; in fine, keep aloof from factions, hatreds, superstitions, injuries, lusts, and plunders." [Vol. 8, pp. 239, 251]

Not sovereignty, therefore, is the end of heroic action, but that empire of reason and faith which is to be realized in and through the free will of a whole people, a noble and puissant nation, released from the fetters of authority to govern itself in the sight of God. And the heroic quality in Cromwell is just that which makes him the supreme representative of these forces of inward liberation. Hence the solemn warning addressed to Cromwell: "But if the patron himself of liberty, and as it were, her tutelary genius—if he, than whom none is esteemed a more just, a holier, or a better man, should at last offer violence to her whom he has defended, this must, of necessity, be destructive and deadly not to himself alone, but, in a manner, to the very cause of all virtue and piety. Honour and virtue themselves will appear to have faded away; henceforward, religious faith will be narrowed; reputation will be a poor thing indeed; and a deeper wound than this, after that first, it would not be possible to inflict upon human kind." [Vol. 8, p. 227]

Thus it would seem true to see in Milton's enthusiasm for Cromwell as hero a particular application of his abiding concern with the nature of heroic reformation.[18] When he finds, therefore, that the ultimately heroic resides in self-conquest, self-dedication, it is not the regular, classical control of self traditionally attributed to *virtu*, but the self-abnegation of an ideal and representative leader of a people. It is a strenuous and prophetic conception of the heroic, and one which can spring only from faith in a purpose in history beyond the rise and fall of dynasties: "You have taken upon you by far the heaviest burden, which will try you thoroughly; it will search you through and through, and lay open your inmost soul; it will show what is the predominant disposition of your nature, what is your strength, what is your weight; whether there is indeed in you that living piety, that faith, justice, and moderation of mind, for which we have thought that you above all others deserved, by the will of God, to be elevated to this sovereign dignity." [Vol. 8, p. 228–229]

Among Milton's contemporaries, only his secretary, Andrew Marvell, whose *Horatian Ode* in fact precedes the two *Defenses,* was capable of articulating with equal clarity a com-

---

[18] Frank Kermode has analyzed "Milton's Hero" in *RES.*, Vol. IV (1953). Further discussion is to be found in M. Y. Hughes, "The Christ of *Paradise Regained* and the Renaissance Heroic Tradition," *SP.*, Vol. XXXV (1938); and in E. Pope, *The Tradition and the Poem* (Baltimore, 1947).

parable sense of the momentous in history and a similar vision of the subordination of the personal insight and resolution of the leader to the appointed end of his heroic action—that end which is not a royal, but a "civicke" crown.

CHAPTER FOUR

"If these the Times, then this must be the Man"

HISTORY AS PROCESS

IF THE impact of the career of Cromwell upon the convinced Roundhead was complex, how much more so was it upon the more detached, or uncommitted, or moderate minds of the age. As late as 1659, Richard Flecknoe reveals, with unwitting clarity, the bewilderment still induced by the attempt to assess the role of the Protector and its significance. In *The Idea of His Highness Oliver, Late Lord Protector* [1] the traditional terms Virtue and Fortune serve to define for Flecknoe the question which puzzles him: whether the power to effect mutations in history truly belongs to the hero, or to that mysterious concatenation of accidents in things over which there is no control. In Flecknoe's own phrase: Whether "Fortune or Vertue had had the greatest share in all his Actions. . . ."

"But whether the Stars command us, or we command the Stars, may be a probleme, as well as whether the *Suns* motion or *Earths* occasions our dayly revolutions. Certain it is, he had such a commanding *Genius* as by gentle force made everyone obey; nor did he ever finde difficulty or opposition, that by avoiding or incountring he did not overcome. [p. 51]

"That he should finde the wheel of things in so vehement commotion was *Fortune* ('tis true) but that (once mounted to the top) he should stop, and fix it so suddainly as he did, appears the work of some more than human hand; so that he should finde the Body and Frame o'th'State all shatter'd in

---

[1] London (1659). The rarest of Flecknoe's pieces, probably suppressed at the Restoration.

pieces, and those pieces all scatter'd about, was Fortune too, but to recollect all those scatter'd pieces, and compose them all into one intire body and frame, was such a masterpiece as none but so great a Master could ever have perform'd. . . ." [p. 53]

"Thus have we . . . by brief glimpses and reflexions given light to see how great a person he was, no humain body being scarcely capable of a greater Soul; how fortune and vertue, never more concurr'd to the advancement of a man; how never any past to the temple of honor by more directer ways, through that of his own vertue and Heroick deeds. . . ." [p. 68]

Flecknoe, it seems, despite a certain hesitation, chooses the heroic view of Cromwell's career. His hesitation vanishes in the *Heroick Portraits* of 1660 where the portrait of Cromwell is recast in accordance with royalist requirements, and the problem solved through the conception of *virtu* which defined the machiavellian Cromwell of the royalist imagination: "For the rest, he was of strong and able parts, and if ever any was Artificer of his own Fortune, it was he: valiant of his person, but never using force, when stratagem would suffice: bold and resolute and what he once to do, none could hinder him from doing it; nor ever met he with any obstacle, but by force or sleight he would remove it straight. . . ." [2]

However, Flecknoe finally apportions credit for Cromwell's actions, and however that "credit" is interpreted, it is clear that in the passages quoted his mind is fixed within the classical frame of reference. He has "the ancient's way of viewing things; it does not see forces, it sees virtues and vices, successes and mistakes" as creators of history.[3] What is significant in his *Idea*, however, is the occasional intimation, as he grapples with the apparent mutual exclusiveness of the two causes, Virtue and Fortune, of a third, a larger category, which will transcend them. "His minde," he says at one point, "was too great and high to be contain'd within the narrow limits of his Estate; but

---

[2] London (1660), H v.
[3] Erich Auerbach, in *Mimesis,* analyzes most profoundly the effect of ways of viewing history upon the representation of reality in Western literature.

it was still breaking forth, till the same Fortune or better Providence provided him with an Estate (at last) proportionable to the greatness of his minde. . . ." [p. 8] "Providence," however, the idea of a divine plan, cannot carry conviction for Flecknoe as it could for the devout republican. We come nearer to his own account of the causes and complexities of events in the following passage: ". . . all things in this world being in perpetual revolution, tis impossible from the beginning to see the end of things; besides, that which is ones end, is but anothers meanes to the attaining his: Onely, there are certain *periods* of things, and who has the carrying of them on when they are next that *period*, is alwayes accounted most happy and fortunate." [p. 19]

I have quoted Flecknoe at some length here not for any intrinsic merit in his contribution, but because of the interest to be derived from a work which stands, as it were, at the very point of emergence of a new idea. In *The Idea of His Highness* we watch the emergence of the conception of "forces" in history from within the old framework of "virtues and vices, successes and mistakes."

The next two chapters will deal with the work of two poets, each of whom, in his own way, hammers out a new and personal evaluation of the great mutation of his time. Both Andrew Marvell and Abraham Cowley are poets of no mean stature; and Marvell was possessed of remarkable subtlety and sensibility. Thus their response to the experience of their time is marked by a greater precision and depth of implication than any we have hitherto encountered; and the range and delicacy of discrimination which informs their historical judgment is unusually great.

While the one is a royalist turned republican, and the other, except for a period of "enthusiasm," a loyal Cavalier, both find their views settling into deterministic patterns which nevertheless find room for heroic endeavour, however differently this may be interpreted by each. Both are aware of the relativity of character and action to social structure, and both are concerned to give the old abstractions, Virtue and Fortune, a more precise and meaningful content. It is worth noticing how full were the years of their most intense activity, the years of the interregnum, of intuitions of a social-deterministic, "materialist" kind in various fields of political and literary thought. One remembers Hobbes's explanation (undreamed of by a Renaissance critic like Puttenham, for instance), of the origin of the "kindes" according to the three regions of poetry—Court, City, and Country—each of which produces, by virtue of its material nature, its proper kind: Epic and Tragedy, Comedy and Satire, and Pastoral, respectively.[4] Or there is Harrington's original analysis of political history and government in terms of land-ownership: "As is the proportion or balance of Dominion or property in land, such is the nature of the Empire." [5] Cowley was associated with Hobbes during the exile of the court; Harrington was a close friend of Marvell. *Oceana*, indeed, was generally influential, and the name of its imaginary republic much used in republican polemic.

Thus the crucial idea of "period" adumbrated by Flecknoe is one of many contemporary attempts to seek beyond the traditional notions of history (as perennial rise and fall external to the fixed and immutable structure of society and morality) towards the notion of a cause of events in dynamic movements within society, within history itself. We watch, in the work of Marvell and Cowley, the birth of this new conception—the emergence of what is, in fact, the modern, post-Romantic conception of history. Hesitant and still vaguely outlined though it may be, it stands squarely opposed to the Medieval and Renaissance view of history as illustration, a mirror for magistrates, a collection of moral exempla, eternally valid for the present as for the past. What the eruption of Cromwell, and the consequent turmoil and mutation in the body politic precipitates is the idea of history *as process.* "Period" may involve the idea of the tidal or cyclic, as it came to do for Cowley; and social determinism served him to refute, rather than to affirm, the Protector's "prodigious merits" as a catalytic agent in history. For Marvell, on the other side, through the republican

---

[4] "Answer to the Preface to Gondibert," in Spingarn, p. 55.
[5] *Oceana* (1656).

idea which inflamed his imagination, the historical and social dynamic was seen to be on the point of culmination in an almost messianic *"Clymacterick."* [6] The idea, at all events, is portentous, and the full weight of it is expressed in the assertion which heads this chapter: "If these the Times, then this must be the Man." [7]

MARVELL'S "HORATIAN ODE" [8]

The poem is well known and has been much analyzed. Though most critics agree in their recognition of the poem's complexity and irony, there are considerable divergences as to its final bearing. Margoliouth, discussing George Clarke's attribution of *An Elegy on the Death of my Lord Francis Villiers* to Marvell, comes to the conclusion that, if it is his, this "one unequivocally royalist utterance . . . throws into strong relief the transitional character of *An Horatian Ode* where royalist principles and admiration for Cromwell the Great Man exist side by side." [9] Ruth Wallerstein [10] disagrees with Muriel Bradbrook's [11] Hegelian interpretation, on the grounds that such a reading is not consistent with seventeenth century rhetorical conceptions, and finds in the poem an unresolved conflict of feeling: a turning away, under the stress of anxiety and the hunger for order, from the older loyalties which had been expressed or hinted at in the Lovelace and Hastings poems, and in *Tom May's Death*. Cleanth Brooks [12] analyzes the ironies, and finds that Marvell is seeking in a "unified total and complex attitude" to find a meaningful and responsible relationship between the praiseworthy elements of both sides in the conflict. Recently the Hegelian theme has been taken up again by L. D.

[6] "An Horatian Ode" (1650), l. 104.
[7] "The First Anniversary" (1655), l. 144.
[8] "An Horatian Ode Upon Cromwell's Return from Ireland" (1650). Problems of dating are dealt with by Margoliouth in his definitive edition of *The Poems*, Vol. I (Oxford, 1927).
[9] Margoliouth, p. 334.
[10] *Studies in Seventeenth Century Poetic* (Wisconsin, 1950).
[11] M. C. Bradbrook and M. G. Lloyd-Thomas, *Andrew Marvell* (Cambridge, 1940).
[12] *Sewanee Review*, Vol. LXI (1953), p. 129.

Lerner [13] once more with a stress upon ironies, Mr. Lerner finds the explanation and the resolution of these ironies in a near-Marxist acceptance by Marvell of Cromwell as a "revolutionary force, destroying the order of things but ultimately produced by that order." "The previous state of society," contends Mr. Lerner, "has thrown up a force that disrupts, not gradually, but suddenly; . . . the contrast ancient Rights/greater Spirits is satisfactorily Marxist, so is the recognition that justice rests on power. All that is missing is the recognition of an ultimately economic source of the apparently military power."

Though there are indeed illuminating parallels to be drawn between Marvell's Cromwell, who "does both act and know," and the Plekhanovian hero, whose "free" power to initiate events is inherent in his recognition of, and obedience to, historical necessity, it is none the less as unhistorical to attribute any kind of formal Marxist categories to a seventeenth century mind as it is misleading to apply such categories to the interpretation of a seventeenth century poem. Nor do the alternative readings, "transition," "unresolved conflict," "inclusive attitude," quite seem to fit the case, suggestive and acute as the comment accompanying them is. Placed in its proper context—that of contemporary panegyric and the contemporary preoccupation with the problem of history and the hero—the *Horatian Ode*, the first of the Cromwellian poems, will be seen to be both more simple and more central, and also, perhaps more satisfactory, than is often acknowledged.

The poem, then, in the last analysis, is a most scrupulous record of a profound mind comprehending to the full the fact of social revolution. It is Cromwell who has precipitated in that mind, formerly reserved and fastidious towards the popular upsurge and turmoil in the depths of its society, the conviction of a purposeful and providential direction in events. And thus the salient feature of the panegyric, from its opening in an analysis of the "now"—the particular moment of history with which he deals, to its end in an invocation of the future—is an

[13] *Mandrake*, Vol. II (1954-1955). Reprinted in *Interpretation*, ed. John Wain (London, 1955).

overwhelming sense of the significance of the historical moment.

The poem turns upon this sense of history and of man's (Cromwell's or citizen's) right relation to it.[14] The sense is that of a moment in time which is portentous, big with the future, crucial—hence, for "forward" spirits " 'Tis time to leave the Books in dust," as Cromwell left his Bergamot; hence the rich ambiguity of "restless" in

> So restless *Cromwel* could not cease
> In the inglorious Arts of Peace . . . [l. 9]

where the restlessness, both in the sense of "ever-seeking" and in the sense of "indefatigable," is made a necessary consequence of the times; and hence the all-but-awed insistence upon the magnitude, significance, and audacity of Cromwell's masterrole: Cromwell who

> Could by industrious Valour climbe
> To ruine the great Work of Time,
> And cast the Kingdome old
> Into another Mold. [l. 33]

The point is made again and more explicitly in *The First Anniversary*, 1655:

> And well he therefore does, and well has guest,
> Who in his Age has always forward prest:
> And knowing not where Heavens choice may light,
> Girds yet his Sword, and ready stands to fight . . .
> [l. 145]

In the *Anniversary*, too, the apocalyptic relation of the hero to time is clarified in terms parallel to "the great Work of Time" and the casting into "another Mold":

> Like the vain Curlings of the Watry maze,
> Which in smooth streams a sinking Weight does raise;
> So man, declining always, disappears

[14] For a similar sense of historical destiny, of personal "calling" in this case, one might compare Milton's Sonnet on "that same lot . . . towards which Time leads me, and the will of Heaven."

In the weak Circles of increasing Years;
And his short Tumults of themselves Compose,
While flowing Time above his Head does close.
Cromwell alone with greater Vigour runs,
(Sun-like) the Stages of succeeding Suns:
And still the Day which he doth next restore,
Is the just Wonder of the Day before.
Cromwell alone doth with new Lustre spring,
And shines the Jewel of the yearly Ring.
'Tis he the force of scatter'd Time contracts,
And in one Year the work of Ages acts . . . [l. 1]

What we have here indeed is Marvell's version of the doctrine "Crownes are for Hero's." In *An Horatian Ode:*

Though Justice against Fate complain,
And plead the antient Rights in vain:
But those do hold or break
As Men are strong or weak.
Nature that hateth emptiness,
Allows of penetration less:
And therefore must make room
Where greater Spirits come. [l. 37]

Moreover, the virtues which distinguish the Cromwell of the first part, at least, of the Ode are familiar to us as *virtu:* valor, industry, resolution, subtle wisdom, or cunning, austere self-discipline. But nevertheless it is *Marvell's* version; it is important to see how deeply the conception of the conquering hero is informed and modified by the definitions of a specific historical context.

The description of Caesar in Tom May's translation, 1627, of Lucan's *Pharsalia* illuminates this point particularly, since verbal resemblances make it clear that Marvell had the passage in mind when he composed the Ode. Lucan's description is of the classic conquering hero of epic quality, arbitrary action, and simple motivation:

But restlesse valour, and in warre a shame
Not to be Conquerour; fierce, not curb'd at all,

Ready to fight, where hope, or anger call
His forward Sword; confident of successe,
And bold the favour of the gods to presse:
Orethrowing all that his ambition stay,
And loves that ruine should enforce his way;
As lightning by the winde forc'd from a cloude
Breakes through the wounded aire with thunder loud,
Disturbes the Day, the people terrifyes,
And by a light oblique dazels our eyes,
Not *Joves* own Temple spares it; when no force,
No barre can hinder his prevailing course,
Great waste, as foorth it sallyes and retires,
It makes and gathers his dispersed fires.[15]

Marvell's version is subtly modified, through the fork'd
lightning image with its progression from merely natural force
to divine instrument, and through the active star image which
fuses the two traditional sources of mutations in history—
Virtue and Fortune—in one controlling and transcendent act.
The poem is thus neither simply a paean to republican Providence nor to the individual heroic role, which Marvell will not
let us forget. The idea which emerges is of a providentially
directed human agency.

> So restless *Cromwel* could not cease
> In the inglorious Arts of Peace,
>   But through adventrous War
>   Urged his active Star.
> And, like the three-fork'd lightning, first
> Breaking the Clouds where it was nurst,
>   Did thorough his own Side
>   His fiery way divide . . .
> Then burning through the Air he went,
> And Pallaces and Temples rent:
>   And *Caesars* head at last
>   Did through his Laurels blast.
> 'Tis Madness to resist or blame
> The force of angry Heavens flame:

[15] See Margoliouth, p. 237.

And, if we would speak true,
Much to the Man is due . . .   [l. 9]

The final couplet is the more effective for the tone of consideration, the unemphatic but insistent precision. The remark forms
the transition from the forked lightning passage to the account
of Cromwell's progress from private garden to triumphant
power. Alone among republican pieces the *Ode* keeps in perfect balance the decisively heroic nature of the agent and the
transcendant nature of his agency. Ripeness is all; it is the
ripeness of the hero and his times, or, to put it more clearly, the
hero's knowledge of the meaning and direction of emergent
history, which turns a random, classical *virtu* into a messianic
election.[16]

So much one Man can do,
That does both act and know.   [l. 75]

It is the knowing, the knowing of ends, which gives to Marvell's
version of "Crownes are for Hero's" its seriousness and its
morality—as opposed to the abdication of morality in a pure
might-is-right doctrine. He bows before the inevitable ruinous,
rending power; there is no room in Nature for the Ancient
Rights and the Greater Spirits simultaneously; but the source
of the power is not presented as the arbitrary cruelty of a
natural law, but as a divinely sanctioned necessity. And this
idea—that it is a final cause, a millennial task,[17] to which this
greater spirit climbs—is prepared for through the placing of
Cromwell's activities in a perspective of historical change. One
of the most significant points in the poem is the transition from
the execution of the King to Cromwell's triumph. It is the
point at which the poem turns from recounting the immediate
past to an assessment of the present and a prophecy for the
future, and the transition is marked by the near repetition of a
phrase:

[16] Cromwell is "th'Elected" in "The First Anniversary."
[17] It is worth remembering that Marvell's poem was written in the
period which witnessed not only the expectation of Christ's Kingdom
come by the Saints in England, but also the Messianism of Shabtai Zvi
in Europe. Latter-day excitement ran high, through many channels, and
could not but have affected an "amphibian" like Marvell.

> He nothing common did or mean
> Upon that memorable Scene: . . . [l. 57]

> This was that memorable Hour
> Which first assur'd the forced Pow'r . . . [l. 65]

Nothing could bring out more strongly Marvell's sense of the historically dynamic in Cromwell's career than this exchange of the static, spatial "scene," for the dynamic, temporal "hour."

The two passages are significant in another way as well. They bring to a point of maximum clarity the great central tug-of-war in the poem, source of all the implications, ambiguities, and reservations, in fact, which inform Marvell's account of the great man of his age. For, that the election and the task, the rearing of God's trophies upon crowned Fortune's neck, as Milton was two years later to put it,[18] is a demanding undertaking, for which a high price has to be paid, no one was better qualified than Marvell to perceive; no one discussed in these pages was more conscious of the high cost of the "clymacterick" in history, because no one was more aware, or more sensitive, a product of the civilization that was about to be replaced. What is interesting is the degree of his consciousness of this high cost, the profoundly deterministic terms in which he casts his analysis, and the prophetic republican nature of his resolution.

It was Cowley who, in the preface to his poems wrote: ". . . a warlike, various, and a tragical age is best to *write of*, but worst to *write in*. . . . There is nothing that requires so much serenity and chearfulness of *Spirit*; it must not be either overwhelmed with the cares of *Life*, or overcast with the *Clouds of Melancholy* and *Sorrow*, or shaken and disturbed with the storms of injurious *Fortune*; it must, like the *Halcyon*, have *fair weather* to breed in. The *Soul* must be filled with bright and delightful *Idàea's*, when it undertakes to communicate delight to others, . . . So that 'tis almost as hard a thing to be a *Poet* in despight of *Fortune*, as it is in despight of *Nature*." [19]

[18] Sonnet to Cromwell (1652).
[19] Preface to *Poems* (1656), in Spingarn, Vol. II, p. 80.

It is with a sense almost of an antiphonal contrast that, with such a passage in mind, we re-read the opening of the *Ode:*

> The forward Youth that would appear
> Must now forsake his *Muses* dear,
> Nor in the Shadows sing
> His Numbers languishing.
> 'Tis time to leave the Books in dust,
> And oyl th'unused Armours rust:
> Removing from the Wall
> The Corselet of the Hall.   [l. 1]

The shadow of regret that lies upon these lines is counter-balanced both by "languishing" with its suggestion of indolence, and by "the Hall," evoking memories of a martial way of life which has been nevertheless a source of liberal culture.[20] This regret, this nostalgia for a more gracious and individualistic past which he shares with Cowley, has a natural history in Marvell's own previous analysis of their "warlike, various, and tragical age." "Our times," he writes to Lovelace,[21]

> are much degenerate from those
> Which your sweet Muse which your fair Fortune chose,
> And as complexions alter with the Climes,
> Our wits have drawne th'infection of our times.
> That candid Age no other way could tell
> To be ingenious, but by speaking well. . . .
> These vertues now are banisht out of Towne,
> Our Civill Wars have lost the Civicke crowne. . . .
> The Ayre's already tainted with the swarms
> Of Insects which against you rise in arms.
> Word-peckers, Paper-rats, Book-scorpions,
> Of wit corrupted, the unfashion'd Sons.
> The barbed Censurers begin to looke
> Like the grim consistory on thy Booke;
> And on each line cast a reforming eye,
> Severer then the yong Presbytery . . .   [l. 1]

[20] J. F. Danby gives an excellent account of the civilizing values of the "Great House" in *Poets on Fortune's Hill* (London, 1952).

[21] "To his Noble Friend, Mr. Richard Lovelace, upon his Poems." Printed in the 1st edn. of *Lucasta* (1649).

And again, in *Upon the Death of the Lord Hastings*,[22] he sums up, in one witty image, all the distaste and contempt felt by the inheritor of a high and liberal civility for the confining austerities of revolutionary Puritanism:

> Had he but at this Measure still increast,
> And on the *Tree of Life* once made a Feast,
> As that of *Knowledge;* what Loves had he given
> To Earth, and then what Jealousies to Heaven!
> But 't is a *Maxime* of that State, That none,
> Lest he become like Them, taste more then one.
> Therefore the *Democratick* Stars did rise,
> And all that Worth from hence did *Ostracize.* [l. 19]

The opposition felt by both Marvell and Cowley reflects the major social and political conflict of the time—that for which the closing of the by now predominantly courtly theatres by a Puritan parliament may serve as a convenient symbol. Marvell's terms generalize the issue and define the antagonistic values: the Muses, standing for the cultivation of the arts and graces of civilization, free individualistic "wit" and aesthetic values; against the "unfashion'd Sons" of the illiberal, ideological, "democratic" new age.[23]

The "unfashion'd Sons" appear in the *Ode.* They are the armed bands who clap their bloody hands; they bear the same relation to the scene they witness as an audience at a theatre; and like an audience they are partly responsible, by virtue of their demand and their participation, for the grim spectacle they watch—the spectacle of a king's exit from history. The Muses too, are present—in the formal but instinctive nobility with which the Royal Actor makes his abdication:

[22] Printed in *Lachrymae Musarum* (1649).
[23] Lionel Trilling has recently described F. R. Leavis as a latter-day Cromwellian for his insistence upon "tension, organized consciousness and moral direction" as against the qualities of "excess, performance, virtuosity, the delight of the mind in itself and the game of freedom from law and order" (*A Gathering of Fugitives*, Boston, 1956, p. 104). This twentieth century analysis of Puritanism aptly accords with Marvell's perceptions. It derives, of course, from Matthew Arnold's distinction between Hellenic spontaneity of consciousness and Hebraic strictness of conscience.

> *He* nothing common did or mean
> Upon that memorable Scene:
> But with his keener Eye
> The Axes edge did try:
> Nor call'd the *Gods* with vulgar spight
> To vindicate his helpless Right,
> But bow'd his comely Head,
> Down as upon a Bed. [l. 57]

Thus Cromwell's irresistible lightning flashes across a world which is ordered by the traditional, perennial attitudes of aristocracy towards the common multitude; and it is the particular virtue of the *Horatian Ode* that Marvell can present with such scrupulous and concrete objectivity, with such simultaneity, the conflicting sets of values which could issue in a view either of providential hero or of upstart usurper. The result is that the figures of Charles and Cromwell in the *Ode* are no longer set one against the other as rightful king and ambitious usurper, or as disabled king and mighty hero. They become more universal antagonists: the impotent grace of an ancient and noble civilization, on the one hand, against the ruthless idealism and sacrifice of a social revolutionary force on the other.

If the first part of the poem presents the dialectical relation between "nothing common or mean" and "forced Power," it is the latter part that presents the acceptance, the resolution, and the prophecy, though these have been prepared for from the beginning. For it is the conception of the "forward Youth" in the very first line which has enabled Marvell's thought to transcend the opposition between the Muses and the unfashion'd Sons. The forward youth, in effect, is he who is aware of history as consequent not upon the "virtues and vices, successes and mistakes" of its ruling figures, but upon the movement of great inner forces:

> And well he therefore does, and well has guest,
> Who in his Age has always forward prest:
> And knowing not where Heavens choice may light,
> Girds yet his Sword, and ready stands to fight . . .[24]

[24] "The First Anniversary," l. 145.

It is through the mediation of such a conception that the modern republican idea can come to birth at all. It is only when the plebeian rabble becomes the "Publick" that it can be taken seriously enough to become the bearer of a new order. It is because this has happened in the *Ode* that the lines

> He to the *Commons Feet* presents
> A *Kingdome*, for his first years rents.
> And, what he may, forbears
> His Fame to make it theirs:
>
> And has his Sword and Spoyls ungirt,
> To lay them at the *Publick's* skirt . . . [l. 85]

are not utterly ridiculous, as they might easily be in the older view. Marvell has reinterpreted his "Civicke crowne." It is no longer, as it were, the bloom upon the face of privilege, but the mark of one of whom the following can be said:

> Nor yet grown stiffer with Command,
> But still in the *Republick's* hand:
> How fit he is to sway
> That can so well obey. [l. 82]

The turning point of the poem is the acceptance of a bleeding head at the base of the new structure:

> So when they did design
> The *Capitols* first Line,
> A bleeding Head where they begun,
> Did fright the Architects to run;
> And yet in that the *State*
> Foresaw it's happy Fate. [l. 67]

It will be clear from this reading that I do not find "Foresaw it's happy Fate" [25] ironic; nor do I think it historically likely that it should be so, in 1650, no matter how prescient the author. What applies to this line applies also to the "Nor

[25] L. Lerner, in the article cited, suggests that it might be; Cleanth Brooks also refers to the "sinister" implications of ll. 82–83, as well as of such words as "restless," "forward," "climb" etc. (*loc. cit.*).

yet . . ." and to the "But still . . ." in the lines quoted above: reservation, or rather a wise knowledge of fallibility, of the possible transformation of republican virtue into ambitious self-regarding *virtu*. Thus, as the "lightning" series forms the main operative image in the first part, so the "falcon" image conveys in the latter part the taming, disciplining, and controlling of the great power of leadership through obedience to an idea and a mission greater than itself. Milton too insisted upon the "sifting and winnowing" of motive and action to be undergone by the republican hero in the performance of his appointed task. Marvell treats the bridling of power emblematically:

> So when the Falcon high
> Falls heavy from the Sky,
> She, having kill'd, no more does search,
> But on the next green Bow to pearch;
> Where, when he first does lure,
> The Falckner has her sure.   [l. 91] [26]

And now the exhortation, which has been found puzzling, falls perfectly into place, as a solemn and prophetic admonition to the chief executive of revolution:

> But thou the Wars and Fortunes Son
> March indefatigably on;
> And for the last effect
> Still keep thy Sword erect:
> Besides the force it has to fright
> The Spirits of the shady Night,
> The same *Arts* that did *gain*
> A *Pow'r* must it *maintain*.   [l. 113]

An erect sword forms the shape of a cross; the ambiguity of the lines is of the same kind as that of "Urged his active Star": an identification in one comprehensive act of the mind, of the heroic power and its controlling destiny. The meaning of the last quatrain, which has been found difficult, would seem to lie in the relation between the charismatic power of the cross, and

[26] It is not without significance that Marvell's word "green," so often expressive for him of harmonious fulfilment or security, appears here.

the creative power of the sword-cross in the hands of the revolutionary hero. A parallel relation, this time between mundane origin and transcendental end, is implied in "Thou the Wars and Fortunes Son" as against "for the last effect. . . ." There is a very rich ambiguity in the word "Arts," glancing as it does both at the Muses and at Machiavellian "policy," while its meaning in context is the state-craft of a dedicated virtue. This is the "wish'd conjuncture" of "high Grace with highest Pow'r," power constantly chastened by awareness of the final cause, the mysterious work, the latest and blest day.

"THE FIRST ANNIVERSARY"—A REPUBLICAN MANIFESTO

The best gloss upon the *Horatian Ode* is Marvell's own later *First Anniversary:*

> Hence oft I think, if in some happy Hour
> High Grace should meet in one with highest Pow'r,
> And then a seasonable People still
> Should bend to his, as he to Heavens will,
> What we might hope, what wonderful Effect
> From such a wish'd Conjuncture might reflect.
> Sure, the mysterious Work, where none withstand,
> Would forthwith finish under such a Hand:
> Fore-shortned Time its useless Course would stay,
> And soon precipitate the latest Day.[27]
> But a thick Cloud about that Morning lyes,
> And intercepts the Beams of Mortal eyes,
> That 'tis the most which we determine can,
> If these the Times, then this must be the Man. [l. 131]

The "Times" however, were none the less troubling, nor did they cease to be so as time went on. The deep conflict between the Muses and the forward spirit is resumed by Marvell in his Nun Appleton poems in the period between the *Ode* and the *First Anniversary.* Their theme is the opposition between the

[27] It would be worth exploring Marvell's preoccupation with the conquest of time whether in contemplative withdrawal, the ecstasy of lover or philosopher, or through the power of the heroic agents of history.

personal virtues of retreat and the public virtues of the active life.[28] Fairfax chose retirement. Cromwell resigned his privacy so dear to yield to rule. Marvell's *Garden* and the forest stanzas of "Upon Appleton House" are sufficient indication that he felt the full pressure and burden of the choice between public and private, active and contemplative life, and he makes the point explicit in the *Anniversary:*

> For all delight of Life thou then didst lose,
> When to Command, thou didst thy self Depose.
>
> [l. 221]

Moreover the "Chammish issue" passage shows how deeply condemnatory Marvell was of the "rage of Sects"—the extreme frenzy of "democracy":

> Accursed Locusts, whom your King does spit
> Out of the Center of th'unbottom'd Pit;
> You who the Scripture and the Laws deface
> With the same liberty as Points and Lace;
> Oh Race most hypocritically strict!
> Bent to reduce us to the ancient Pict;
> Well may you act the *Adam* and the *Eve;*
> Ay, and the Serpent too that did deceive   [l. 311]

The *First Anniversary* marks, not so much a subsequent stage in Marvell's thought, as an amplification of the republican idea stated in the *Ode.* In the form of praise for the hero who has deposed himself, renounced "delight of life," it is an extended examination of the operation and effect of republican leadership and of a "sober liberty." In it he returns, it is significant to notice, to the heroic couplet which Waller had established for panegyric, and in which Denham had written *Cooper's Hill,* a

[28] M. S. Røstvig, *The Happy Man* (Oslo, 1954), has fully examined the Stoic theme of "retreat" and its significance in seventeenth century poetry. D. C. Allen, *Image and Meaning* (Johns Hopkins, 1960), has an illuminating chapter on "Upon Appleton House," in which he sets out the metaphoric traditions behind Marvell's "poetic allegories" of garden, field and forest, and throws particular light on the harvest and flood stanzas (XLVII–LXI) which represent "a masque . . . of war and social chaos." (p. 129 ff.)

royalist panegyric bearing comparison with Marvell's in its judicious treatment and philosophically generalizing level. A further settling of Marvell's mind is thus indicated, after the highly individual, indeed unique, measure of the *Ode*, whose shorter lines contribute to an effect of excitement held in firm control by the rhymes.

The emotional and symbolic center of the poem is the image of the order-creating constitution—(the "ruling Instrument")—which, in the hands of this Amphion of state,[29] becomes the means whereby the minds of men, that stubbornest of all matter, are built into the forms of concord:

> Such was that wondrous Order and Consent,
> When *Cromwell* tun'd the ruling Instrument;
> While tedious Statesmen many years did hack,
> Framing a Liberty that still went back;
> Whose num'rous Gorge could swallow in an hour
> That Island, which the Sea cannot devour:
> Then our *Amphion* issues out and sings,
> And once he struck, and twice, the pow'rful Strings.
> The Commonwealth then first together came,
> And each one enter'd in the willing Frame; . . .
> The Common-wealth does through their Centers all
> Draw the Circumf'rence of the publique Wall;
> The crossest Spirits here do take their part,
> Fast'ning the Contignation which they thwart;
> And they, whose Nature leads them to divide,
> Uphold, this one, and that the other Side;
> But the most Equal still sustein the Height,
> And they as Pillars keep the Work upright;
> While the resistance of opposed Minds,
> The Fabrick as with Arches stronger binds,
> Which on the Basis of a Senate free,
> Knit by the Roofs Protecting weight agree. [l. 67]

In this central conception, the musical and architectural harmonies fuse in an image of parliamentary *concordia discors,*

[29] cf. Waller, p. 26 above.

which gives both perspective and a proper limitation to passages which would otherwise overbalance the poem in the direction of adulation or Carlylean hero-worship:

> When for his Foot he thus a place had found,
> He hurles e'r since the World about him round;
> And in his sev'ral Aspects, like a Star,
> Here shines in Peace, and thither shoots a War.   [l. 99]

> Thou Cromwell falling . . .
> . . . all about was heard a Panique groan,
> As if that Natures self were overthrown.
> It seem'd the Earth did from the Center tear;
> It seem'd the Sun was faln out of the Sphere:
> Justice obstructed lay, and Reason fool'd;
> Courage disheartn'd, and Religion cool'd.   [l. 201][30]

Indeed it must be Marvell's vividly grateful sense of Cromwellian order subduing the chaos of the sects which makes him reanimate the ancient cosmic sun-king imagery at the very moment when he is insisting that to be Cromwell

> . . . was a greater thing,
> Then ought below, or yet above a King.   [l. 225]

For, in contradistinction to the simple doctrine of "Crownes are for hero's," he insists that

> He seems a King by long Succession born,
> And yet the same to be a King does scorn.
> Abroad a King he seems, and something more,
> At Home a Subject on the equal Floor.   [l. 387]

For kings, in their regal state, strong only against their subjects, building no temples in their days, consulting no prophecies but

---

[30] This passage refers to a well-known carriage accident undergone by Cromwell. The lines call to mind Milton's later description of the moment of the Fall of Man (*P.L.*, Bk. 9, l. 1000). Milton may have remembered the poem of his friend and colleague when, some time before 1667, politics became for him subsumed in theology, and he turned from the particular problems of contemporary Englishmen to the universal problems of mankind.

those which augur their personal fate, are unlike the forward
spirits in their relation to history. The kings

> Thus (Image-like) an useless time they tell,
> And with vain Scepter, strike the hourly Bell;
> Nor more contribute to the state of Things,
> Then wooden Heads unto the Viols strings.   [l. 41]

It is the forward spirits, through their foresight and guiding
power, who "contribute to the state of things" and are enabled
to "contract the work of ages in a year."

The substitution of the hero, the master of time, for such
kingly puppets of time forms one of the main themes of the
poem. It is conveyed, with a kind of poetic justice, through
traditional, if reanimated, sun imagery, in the long sunset-sun-
rise passage (ll. 325–342), for example. Once again we have an
amplification of the "Crowns are for hero's" doctrine; but the
old coins crown-king-sun have been given a different value.

The rest of the poem is concerned with the nature of the
leader's mastery of time, which consists of so realizing the
direction of the historic present as to determine the future. His
own inalienable power of judgment and choice imposes his will
on events, while he conforms to the will of the "higher Force,"
which expresses itself in the movement of history. The "Chari-
oteer" and "Captain" metaphors convey the idea of the Protector's decisive powers of judgment, guidance, and control,
and this is recapitulated in a second image from the art of
building:

> But walk still middle betwixt War and Peace;
> Choosing each Stone, and poysing every weight,
> Trying the Measures of the Bredth and Height;
> Here pulling down, and there erecting New,
> Founding a firm State by Proportions true . . .   [l. 244]

The same dual faculty is revealed in the lines on freedom and
tyranny:

> 'Tis not a Freedome, that where All command;
> Nor Tyranny, where One does them withstand:

But who of both the Bounders knows to lay
Him as their Father must the State obey.   [l. 279]

It is worth noticing, however, that praise of Cromwell's specifically personal qualities, as well as his intimidating military
power, is placed as dramatic speech in the mouths of the aston-
ished princes of the world. That is the aspect of the hero that
strikes the public eye, captures the popular imagination. The
poet, in his own voice, insists upon the huge, suprapersonal
movement of events to which the hero is servant and instrument:

What since he did, an higher Force him push'd
Still from behind, and it before him rush'd,
Though undiscern'd among the tumult blind,
Who think those high Decrees by Man design'd.
                                                    [l. 239]

The true inward nature of the heroic role is presented in a final
brilliant metaphor of intelligent mission:

And as the *Angel* of our Commonweal,
Troubling the Waters, yearly mak'st them Heal.
                                                    [l. 401]

Except for the elegy on Cromwell's death, which, significantly enough, deals almost entirely with the private and domestic aspects of the Protector's death, Marvell's last Cromwellian panegyric was written in 1657 on Blake's victory over
the Spaniards. And that poem too reaches a climax with the
idea of conscious mission as opposed to blind Fortune:

Fate these two Fleets, between both Worlds had brought,
Who fight, as if for both those Worlds they fought.
Thousands of wayes, Thousands of men there dye . . .
Far different Motives yet engag'd them thus,
Necessity did them, but Choice did us.
A choice which did the highest worth express,
And was attended by as high success.
For your resistless Genius there did Raign,

By which we Laurels reapt ev'n on the Mayn.
So prosperous Stars, though absent to the sence,
Bless those they shine for, by their Influence.   [l. 125 ff.]

WALLER'S PANEGYRIC—THE PERSISTENCE
OF CONSERVATIVE ATTITUDES

It is instructive to compare Marvell's *On Blake's Victory*
with Waller's *Of a War with Spain and a Fight at Sea*, written
upon the same occasion. Both writers refer, and in similar terms,
to "fatal gold"—war's chief support, the pay of armies, the
pride of courts, troubler of the people's quiet—as the determining cause of the conflict. Marvell sees the battle and the
loss of the Spanish treasure as one more decisive link in the
blessed chain of events forged by the influence of Cromwell's
resistless genius:

> Ages to come, your conquering Arms will bless,
> There they destroy, what had destroy'd their Peace.
> And in one War the present age may boast,
> The certain seeds of many Wars are lost.   [Marvell, l. 157]

Waller by contrast expresses a traditional Renaissance criticism
of worldly vanity:

> Vain man! whose rage buries as low that store,
> As avarice had dig'd for it before:
> What earth in her dark bowels, could not keep
> From greedy hands, lies safer in the Deep,
> Where THETIS kindly does from mortals hide
> Those seeds of luxury, debate and pride.
>   [Waller, p. 123]

It is indicative that Marvell points forward from that moment
in the present which is pregnant with the future, while Waller
points back to the static concepts of a fixed and perennial order.
For the royalist poet too, the true hero of the action is the
noble courtier-lover, although he is in fact the conquered
enemy. The center-piece of Waller's miniature epic—the chivalric and courtly action of the defeated Marquis, incapable of
affecting history, affects the sentiments of the English soldiers:

The Marquis . . . laid him by his burning lady's side;
And, since he could not save her, with her dy'd.
Spices, and gums, about them melting fry,
And phoenix-like, in that rich nest they Dye.
Alive, in flames of equal love they burn'd;
And now, together are to ashes turn'd: . . .
Beauty, and youth, about to perish, finds
Such noble pity in brave English minds;
That, (the rich spoil forgot, their valors Prize,)
All labor now to save their enemies . . .
And, their young foes endeav'ring to retrieve,
With greater hazard than they fought, they dive.

[pp. 123–124]

Fenton says of this poem that it was written in gratitude for the leniency with which the author's part in "Waller's Plot" was treated, and that it was designed "to persuade the nation to think itself safe, and happy, under the new Protector. . . ."[31] Whatever the personal motivation of the poet, the poem interestingly reveals the royalist patterns of allegiance, and evaluations of the heroic. And when these are applied to the great opponent himself, as in Waller's panegyric to Cromwell,[32] the contrast with the republican content of Marvell's Cromwellian poems is thrown strongly into relief. Here there is no millennial vision of civic order and consent, no sober liberty of a free people. The real subject of Waller's panegyric is England as a glorious state, the seat of empire, balance to the awed countries of Europe, unified, fortified, mistress of the seas and their commerce. The Protector, by his personal authority author of this happy state of affairs, is lauded in terms which stress his fitness to rule a submissive flock. The contrast with Marvell's "At Home a Subject on the equal Floor" is crucial. And the princely virtue, the fitness to rule, is seen as the traditional quality of the well-born descendant of a noble line.

. . . so much pow'r and piety in one.
One! whose extraction from an antient line,

[31] *Works of Waller,* ed. Fenton, p. cxiii.
[32] "Panegyric to my Lord Protector," 1655.

Gives hope again that well-born men may shine:
The meanest, in your nature, mild and good;
The Nobles rest secured in your Blood.
Oft have we wonder'd, how you hid in peace
A mind proportion'd to such things as these;
How such a ruling spirit you could restrain,
And practise first over your self to reign . . .
Born to command, your Princely virtues slept
Like humble *David's*, while the flock he kept.

But when your troubled country call'd you forth,
Your flaming courage, and your matchless worth,
Dazzling the eyes of all that did pretend,
To fierce contention gave a prosp'rous end.
Still as you rise, the state, exalted too,
Finds no distemper while 'tis chang'd by you;
Chang'd like the world's great scene when, without noise,
The rising sun night's vulgar lights destroys.   [p. 118]

It is at once a reminder of Marvell's point of departure in generally similar attitudes and a measure of the distance he travelled, that the last line recalls his "Democratick stars" in the poem on Lord Hastings.

It is also worth remarking in this connection that Waller's alteration of *The Maid's Tragedy* [33] is such as to bring about a happy ending for the play's legitimate monarch through a noble and chivalrous gesture on the part of the King. Melanthius is touched and disarmed, as were the English soldiers by the Marquis, or the pretenders to fierce contention in the *Panegyric*. Sheer flattery though the latter may be, it is significant in revealing the courtly-chivalric values of the Cavalier conception of the political hero. Naturally enough, these are persistent, and exist side by side with the formulation in other minds of newer notions of leadership and its destined social objectives.

By the end of his life Marvell, too, ceased to believe in the power of great men to mould social destiny. His sense of the

[33] *Ibid.*, p. 217.

immutable process of history remains, but his sense of the sovereignty over time of the elect vanishes. During the high days of the Commonwealth he had felt that the blest conjunction of great man and right time could bring about the millennium. By 1672, however, he expresses in a tone of resigned acceptance the view that history cannot be speeded up by the heroic will, and that the millennium is as far off as ever.

"Whether it be a war of religion or of liberty, is not worth the labour to enquire. Whichsoever was at the top, the other was at the bottom; but upon considering all, I think the cause was too good to have been fought for. Men ought to have trusted God; they ought and might have trusted the King with that whole matter. 'The arms of the Church are prayers and tears;' the arms of the subjects are patience and petitions. The King himself, being of so accurate and piercing a judgement, would soon have felt where it stuck. For men may spare their pains where nature is at work, and the world will not go the faster for our driving. Even as his present Majestie's happy Restauration did itself, so all things else hapen in their best and proper time, without any need of our officiousness." [34]

This view expresses not only the changing outlook of an aging, though still energetically polemical Marvell, but a reversal of values undergone by an entire period. The decades which produced the ideas and forms, no longer of the heroic, but of a retreat from the heroic, will be treated in a separate chapter.

[34] *The Rehearsal Transpros'd* (1672), p. 213.

CHAPTER FIVE

"*With his own Fasces he shall make him Fires*"

COWLEY'S SKEPTICISM

For Cowley as well as for Marvell the problem raised by Cromwell's heroic career was a central one. It is not by chance that Cowley, bound by personal loyalty to the royalist party, was suspected by the Cavaliers of being a renegade and by the Roundheads of being a spy.[1] But whether his abortive and confused political activities were the cause or the result of the profoundly pessimistic skepticism which is the keynote of his poetry—a skepticism which only towards the end of his life settled into a rationalistic Epicureanism in the "retreat" tradition [2]—is perhaps impossible to say. It is, at all events, important to notice the terms in which, in 1656, he sets about to "*dismantle . . . our Cause . . . of all the Works and Fortifications of Wit and Reason by which we defended it.*" [3]

The Brutus Ode, published in the 1656 collected edition of his works which Cowley prepared in prison, is as fervent in its admiration of the archetypal republican "usurper" as is the *Anniversary* of Marvell (himself, it will be remembered, once a royalist). It offers a view of Brutus' virtue as a central, order-creating moral force just as does the *Anniversary*, of Cromwell's:

[1] The best biography of Cowley is A. H. Nethercot, *The Muses' Hannibal* (London, 1930). There is an account of his philosophical views in general, as they were influenced by Montaigne and Gassendi, in W. K. Jordan, *The Development of Religious Toleration in England* (Harvard, 1932).
[2] Discussed fully in M. S. Røstvig, *The Happy Man*.
[3] Preface to *Poems* (1656), in Spingarn, Vol. II, p. 84.

Excellent *Brutus*, of all humane race
The best till Nature was improv'd by *Grace*, . . .
Virtue was thy *Life's Center*, and from thence
Did *silently* and *constantly* dispense
The gentle vigorous *Influence*,
To all the wide and fair *Circumference:*
And all the parts upon it lean'd so easily,
Obey'd the mighty *force* so *willinglie*
That none could discord or disorder see
In all their *Contrariety.*
Each had his motion natural and free,
And the *Whole* no more *moved* then the *whole World*
    could be.[4]

Moreover, Cowley, in one respect, goes further than Marvell. If Marvell's "forward spirit" could be read as the answer to the nostalgic demand of Cowley's halcyon poesie for fair weather to breed in, Cowley's defense of Brutus reads like a response, in a mind working over a similar area of experience, to the aesthetic regret implicit in Marvell's description of his Royal Actor, who "nothing common did or mean Upon that memorable Scene":

From thy strict rule some think that thou didst swerve
(*Mistaken Honest men*) in *Caesars* blood;
What *Mercy* could the *Tyrants life* deserve,
From him who kill'd *Himself* rather then *serve?*
Th'*Heroick Exaltations* of the *Good*
Are so far from *Understood,*
We count them *Vice* . . .
Can we stand by and see
Our *Mother* robb'ed, and bound, and ravish't be,
Yet not to her assistance stir,
Pleas'd with the *Strength* and *Beauty* of the *Ravisher?*

            [p. 195]

Yet in this very ode the characteristic oscillation of Cowley's thought between admiration for heroic prowess and pessimistic

---

[4] *Poems*, ed. A. R. Waller, p. 195. Reference is to this edition, unless otherwise indicated.

fatalism is evident. He is, it seems, by tradition and temperament too much a royalist, too committed to the idea of government invested in personal power, to be capable of a Marvell's Commonwealth vision. His enthusiasm is a forced growth, and cannot withstand a native defeatism. The result is a recoil on the part of the poet from belief in the efficacy of heroic virtue:

> What joy can *humane things* to us afford,
> When we see perish thus by odde events,
> *Ill men,* and wretched *Accidents,*
> The best *Cause* and best *Man* that ever drew a *Sword? . . .*
> What can we say but thine own *Tragick Word,*
> That *Virtue,* which had worshipt been by thee
> As the most solid *Good,* and greatest *Deitie,*
> By this fatal proof became
> An *Idol* only, and a *Name . . .* [p. 196]

The reservation implied by "The best till Nature was improv'd by Grace," is seen to be, after all, sovereign in the poem. It expresses an ambivalent attitude to the hero and heroic power which is consistent with the skepticism expressed previously in several poems which had appeared in *Miscellanies* in 1651.

In *The Tree of Knowledge,* for example, man goes "Ignorantly on to Know," grows by so doing "more blind," and acquires no science through the eating of the apple but "to know he nothing (knows)."

> A certain *Death* does sit,
> Like an ill *Worm,* i'th'*Core* of it.
> Ye cannot *Know* and *Live,* nor *Live* or *Know* and *Eat.*
> [p. 65]

In *Reason* even the highest human faculty is limited to the function of a compass which can show only where truth's mysteries are; it cannot see through them; and it, like Moses,

> by a sad command
> Must not come into th'*Holy* Land, . . . [p. 47]

The address to Brutus employs the irony of historical hindsight to make the complementary point:

The *Time's* set forth already which shall quell
Stiff *Reason*, when it offers to *Rebell* . . .
A few years more, so soon hadst thou not dy'ed,
Would have confounded *Humane Virtue's* pride,
And shew'd thee a God crucifi'ed . . . [p. 197]

Cowley's constant sense of the limitations of Reason and
Virtue throws his mind strongly towards a belief in the impo-
tence of human action and intention in the face of Fortune.
There can be no Fortune-quelling hero for him; no finally
conclusive event-making act. His retreat from politics and the
world to his own Sabine farm, where he composed his essays
in Horatian vein upon the theme of the mean estate which does
not tempt providence, is consistent with the melancholy skepticism expressed in even so enthusiastic a poem as *Brutus*. But
before he reached the point of retreat, there was a stage when
Cowley's mind was evidently drawn strongly towards belief
in the capacity of outstanding men to overcome Fortune and
to determine the course of events. While his skepticism led him
to doubt whether the hero could ultimately succeed, he nevertheless maintained the worthwhileness of the challenge which
the great man issues to Fortune in the attempt to impose his
will, tutored by virtue, upon circumstance. Thus his *Dream of
Elysium* is a vision of the valiant heroes who will in Elysium
find the rewards denied them on earth; and they are defined
as those who "sterne Death and perils did imbrace for Vertues
cause." [5]

It was the *Davideis* [6] which enabled Cowley to escape the
dilemma in his mind between doubt of the effectiveness of the
heroic and affirmation of its validity. Basil Willey sees his well-
known defense of Holy Scripture as a legitimate source of epic
poetry in the context of the seventeenth century debate on the
limits of truth and fiction, science and poetry. It is evidence,
he says, "of a realisation . . . that the Bible was a poetic source
of unique value, inasmuch as its contents could not, even by

[5] *Essays, Plays and Sundry Verses,* ed. A. R. Waller, p. 43.
[6] 1656.

modern philosophy, be dismissed as fabulous." [7] No less, however, would it seem to spring from his own particular need for an heroic which is not subject to the frustrations of Fortune and historical circumstances. The heroes of Revelation are firmly established within the framework of Providence. The heroes of Reason, like Brutus, imagine that their mere human virtue, without benefit of Divine Grace, is sufficient to ensure success in the great conflicts of history. Thus only in the heroic subjects which Scripture affords can "the Glory of God be joyned with the singular utility and noblest delight of Mankind. . . ." [8] Accordingly, Cowley's belief in the heroic in the field of contemporary history becomes progressively weaker. Henceforth the idea of men, as mere puppets whose strings are twitched by the unseen hands of destiny—and this whether public hero or private citizen—is to be explicitly stated. Cowley's own decisive turn from the aspirations of the grand to the austerities of the mean estate is indirectly expressed in his translation *On the Uncertainty of Fortune:*

> If *Fortune* knit amongst her Play
> But seriousness; he shall again go home
> To his old Country-Farm of Yesterday,
> To Scoffing People no mean Jest become;
> And with the *Crowned Ax,* which he
> Had rul'd the World; go back and prune some Tree;
> Nay, if he want the Fuel Cold requires,
> With his own *Fasces* he shall make him *Fires.* [9]

Once more, as so often in the works of Cowley and Marvell, one is aware of an effect as of antiphonal response in the "Crowned Ax," irresistibly reminiscent of Marvell's "But with his keener Eye The Axes edge did try. . . ."

The finally dominant bent of his mind is fully revealed in the Ode *Destinie,* of 1656, and in an ode attached to the essay On

[7] B. Willey, *The Seventeenth Century Background* (London, 1934), p. 231.
[8] *Poems,* ed. Waller, p. 12.
[9] *Works,* ed. Tonson, Vol. III, p. 48.

Libertie, which may be regarded as a companion piece to the *Destinie*, dating from the latter period of his life.

Retreat to Liberty

Destinie, together with *Brutus* and the "recanting" preface of 1656, accounted, no doubt, for Clarendon's famous reply to Cowley's request for recompense after the Restoration.[10] It makes its major point with the utmost clarity.

1.

Strange and *unnatural!* Let's stay and see
This *Pageant* of a *Prodigie.*
Lo, of themselves th'enlivened *Chesmen* move,
Lo, the unbred, ill-organ'd *Pieces* prove,
As full of *Art*, and *Industry*,
Of *Courage* and of *Policie*,
As *we our selves* who think ther's nothing *Wise* but *We,*
Here a proud *Pawn* I'admire,
That still advancing higher
At top of all became
Another *Thing* and *Name.*
Here I'm amaz'ed at th'Actions of a *Knight,*
That does bold Wonders in the Fight.
Here I the losing Party blame
For those false *Moves* that break the *Game,*
That to their *Grave* the *Bag*, the conquered *Pieces* bring,
And above all, th'*ill Conduct* of the *Mated King.*

2.

Whate're these *seem*, whate're *Philosophie*
And *Sense* or *Reason* tell (said I)
These Things have *Life, Election, Libertie;*

[10] "Your pardon Sir, is your reward." Cowley's note on the "ill-conduct of the Mated King," though consonant with the view of Fate and Virtue expressed in the poem, was apparently not considered sufficently conciliatory! The note reads: "When the *Fates* lay hold on a Man, when they arrest him, he's confounded, and loses his Wits. . . . Fatality grew too strong for *Humane Counsels*, and dazled the sight of his judgement, for so it also happens, that the *designs* and *counsels* are corrupted of the *Man that is to perish.*"

'Tis their own *Wisdom* molds their *State*,
Their *Faults* and *Virtues* make their *Fate.*
They do, they do (said I) but strait
Lo from my'enlightned *Eyes* the Mists and Shadows fell
That hinder *Spirits* from being *Visible.*
And, lo I saw *two Angels* plaid the *Mate.*
With Man alas, no otherwise it proves,
An unseen *Hand* makes all their *Moves.*
And some are *Great*, and some are *Small*,
Some climb to *Good*, some from *good Fortune* fall,
Some *Wisemen*, and some *Fools* we call,
Figures, alas, of *Speech*, for *Desti'ny plays us all.* [p. 192]

In the third strophe the poem shifts from the public theme to
the private. The shift will not seem arbitrary when it is remembered how closely connected are poetry and politics for
Cowley, as for Marvell. So, Destiny plays us all; Destiny, in the
shape of the Midwife Muse, "Me from the *womb* . . . did take.
. . . Such I *began*, such *am*, and so must *end.*"

> *Hate* and *renounce* (said she)
> *Wealth, Honor, Pleasures*, all the *World* for *Me.*
> Nor at th'*Exchange* shalt be, nor at the wrangling *Bar.*
> Content thy self with the small *Barren Praise*,
> That neglected *Verse* does raise. [p. 193]

In the fine Ode *Upon Liberty*,[11] Cowley comes at last to
terms with his destiny:

> Freedome with Virtue takes her seat,
> Her proper-place, her onely Scene,
> Is in the Golden Mean.
> She lives not with the Poor, nor with the Great.
> The Wings of those Necessity has clipt,
> And they'r in Fortunes Bridewell whipt,
> To the laborious task of Bread;
> These are by various Tyrants Captive lead.
> Now wild Ambition with imperious force

[11] *Essays*, etc., ed. Waller, p. 388 ff.

Rides, raines, and spurs them like th'unruly Horse.
And servile Avarice yoakes them now
Like toilsome Oxen to the Plow . . .
If any Few among the Great there be
From these insulting Passions free,
Yet we ev'n those too fetter'd see
By Custom, Business, Crowds, and formal Decency . . .

He's no small Prince, who every Day
Thus to himself can say,
Now will I sleep, now eat, now sit, now walk,
Now meditate alone, now with Acquaintance talk . . .
Make an Escape; out at the Postern flee,
And get some blessed Hours of Libertie,
With a few Friends, and a few Dishes dine,
And much of Mirth and moderate Wine.
To thy bent Mind some relaxation give,
And steal one day out of thy Life to Live.

One of Cowley's best extended images—that of the birds, those
"Freeborn Nations of the Air"—serves to modulate the poem
from general reflection to personal position:

Never did Bird a spirit so mean and sordid bear,
As to exchange his Native Liberty . . .
For a more plentiful or constant Food.
Nor ever did Ambitious rage
Make him into a painted Cage; . . .
Now, Blessings on ye all, ye Heroick Race,
Who keep their Primitive powers and rights so well,
Though Men and Angels fell . . .

If Life should a well-order'd Poem be, . . .
The more Heroique strain let others take,
Mine the Pindarique way I'le make.
The Matter shall be grave, the Numbers loose and free . . .
A thousand Liberties it shall dispense, . . .
When the wide Air's a Road for it.
So the Imperial Eagle does not stay,
Till the whole Carkass he devour

That's fallen into its power.
As if his generous Hunger understood
That he can never want Plenty of Food, . . .

The conquest of destiny is not to be achieved through greatness of action. On the contrary, renunciation of great ambi-
tions is required; and heroic virtue, heroic freedom, become
the fruits of a stoic self-restraint. Nothing could better illustrate
at once the parallelism and the sharp divergence between Marvell's and Cowley's view of the nature of the heroic than a
comparison between the "Falcon high" of the one, and the
"Imperial Eagle" of the other. The two images, in their respective poems, illustrate the essential difference between the heroic
ethos of the Cavalier and that of the republican. For Cowley's
treatment of the theme of liberty, though deeper, has much in
common with the constant Cavalier theme of stoic defiance,
of loyalty as an affirmation of the freedom of the soul. The
images of the caged bird free nevertheless to sing

> The mercy, sweetness, majesty,
> And glories of my King . . .[12]

of the soul "free as ambient air" which finds

> These walls are but my garrison; this cell,
> Which men call gaol, doth prove my citadel . . .[13]

and of poverty as a "royal thing" [14] echo through innumerable
Cavalier elegies and lyrics. Essentially they are all affirmations
of a final freedom which is sought only when the direction of
Fortune and the times is felt to be profoundly inimical, and all
hope of seizing an historical initiative is abandoned.

Cowley has the stoic attitude in common with such Cavaliers,
but his philosophical skepticism leads him to push his investigation of the effect of the heroic upon history further; and the
fruits of that investigation are elucidated in *A Discourse By
Way of Vision, Concerning the Government of Oliver Cromwell*, published anonymously in 1661.

[12] Richard Lovelace, "To Althea from Prison" (1642).
[13] Sir Roger L'Estrange, "The Liberty of the Imprisoned Royalist."
[14] Sir Richard Fanshawe, "The Royalist" (1646).

THE DETHRONING OF THE HERO

The *Vision* is a carefully constructed debate upon the problem of ends and means, set in the frame of a vision following the Protector's funeral, in which each participant is given in the course of his argument a set-piece in verse—in the one case, on the unhappy state of England; in the other, on the theme "Tis God-like to be great," however ruthless the means of attaining the greatness.

The terms of the debate are set in the opening speeches of the opponents. The Protector's spokesman would not have his countrymen:

"fall into the general errour of the World, that detests and decryes so extraordinary a Virtue; what can be more extraordinary than that a person of mean birth, no fortune, no eminent qualities of Body, which have sometimes, or of Mind, which have often raised men to the highest dignities, should have the courage to attempt, and the happiness to succeed in so improbable a design, as the destruction of one of the most antient, and most solidly founded Monarchies upon the Earth? that he should have the power or boldness to put his Prince and Master to an open and infamous death? . . . to oppress all his Enemies by Armes, and all his Friends afterwards by Artifice; to serve all parties patiently for a while, and to command them victoriously at last? to over-run each corner of the three Nations, and over-come with equal facility both the riches of the South, and the poverty of the North? . . . to call together Parliaments with a word of his Pen, and scatter them again with the Breath of his Mouth; . . . to have the Estates and Lives of three Kingdomes as much at his disposal, as was the little inheritance of his Father, . . . to be buried among Kings . . . and to leave a name behind him, not to be extinguisht, but with the whole World, which as it is now too little for his praises, so might have been too for his Conquests, if the short line of his Humane Life could have been stretcht out to the extent of his immortal designs?" [15]

---

[15] *Essays*, etc., ed. Waller, p. 347 ff.

But his countryman is at no loss for a reply:

". . . sure I am, that we must renounce or forget all the Laws of the New and Old Testament, and those which are the foundation of both, even the Laws of Moral and Natural Honesty, if we approve of the actions of that man whom I suppose you commend by Irony. . . . What can be more extraordinarily wicked, than for a person, . . . to endeavour not only to exalt himself above, but to trample upon all his equals and betters? to pretend freedom for all men, and under the help of that pretence, to make all men his servants? to take Armes against Taxes of scarce two hundred thousand pounds a year, and to raise them himself to above two Millions? to quarrel for the losse of three or four Eares and strike off three or four hundred Heads? . . . to pretend the defence of Parliaments, and violently to dissolve all even of his own calling, and almost choosing? to undertake the Reformation of Religion, to rob it even to the very skin, and then to expose it naked to the rage of all Sects and Heresies? to set up Counsels of Rapine, and Courts of Murder? to fight against the King under a commission for him? to draw him into his Net, . . . and . . . to butcher him, with as little shame, as Conscience, or Humanity, in the open face of the whole World? . . . to break his faith with all Enemies, and with all friends equally? . . . to usurp three Kingdoms without any shadow of the least pretensions, and to govern them as unjustly as he got them? . . ." [p. 348 ff.]

This is the familiar material of charge and countercharge which drew the line of civil dissension across the country and the period. But the ideological crux of the conflict is given by way of irony, by the "Protector" himself, in the terms which are central to the thought of the time—*Virtu* and Virtue. These concepts had clarified themselves in Cowley's mind as ambition on the one hand and Epicurean renunciation on the other:

"You seem to pretend extremely, to the old obsolete rules of Virtue and Conscience, which makes me doubt very much whether from this vast prospect of three Kingdoms you can show me any acres of your own. . . . For this I perceive which you call Virtue, is nothing else but either the frowardness of a

Cynick, or the laziness of an Epicurean. I am glad you allow me at least Artfull Dissimulation, and unwearied Diligence in my Hero, and I assure you that he whose Life is constantly drawn by those two, shall never be misled out of the way of Greatness. But I see you are a Pedant, and a Platonical Statesman, a Theoretical Common-wealths-Man, an Utopian Dreamer. Was ever Riches gotten by your Golden Mediocrities? or the Supreme place attained to by Virtues that must not stir out of the middle? Do you study *Aristotles* Politiques, and write, if you please, Comments upon them, and let another but practise *Machiavil,* and let us see then which of you two will come to the greatest Preferments. If the desire of rule and superiority be a Virtue (as sure I am it is more imprinted in human Nature than any of your Lethargical Morals; and what is the Virtue of any Creature but the exercise of those powers and Inclinations which God has infused into it) if that (I say) be Virtue, we ought not to esteem any thing Vice, which is the most proper, if not the onely means of attaining it." [p. 372 ff.]

We have seen that Cowley came more and more to renounce riches and supreme place, rule and superiority as the proper ends of heroic virtue. Yet he is not in fact a "Theoretical Common-wealths-Man" and therefore has no alternative conception of a supreme political virtue to offer. Thus the basis of his refutation of the "Protector's" claims lies elsewhere than in the sphere of political morality. His argument probes towards a philosophy of history which questions the validity of the hero's claim to affect events for good or ill at all. And while no doubt originating in the fatalistic and skeptical bent of his mind, it comes close to being a completely secular and rational statement of social determinism in a context of historical process:

"But because the general ground of your argumentation consists in this, that all men who are the effecters of extraordinary mutations in the world, must needs have extraordinary forces of Nature by which they are enabled to turn about, as they please, so great a Wheel; I shall speak first a few words upon this universal proposition, which seems so reasonable, and is so popular . . .

"I have often observed (with all submission and resignation of spirit to the inscrutable mysteries of Eternal Providence) that when the fulness and maturity of time is come that produces the great confusions and changes in the World, it usually pleases God to make it appear by the manner of them, that they are not the effects of humane force or policy, but of the Divine Justice and Predestination, and though we see a Man, like that which we call Jack of the Clock-house, striking, as it were, the Hour of that fulness of time, yet our reason must needs be convinced, that his hand is moved by some secret, and to us who stand without, invisible direction. And the stream of the Current is then so violent, that the strongest men in the World cannot draw up against it, and none are so weak, but they may sail down with it. These are the Spring-Tides of publick affairs which we see often happen, but seek in vain to discover any certain causes, . . . and one man then, by malitiously opening all the Sluces that he can come at, can never be the sole Author of all this (though he may be as guilty as if really he were, by intending and imagining to be so)." [pp. 360–361]

The contrast with Marvell's view is made the more conspicuous by the Jack of the Clock image they both employ:

> Thus (Image-like) an useless time they tell,
> And with vain Scepter, strike the hourly Bell;
> No more contribute to the state of Things,
> Than wooden Heads unto the Viols strings.[16]

For Marvell the impotent Jack is the merely hereditary king, thus distinguished from the republican hero who is master of time and of men's minds by virtue of his insight into the hidden providential workings of history. For Cowley the image underlines the illusory nature of all heroic action either with or against the spring-tides of public affairs. And while these tides are not ultimately autonomous—"it is God that breaks up the Flood-gates of so general a Deluge, and all the art then and industry of mankind is not sufficient to raise up Dikes and Ramparts against it . . ."—yet, for Cowley, God's hortatory

---

[16] "The First Anniversay," ll. 41–44.

system of reward and punishment is remote, and mediated in fact by a relatively independent process which he calls "the fulness and maturity of time."

It is worthwhile once more to review the curiously related stages in the thought of Cowley and Marvell, epicurean Cavalier and Puritan republican, with regard to the tumultuous events of their time. Cowley, doubtful from the beginning of the possibility of success attending heroic revolutionary action, nevertheless at first affirms the value of the endeavor. From this position he moves to a pessimistic defeatism in which he finds the willed effort and aim of the active life illusory, since in fact, "Desti'ny plays us all." When, however, he shifts the focus of attention from the public to the private life, he finds a steady if limited optimism in the freedom from fortune of the contemplative life of the Garden, the mean estate which avoids those extremes either of eminence or obscure poverty which are subject to the tyranny of passions or circumstances. Destiny, for him, is finally identified as that historical process upon which men can have no effect though they are blame- or praise-worthy insofar as they act in the illusion that they can form or alter its course. Marvell, on the other hand, begins as the spokesman of the graces of established culture against the harsh realities emerging with the new forces in society. He then becomes aware of what he feels to be a purposive pattern in history, and affirms the validity of the call to play an active part in the shaping of the Commonwealth. Thus his heroically "forward spirit" leaves his Bergamot, resigns "delight of life," the private virtues and freedoms of the contemplative life, for the public good, the public virtues of leadership and the active struggle to realize a new order. Much later, when Marvell expresses the view that "things . . . happen in their best and proper time, without any need of our officiousness," it might seem that the wheel has come full circle and that Marvell too, like Cowley, is finally rejecting the possibility of man-made change or reform. There is, however, a radical difference between them. Where Cowley has lost faith in the outcome of political action, Marvell has retained his belief in the ultimate happening of things in their best and proper time, though that time may be far from imminent. Providence is appealed to by both. But the true content of Cowley's view is indicated by his use of the tidal image. History for him is repetitive, cyclic. It is the classical intuition of natural cycles indifferent to mankind, and therefore quite contrary to Marvell's sense of God's purposes progressively revealed in history. It is only in the speed and imminence of this progress that he is disillusioned, not in its direction. And he does not himself withdraw from active political life despite his delight in the respites afforded by the Garden with its transcendental vision. On the contrary, the Restoration witnessed his most notable prose contributions, and his tireless political activities as member of parliament for Hull.

PROTECTOR IN THE ROYALIST IMAGE

Cowley's view, radically opposed to that of the militant republican who would find that the ordained will of God in history had chosen the best and most fitting instrument—a paragon of virtue—to effect its ends, or that the career of Cromwell exemplified or at least presaged virtue triumphant in the world, was nevertheless also a notable departure from the established royalist position. It was his skepticism rather than his royalism which denied in the last resort both to virtue and *virtu* the power to determine the course of history. For the royalist mind was necessarily committed to the view of a ruling class which, if defeated, cultivates the noble gesture, but in victory celebrates the absolute power of its great to create and mould events. This conviction is fundamental to a monarchist *weltanschauung*, whether it be that of the intransigant, who excoriates Cromwell for ruthless *virtu*, machiavellian and damnable, or of the more moderate or adaptable, willing to acknowledge and pay tribute to the political and imperialistic achievements of the conqueror. Having successfully demonstrated his might, he could then be accredited with all the usual moral qualities. This is exactly what we find characterizing the work of the three royalist panegyrists, Dryden, Sprat, and Waller, who wrote elegies upon the death of Oliver Cromwell.

Dryden's *Heroic Stanzas . . . To The Glorious Memory
. . . Of the Late Lord Protector,* 1659,[17] is unequivocal in its
insistence on the superiority of heroic virtue, the virtue of
the good conqueror, over circumstances:

> His name a great example stands to show
> How strangely high endeavours may be blest,
> Where piety and valor jointly go. [st. 37]

> When such heroic virtue Heav'n sets out,
> The stars, like commons, sullenly obey; . . .
> [st. 27] [18]

> His grandeur he deriv'd from heav'n alone;
> For he was great ere fortune made him so:
> And wars like mists that rise against the sun,
> Made him but greater seem, not greater grow. [st. 6]

> He fought secure of fortune as of fame;
> Still, by new maps, the island might be shown,
> Of conquests, which he strew'd wher'er he came,
> Thick as the galaxy with stars is sown. [st. 14]

Dryden, however, goes beyond the mere enumeration of attributes—majesty, military ability, skill in counsels, modesty,
piety, and knowledge of men—which may be said to account
for Cromwell's superiority over Fortune. He dwells upon the
heroic quality itself as something mysterious, awe-inspiring,
and transcendent:

> Such was our prince; yet own'd a soul above
> The highest acts it could produce to show:
> Thus poor mechanick arts in public move,
> Whilst the deep secrets beyond practice go. [st. 32]

> 'Tis true, his count'nance did imprint an awe;
> And naturally all souls to his did bow,

[17] *Poetical Works,* ed. Noyes, p. 4 ff.

[18] It is worth noting the recurrence of this image, used by Marvell in
his royalist poem on Lord Hastings, and by Waller as well as Dryden.

> As wands of divination downward draw,
> And point to beds where sov'reign gold doth grow.
>
> [st. 19]

Similarly, Thomas Sprat describes the especial nature, esoteric in its rarity, of the hero's power: [19]

> Great Life of wonders, whose each year
> Full of new Miracles did appear! . . .
> All that thou didst was so refin'd,
> So full of substance, and so strongly join'd,
> So pure, so weighty Gold,
> That the least Grain of it,
> If fully spread and beat,
> Would many Leaves and mighty Volumes hold.
>
> [p. 19]

It too insists upon the existence of the heroic virtue in itself, regardless of the events upon which it exerted itself and through which it was made manifest.

> The Sun doth only shew
> That they are bright, not make them so: . . .
>
> [p. 16]

While conquest and victory and sea-power are naturally made much of, Sprat's main emphasis is upon the purity of Cromwell's motives:

> Though Fortune did hang on thy Sword,
> And did obey thy mighty Word;
> Though Fortune for thy side and thee,
> Forgot her lov'd Unconstancy;
> Amidst thy Arms and Trophies thou
> Wert valiant and gentle too . . .
> Thou fought'st not to be high or great,
> Not for a Scepter or a Crown,

[19] Sprat, "To the Happy Memory of the Most Renowned Prince" (1659). In *Poems on Affairs of State* (1697), p. 15 ff. (As . . . " of the Late Usurper.")

> Or Ermyn, Purple, or the Throne;
> But as the Vestal Heat,
> Thy Fire was kindled from above alone . . .
>
> > [p. 20]

> Thou fought'st not out of Envy, Hope or Hate
> But to refine the Church and State . . . [p. 19]

Waller's chief reason for praising Cromwell, on the other hand, is, as it had been before in the *Panegyric*,[20] the enlargement of England's empire:

> From civil broils he did us dis-engage;
> Found nobler objects for our martial Rage:
> And, with wise conduct, to his country show'd
> The ancient way of conquering abroad.[21]

His whole panegyric, indeed, is assimilated to the theme of sea-power, so that even the storm which occurred on the night of Cromwell's death is presented as a sign of upheaval in nature at the loss of the sea's sovereign:

> Nature her self took notice of his death,
> And, sighing, swell'd the sea with such a breath,
> That, to remotest shores her billows roul'd,
> Th'approaching fate of their great ruler told.

The elegies of Dryden, Sprat, and Waller mark the end of the epoch of the Cromwellian panegyric. It is not merely that they were in fact written after his death; in their content and approach there is every indication of the subsiding of conflict, the lessening of acute ideological tension. There is evident in them an abstraction of the idea of heroic virtue from the mesh and tug of revolutionary political events, revolutionary decisions. In this abstraction is to be found the germ of the grandiloquent and fanciful heroic drama of the Restoration. The importance of the historic milieu and the philosophy of history have receded. What emerges is an idea of the heroic, which,

[20] See p. 115 ff., above.
[21] *Works*, ed. Fenton, p. 125 ff.

[136]

divorced from specific historical or political contexts, can henceforth be applied to fictitious characters in imaginary situations, as in the heroic drama. In this it differs significantly from Elizabethan and Jacobean tragedy—written for a popular and national, rather than a restricted, court audience—whose heroes are historical figures; "historical" perhaps often in a sense which the modern historian, with his sharper distinction between history and legend, finds difficult to accept, but nevertheless historically conceived in terms of actualities, whether past, present, or future, of a real prince or a real people. The baroque hero,[22] on the other hand, is detached from history. Abstracted from real events, the hero's great exploits, his great acts, his large gestures alone define him, and are sufficient to establish his validity. Public ceremonious affirmation resolves the private agonies of ideological decision. Since such emperor-worship informed the attitude and temper of the royalist supporters Cromwell gained, one is tempted to adapt the maxim of Voltaire: if the Restoration had not occurred, it would have had to be invented.

[22] The idea of the baroque in literature is lucidly expounded by W. Sypher, *Four Stages of Renaissance Style* (New York, 1955).

CHAPTER SIX

"An Heroick,
and a lawful King . . ."

THE UNANIMITY OF RESTORATION PANEGYRIC

"IT HAS been an Antient and laudable custome . . . to celebrate the Inaugurations, Triumphs and Vertues of Princes, upon every happy Turn of State, memorable Success, or glorious action . . . by way of Panegyrick, or Laudatory Oration. . . . Let us therefore now celebrate our Countries Redemption, Joy and Dignity, and forget her old bondage, wounds and afflictions . . . restored to a flourishing kingdom under the blessed government of an Heroick, and a lawful King. . . . A Prince who has not only, and that fearless, opposed his magnanimous brest to all these (blows of force and fortune) but which is more, and still more shining, even in the midst and fury of mischance, and in the lowest ebbe of his greatest necessities, through the purety of his innocence . . . and the constancy of his Vertue, has defended himself from the snares of insinuating policy. . . ."

Thus Charles Cotton, in his *A Panegyric on the King's Most Excellent Majesty*, 1660,[1] provides a definition of the occasion, motivation, and theme of the panegyrics of Restoration. The works of all three major panegyrists who welcomed King Charles home are easily distinguishable by individual talent, style, and personal preoccupation. Dryden's analytic couplets are markedly his own; Waller fawns for forgiveness, and reveals in the poem more anxiety over past sins of defection than was evident in the self-confident assurance of his reply to the King when the latter acidly noted the superiority of the

[1] London (1660), pp. 2–6.

panegyric to Cromwell;[2] Cowley expresses a deep personal
relief at the return of "felicity and innocence" after the period
of moral tension and confusion created by the "proud Gigantick Son of Earth."[3]

Yet in all three a common pattern of thought is to be discerned, which is shared also by the many minor panegyrists
whose treatment is less full and less sustained. Each reviews
the troubled times which have passed, praises the King's
fortitude in exile and the uses of adversity, expresses relief and
gratitude at the bloodless revolution of his return, dilates upon
the rejoicing of the people, pleads guilty, as the nation's spokesman, of its previous falling off, invokes the King's clemency and
forgiveness, and prophesies the birth of a new and better age,
an age of empire, unity, and the arts. The last is particularly
stressed by the former laureate Davenant,[4] who praises the
King's taste and care for harmony and ornament, his restraint
of licence in the arts and his refinement of ancient drama, thus
expanding, in terms of his own especial interests, the general
panegyric pattern, which for the rest he too follows.

In his review of the past and his expectations for the future
Dryden is the most succinct of the four poets.

> For his long absence Church and State did groan;
> Madness the pulpit, faction seiz'd the throne:
> Experienc'd age in deep despair was lost,
> To see the rebel thrive, the royal cross'd: . . .
> The rabble now such freedom did enjoy,
> As winds at sea, that use it to destroy:
> Blind as the Cyclops, and as wild as he,
> They own'd a lawless salvage liberty . . .[5]

> And now Time's whiter series is begun,
> Which in soft centuries shall smoothly run: . . .
> Our nation, with united int'rest blest,
> Not now content to poise, shall sway the rest.

[2] "We poets, Sir, never succeed so well in writing truth as in fiction."
[3] Cowley, "Ode Upon his Majesty's Restoration and Return."
[4] "Poem to the King's Most Sacred Majesty" (1663).
[5] "Astraea Redux," *Poetical Works*, ed. Noyes, p. 7.

Abroad your empire shall no limits know,
But, like the sea, in boundless circles flow . . .
Their wealthy trade from pirates' rapine free,
Our merchants shall no more advent'rers be; . . .
At home the hateful names of parties cease,
And factious souls are wearied into peace . . .
O happy age! O times like those alone
By fate reserv'd for great Augustus' throne!
When the joint growth of arms and arts foreshew
The World a monarch, and that monarch *you.*

[l. 292]

Cowley's greater sensitivity of feeling is evident in many a passage which is more than "occasional" in that it bears the imprint of the poet's whole mind as this is disclosed in the body of his work:

Will *Peace* her *Halcyon Nest* venture to build
Upon a Shore with *Shipwrecks* fill'd?
And trust that *Sea,* where she can hardly say,
Sh'has known these twenty years one *calmy day,*
Ah! mild and gaulless *Dove,*
Which dost the *Pure* and *Candid* Dwellings love:
Canst thou in *Albion* still delight?
Still canst thou think it *white?* . . .
Will *Justice* hazard to be seen,
Where a *High Court* of *Justice* e're has been? [6]

Vain men! who thought the Divine Power to find
In the fierce *Thunder* and the violent *Wind:*
God came not till the storm was past,
In the *still voice of peace* he came at last . . . [st. 7]

He's come, he's safe at shore; I hear the noise
Of a whole *Land* which does at once rejoyce,
I hear th'united *People's sacred voice* . . .
The *Starry Worlds* which shine to us afar,
Take *ours* at this time for a *Star.*

[6] "Ode Upon his Majesty's Restoration and Return," *Poems,* ed. Waller, p. 420, st. 3.

With *Wine* all *rooms*, with *Wine* the *Conduits* flow . . .
There is no *Stoick* sure who would not now,
Ev'n some *Excess* allow;
And grant that one *wild fit of chearful folly*
Should end our twenty years of *dismal Melancholy*.

[st. 16]

Waller's ulterior motive pervades his panegyric, whether he is cunningly pointing out the resemblance between Charles and his "Great Master, (who) the storm withstood, And pity'd those who love with frailty shew'd . . ." or whether he is engaged in giving a sophisticated turn to the plea:

Your youth, and all the splendor of your state,
(Wrap't up, 'till now, in clouds of adverse Fate!)
With such a flood of light invade our eyes,
And our spread hearts with so great joy surprize;
That, if your grace incline that we should live,
You must not SIR! too hastily forgive.[7]

The latter passage contrasts amusingly with Dryden's considerably more self-respecting treatment of the forgiveness theme:

Not tied to rules or policy, you find
Revenge less sweet than a forgiving mind . . .
And as those lees that trouble it, refine
The agitated soul of generous wine:
So tears of joy, for your returning split,
Work out and expiate our former guilt. [l. 260]

Thus there is a remarkable uniformity, almost unanimity, in the panegyrists' response to the King's return, despite the fairly clearly marked divergences of approach and motivation. Flattery in the hope, no doubt, of reward or favor under the new dispensation would seem to be the dominant motive of a number of the ephemeral panegyrics of the time. For example:

Your mind's a Constellation fixt above
The Orbes, where Kepler, and where Tycho rove . . .

[7] "To the King, upon His Majesty's Happy Return," *Works*, ed. Fenton, p. 126.

You are yourself a Senate, Diet, One,
A single Council, Parliament alone . . .
The Volatile Spirits of the Region
Shall here be fixt beyond Reduction.
So the keen Winde (as Muscovites relate)
Quick with Refining Force does operate
And make a gem which can't apostatize
From solid chrystal into brittle ice . . .[8]

One can, however, distinguish such hyperbolic adulation from another more serious kind of deification, which appears like a theme, with variations, in many of these panegyrics. Two springs of traditional sentiment join to encourage the apotheosis of Charles: faith, now strongly renewed, in divine right; and the sacrificial pathos with which the figure of the martyr-king, Charles I, had become imbued. It will be remembered that Richard II had acquired Christological significance in the popular mind, as indeed according to the findings of modern anthropology, kings who have been killed invariably tend to do. Thus references of some kind or another to Charles' divinity abound. Cowley for instance (it is in him perhaps a refraction of his skepticism regarding merely *human* powers) has:

God did *stamp* first upon one side of *Thee*
The *Image* of his *suffering Humanity:*
On th'other side, turn'd now to sight, does shine
The *glorious Image* of his *Power Divine;* [st. 12]

and Davenant rationalizes the idea of a God upon the throne in terms of "natural" religion:

They seek out *God* in cruel Camps, and boast
They *God* have found, when they have Nature lost;
Nature, the publick Light which is held out
To all dimm Minds who do of *God-head* doubt.
She openly to *all* does *God-head* shew;
Faith brings him, like a *Secret,* but to few.
Sects, who would God by *private Opticks* reach

[8] H. Beeston, London (1660), pp. 4-5.

Invent those Books by *which themselves* they *teach;*
And whilst with Heaven they too familiar grow,
They to the Gods on earth disdain to bow.[9]

On the other hand, there is Martin Lleuelyn's secular and prag-
matic approach to Restoration which issues in a paean scarcely
less fervent:

For though we shiver in a thousand Rents,
Of Querulous Sects, and unappeas'd intents:
Yet in this one we center, and agree;
We still request a King, and that King, thee.
Come then and bind us up with tender hands,
O Thou the Balsome of these bleeding Lands . . .
What Birth, nor Brains, Treasure, nor Force could do,
Our kind Necessity hath rais'd Thee to.
And you attain your long disputed height,
A Glorious Conqueror without a Fight.[10]

The period, then, which royalist and republican alike saw as
characterized by "the itching sweetness for to head a faction" [11]
ended with a hallelujah of universal relief. Not a little of that
relief was due to the possibility of a return to traditional ways
of thought and feeling: habits of mind against which republicanism had pitted itself in vain, and been forced to retreat, or
assimilate, or project itself in a messianic dream, in proportion
as it was still in fact premature. Thus Dryden's revulsion against
"lawless liberty," Davenant's contempt for the "private Opticks" by which the sects would spy out their God, Cowley's
longing for the stasis of peace, the insistence upon the King as
himself a parliament alone, and frequent use of the crystal-ice
image—all imply the re-establishment of the coherence of unity.
The centripetal forces of authority, overcoming the centrifugal
forces of the Commonwealth period, are gladly seen to remove
the burden of the liberty of individual choice which the latter
had imposed. For among other things which the Restoration

[9] "Poem to the King's Most Sacred Majesty."
[10] Lleuelyn, "To the King's Most Excellent Majesty" (1660).
[11] Carew Reynell, "The Fortunate Change" (1661).

was able to restore was the old certitude that the King was the natural repository of the princely virtues as they shed their beneficent influence from the royal apex of society down the whole hierarchical structure. The panegyrist therefore has no longer to be concerned with such re-interpretation of history as will provide for a virtuous usurper, nor indeed to occupy his mind at all with the exact nature and effect of virtue in the Great Man. It seems manifestly proved that royal virtue, buffeted by adversity, has at last attained to its due reward. The result is *ex hypothesi* a return to—a return of—decorum, natural, metaphysical, social, and aesthetic. And for the panegyrist the ancient commonplaces, capricious Fortune and triumphant Virtue, are not only sufficient for his purposes, but self-explanatory.

> So much you suffer e're you could be Great,
> For Fortune alwayes does with Vertue strive.
> But Vertue does at last her power subdue,
> And makes her stoop, as now she does to you.[12]

Providence (or Destiny, in Cowley's skeptical terminology), is once more the ruler of Fortune, and firmly on the side of the ancient rights and privileges and the stoic virtues:

> Those who did hold Success the Cast of Chance,
> And *Providence* the Dream of Ignorance,
> Might in these Miracles Design descern,
> And from wild *Fortune's* looks Religion learn.[13]

> So when the wisest *Poets* seek
> In all their liveliest colours to set forth
> A *Picture* of *Heroick* Worth, . . .
> They chuse some *comely Prince* of *Heavenly Birth*,
> (No proud *Gigantick son* of *Earth*,
> Who strives t'usurp the *god's forbidden seat*)
> They feed him not with *Nectar*, and the *Meat*
> That cannot without *Joy* be eat
> But in the *cold* of *want*, and storms of *adverse chance*

[12] Sir T. Higgons, "A Panegyric to the King" (1660), p. 10.
[13] Davenant, "Poem to the King's Most Sacred Majesty."

They *harden* his *young Virtue* by degrees;
The *beauteous Drop* first into *Ice* does *freez,*
And into *solid Chrystal* next advance,
His *murdered friends* and *kindred* he does see,
And from his *flaming Country* flee,
Much is he *tost* at Sea, and much at *Land,*
Does long the force of *angry gods* withstand.
He does long *troubles* and long *wars* sustain,
E're he his *fatal Birth-right* gain.
With no less *time* or *labour* can
Destiny build up such a *Man.*
Who's with sufficient virtue fill'd
His *ruin'd Country* to *rebuild.*[14]

Confident once more that his hero's greatness is "owing to his virtue," in Fenton's phrase, the panegyrist can undertake without reservation the amplification of that virtue:

Kings like the Sun, in their full Majesties,
Are too resplendent bright for Subjects eyes; . . .
But when Eclipst, then every one can see
(Without that splendor) what their persons be; . . .
For moral virtues then, ha's every one
In their full splendours and perfection . . .[15]

and can thankfully consign his own conscience and his country's welfare to the King's keeping:

Great Sir, 'tis you
That makes us great, and makes us vertuous too.[16]

Thus, shewing what *you are,* how quickly we
Infer what all your Subjects soon *will be!*
For from the Monarch's vertue *Subjects* take,
Th'ingredient which does publick vertue make.
At his bright beam they all their Tapers light,
And by his Diall set their motion right.[17]

[14] Cowley, "Ode Upon His Majesty's Restoration and Return," st. 13.
[15] Flecknoe, *Heroick Portraits* (1660).
[16] Reynell, "The Fortunate Change."
[17] Davenant, "Upon His Sacred Majesty's Most Happy Return" (1660), p. 11.

Such an attitude constitutes a shift back from an historical consciousness, an awareness of great forces at work in society, to a moral-didactic consciousness which posits an ideal norm for society, stable and permanent—"Augustan." Davenant, in the passage quoted, when he presents the relation between King and people in this light has set forth the heart of the matter:

> At his bright beam they all their Tapers light,
> And by his Diall set their motion right.

On this view the panegyrist, in his celebration and illustration of the Dial of virtue in the person of the king, finds himself once more firmly in the didactic-ethical tradition of the Renaissance epic. Courtly makers may be once again moral mentors; "such Priests," in Davenant's phrase, . . . "as figur'd Virtue and disfigur'd Sin." They will then be giving practical effect to Hobbes' dictum: "For there is in Princes and men of conspicuous power, anciently called *Heroes*, a lustre and influence upon the rest of men resembling that of the Heavens. . . ." [18] The author of *Gondibert* had indeed always been a chief spokesman for this view of heroic poetry,[19] and as early as 1631 had expressed his belief that "Charles our King . . . is the example and the law Where-by the good are taught. . . ." [20] Now, in 1660, in the clear light of manifest Order it will be every heroic poet's task to celebrate the glorious virtues of his sovereign and his court, and to anathematize the cursed brood of hypocrites and rebels, so that, under the potent influence of the epic muse, the former is imitated and the latter abhorred. Heroic virtue has no longer to be defined, but exhibited. Now that the King, its proper emblem and exemplar, is back, his poets may devote themselves with a whole heart to the finding of an effective style in which to do so. The result is the development of the baroque heroic.

The Baroque Heroic

The panegyrics of the Restoration express an overwhelming sense of restored rightness, of light out of darkness issuing in a

[18] Hobbes, "Answer to the Preface to Gondibert," in Spingarn, p. 55.
[19] See Chapter 1, above.
[20] "A New Year's Gift to the King" (1631).

universal decorum. The experience was impressive enough, and general enough, to put its stamp upon a whole body of verse, marking it out as belonging to a distinguishable mode or style. When one entitles that style "baroque heroic," as one conveniently may, one is referring to a mode of vision, a kind of imagery, an idiom, a complex of aesthetic attitudes and evaluations which can be traced not only in the heroic poetry of the period but in other forms of its art as well. Wylie Sypher, in his *Four Stages of Renaissance Style,* has set out a persuasive characterization of the baroque which proves most helpful in illuminating the quality of Restoration panegyric. The great theme of Restoration panegryic is the "full splendour and perfection" of royalty emerged from its eclipse and restored to its proper place in a long-accepted scheme of things whose rightness is now freshly and triumphantly perceived. Nothing, it seems, could more clearly demand treatment in what has come to be known as the baroque manner, with its large-scale proportions, its demonstrativeness and its strongly effective sensuous display.

According to Sypher, baroque may be defined as a "secularization of the transcendental" [21] in splendid material images, public acts, great exploits, titanic figures which resolve by overwhelming energy the conflicting impulses which had crisscrossed the art of the Jacobean dramatists, the Metaphysical poets, the Mannerist painters. The baroque image exists "in a powerfully but simply constructed context of obvious values," [22] stimulates to feel rather than to think or discriminate, and prefers simplified emotions of epic grandeur. This last point is aptly illustrated by a comparison between the tensely thoughtful last stanza of Marvell's *Horatian Ode:*

> And for the last effect
> Still keep thy Sword erect:
> Besides the force it has to fright
> The Spirits of the shady Night,
> The same *Arts* that did *gain*
> A *Pow'r* must it *maintain . . .*

[21] Johnson long ago accused Dryden of attempting "to mingle earth and heaven by praising human excellence in the language of religion."

[22] Sypher, p. 232.

and Dryden's simplified and magnified version in the Coronation panegyric:

> A noble emulation heats your breast,
> And your own fame now robs you of your rest:
> Good actions still must be maintain'd with good,
> As bodies nourish'd with resembling food.   [l. 75]

The idolization of Charles already referred to is of course the supreme instance of the "secularization of the transcendental." But the process is pervasive, and nowhere better to be seen than in the frequency and nature of the sun images in the poems of praise to the King. "Time's whiter series," which his reign initiates, is almost always acclaimed in imagery of light, and in sun conceits. We have encountered the eclipse and the dial in Flecknoe and Davenant. Then there is the Russian winter:

> The frozen Samovite, who half the year
> Lives underground, and never sees the sky,
> Feels not that comfort when the Sun is neer,
> At whose approach Darkness and Winter flie;
> As all Great Britain, at your Royall sight,
> After so dismal, and so long a night! . . .[23]

The "kindly heat of lengthened day" to which is likened the peaceful nature of "our blessed change" is a variant, as is crop ecology:

> Your reign no less assures the ploughman's peace,
> Than the warm sun advances his increase.[24]

Cowley compares the Protector to an Ignis Fatuus, "which e're while Mis-led our wandring Isle," his son to a falling star, and the Long Parliament to a fatal comet, with fiery tail of vast

[23] Higgons, "A Panegyric to the King," p. 6.
[24] Waller, "Upon His Majesty's Happy Return." Both anthropologists like Frazer and Cornford and archetypologists like Bodkin and Frye would no doubt find the significance of ritual pattern in such use of sun imagery. The son of the slain king brings back fertility to the earth which has lain waste since the killing of the old king by the powers of darkness. The theme "Resurrection of the Spring" (Cowley, st. 10) recurs repeatedly in these panegyrics.

length, "Insatiate with our Ruine and our Blood." Against these
he sets the light of the sun:

> Already was the *shaken Nation*
> Into a wild and deform'd *Chaos* brought,
> And it was hasting on (we thought)
> Even to the last of Ills, *Annihilation.*
> When in the midst of this confused Night,
> Loe, the blest *Spirit* mov'd, and *there was Light.*
> For in the glorious *General's* previous Ray,
> We saw a new created *Day.*
> We by it saw, though yet in *Mists* it shone,
> The *beauteous Work* of Order moving on.   [st. 7]

What is significant and characteristic in this sun imagery is
that it illustrates a new treatment of the traditional symbol. The
ancient notions of cosmic and hieratic order associated with the
sun are still present in the background of consciousness. In the
foreground, however, now stand the sun's light-endowing values, or its genial and life-giving warmth. These attributes together may be further expanded into the conception of the
creation, or re-creation of form as in Cowley, or in an anonymous poem *Upon His Majesty's Happy Return:*

> As the great World at first in Chaos lay;
> Then darkness yielded to triumphant day;
> And all that wilde and indigested *Mass*
> Did into *Form,* and to *Perfection* pass.[25]

The intensity of the light of the sun provides this poet with a
similitude for the justification of monarchy as a form of government:

> As when Great Nature's Fabrick was begun,
> Expanded Light made Day, and not the Sun,
> But Light diffus'd was to perfection grown,
> When from one Planet, it contracted, shone.   [p. 2]

Comparison with the sun imagery in panegyrics written before
the civil wars will sufficiently make clear the degree to which

[25] Anon, "To the King, Upon His Majesty's Happy Return" (1660), p. 2.

it is the restorative virtue of the sun, and its physical properties
—its impact upon the senses—which is being emphasized in
these poems.

Intensely sensuous appeal, then, mainly visual, though by no
means always so, and a sense of decorum which verges upon a
sense of "decor," both in the interests of a grand assertion of
value—these, pre-eminently, are the features of the baroque
idiom which dominates the panegyric of the sixties, and tran-
scends individual differences of expression. Dryden's two chief
works in this mode, *A Panegyric on his Coronation*, 1661, and
To My Lord Chancellor, 1662; Waller's *Instructions to a
Painter*, 1666; and Marvell's *The Loyall Scot*, 1667, all stand
out in the canon of their respective author's works as marked
by distinctive attitudes, evaluations, and modes of vision. These
we have already seen emerging in the royalist elegies on
Cromwell and shaping directions in the poems of welcome.
Now, in the four main poems presently to be dealt with, the
baroque attitudes become fully articulate, and its stylistic principles receive, in poems and prefaces, however sporadically, a
fair degree of critical formulation.

Dryden's Coronation panegyric [26] fairly answers to Sypher's
description of baroque. The poem is built on a principle of
rhetorical accumulation; it searches the topics of invention,
cause, effect, manner of doing, manner of suffering, quantity
and quality, substance, relation, place, time, circumstance,[27] for
conceits which will amplify and demonstrate the one grand
simple subject—the King's glory. Invention from the topics
produces not only extremely sensuous images but a multipli-
cation of delicious sense impressions:

> Music herself is lost, in vain she brings
> Her choicest notes to praise the best of kings;
> Her melting strains in you a tomb have found,
> And lie like bees in their own sweetness drown'd.

---

[26] "To His Sacred Majesty, A Panegyric on His Coronation," *Poetical
Works*, ed. Noyes, p. 13.

[27] Rosamund Tuve, *Elizabethan and Metaphysical Imagery* (Chicago,
1947), Chapter XI, gives a full account of the logical forming of imagery
in the poetry of the Renaissance.

He that brought peace, and discord could atone,
His name is music of itself alone.   [l. 53]

Wrapp'd soft and warm your name is sent on high,
As flames do on the wings of incense fly: . . .   [l. 51]

It is, moreover, not by chance that Dryden has chosen to
present his panegyric to the King in terms of the ceremonious
pageantry of the Coronation. Nor is the presence in the poem
of the "fair spectators" who "witness" the glorious Cavalcade
with their longing to date a conquest from the day, without
significance. They are certainly newcomers in the panegyric,
and natural inhabitants of this brave new world of splendid
material images, where a royalist poet could relax and bask in
the beams of a safely restored monarchy.

The poem, *To the Lord Chancellor,* 1662,[28] which followed
the *Coronation* is reminiscent in its conceits of Cleveland's
metaphysical manner, or of Dryden's own earlier style in *Upon
the Death of the Lord Hastings,* 1649, but with the difference
that now the conceits are mostly found, to use the terms of
rhetoric, from the places quality, adjunct, or manner of doing—those most fruitful for uncovering the demonstrable nature of the subject, and for praise and amplification. They take
the form of the similitude argument, and range for their content
through the empirical sciences, optics, physiology, astronomy,
geography, and topography in the manner of Denham.[29] The
result is a series of daring, yet exact, and often exactly visualized
assertions, which one is tempted to see as representing a disciplining and redirecting of the frenetic energies exhibited in
Cleveland's pursuit of analogy at all costs.

> In open prospect nothing bounds our eye,
> Until the earth seems join'd unto the sky:
> So in this hemisphere our utmost view
> Is only bounded by our King and you;

[28] *Poetical Works,* ed. Noyes, p. 15.
[29] There are a very few similitudes taken from classical myth or epic
such as burning Troy, l. 18; new-born Pallas, l. 100; Olympus' top, l. 145;
and the Happy Isles, l. 135. Newton's *Opticks,* it will be remembered,
appeared in 1675.

Our sight is limited where you are join'd,
And beyond that no farther heav'n can find.   [l. 31]

By you he fits those subjects to obey,
As heaven's eternal monarch does convey
His pow'r unseen, and man to his designs
By his bright ministers the stars inclines.   [l. 83]

Such is the mighty swiftness of your mind,
That, like the earth's, it leaves our sense behind,
While you so smoothly turn and roll our sphere,
That rapid motion does but rest appear.
For as in nature's swiftness, with the throng
Of flying orbs while ours is borne along,
All seems at rest to the deluded eye,
(Mov'd by the soul of the same harmony,)
So carried on by your unwearied care,
We rest in peace, and yet in motion share.   [l. 109]

Your equal mind yet swells not into state;
But like some mountain in those happy isles,
Where in perpetual spring young nature smiles,
Your greatness shows: not horror to affright,
But trees for shade, and flow'rs to court the sight:
[l. 134]

Your age but seems to a new youth to climb,
Thus heav'nly bodies do our time beget,
And measure change, but share no part of it.
And still it shall without a weight increase,
Like this new-year, whose motions never cease:
For since the glorious course you have begun
Is led by *Charles*, as that is by the sun,
It must both weightless and immortal prove,
Because the Center of it is above.   [l. 148]

Dryden was elected a Fellow of the Royal Society [30] in the
year this poem was written, and it was his belief that "A man
should be learned in several sciences, and should have a reason-

[30] On Nov. 19, 1662.

able, philosophical, and in some measure a mathematical head, to be a complete and excellent poet." [31] The logic of his superlatives is accordingly better than Cleveland's, his premises less fanciful and more securely based in scientific data and method, or at least in speculation. The significant difference, however, is that, with almost the single exception of the final syllogism quoted above, Dryden's similitudes are all directed to "discover" the virtues of this "bright minister" in material, sensible, and spatially grounded images. These are mainly visual, optic theory itself providing the source of at least three main conceits.

In *To My Lord Chancellor* there are two references to Fortune which admirably illustrate the baroque vision and method in Dryden. The idea, or complex of ideas, behind the word "Fortune" is not any longer of dialectical interest, as it had been in the period of the Commonwealth; Fortune has become once more the emblematic figure familiar to the Middle Ages, handled however, in a new manner. She has become decorative, elaborate; her function is auxiliary, like that of sculpture supporting a pedestal, the delicacy and freedom of whose modelling contributes its own energy to the glory of the whole:

> . . . Fortune, conscious of your Destiny,
> Ev'n then took care to lay you softly by;
> And wrapp'd your fate among her precious things,
> Kept fresh to be unfolded with your kings. [l. 95]

> You have already wearied Fortune so,
> She cannot farther be your friend or foe;
> But sits all breathless, and admires to feel
> A fate so weighty that it stops her wheel. [l. 129]

The baroque appeal to the physical and the concrete, the intensity with which the heroic affirmation is made through the material data of the senses, characterizes not only Dryden's

[31] From the postscript to "Notes and Observations of the Empress of Morocco" (1674); *Works*, ed. Scott-Saintsbury, Vol. xv, p. 406. The pamphlet was a joint composition with Crowne and Shadwell, but the postscript is attributed by Malone and Scott to Dryden.

panegyric at this date, but also the slightly later *Instructions to a Painter*,[32] by Waller, and Marvell's *The Loyall Scot*. In the latter, the outstanding feature of the heroic section, which is Marvell's work (as distinct from the discursive or polemic section which was added),[33] is the sensuously saturated image of the valiant Scot, grasped at the moment of his supreme gesture:

> Like a glad lover the fierce Flames hee meets
> And tries his first Imbraces in their sheets.
> His shape Exact which the bright flames enfold
> Like the sun's Statue stands of burnisht Gold:
> Round the Transparent fire about him Glowes
> As the Clear Amber on the bee doth Close;
> And as on Angells head their Glories shine
> His burning Locks Adorn his face divine.
> But when in his Immortall mind hee felt
> His Altred form and sodred Limbs to Melt,
> Down on the Deck hee laid him down and dy'd
> With his dear sword reposing by his side,
> And on his flaming Planks soe rests his head
> As one that Huggs himself in a Warm bed.   [l. 43]

In the *Instructions:*

> The *Duke* (ill-pleas'd that Fire should thus prevent
> The work, which for His brighter Sword he meant,)
> Anger still burning in his valiant breast,
> Goes to complete revenge upon the rest.
> So, on the guardless herd, their keeper slain,
> Rushes a tiger in the *Lybyan* plain.
> The *Dutch* . . .
> Never met tempest which more urg'd their fears,
> Than that which in the Prince's look appears.
> Fierce, goodly, young! *Mars* he resembles, when
> *Jove* sends him down to scourge perfidious men: . . .[34]

---

[32] 1666.

[33] The dating of the several sections of the poem is discussed by Margoliouth, in his Notes, p. 295. The Douglas passage originally formed part of Marvell's "Last Instructions," discussed by Margoliouth, p. 267.

[34] *Works*, ed. Fenton, p. 167.

Again, the treatment of a moving moment during the sea-battle, the death of three at once at the Duke's side, well illustrates the baroque combination of simplified, impersonal, extreme sentiment with a high sense of spectacle:

> Happy! to whom this glorious death arrives;
> More to be valu'd than a thousand lives!
> On such a theatre, as this, to die;
> For such a cause, and such a witness by!
> Who would not thus a sacrifice be made,
> To have his blood on such an altar laid?   [p. 166]

Baroque indeed revives the classical definition *ut pictura poesis*, and endows it with a wider application. The visual arts are constantly invoked, and enlisted in the endeavor to display heroic might to the best advantage. The very conception of Waller's panegyric—Instructions to a Painter—is a case in point, and the poem initiated quite a minor mode in the "Painter" manner. The rationale is given in the poem, *To the King* which was appended:

> Painters express with emblems of their pow'r;
> His club *Alcides, Phoebus* has his bow,
> *Jove* has his thunder, and your navy You . . .   [p. 171]

and the practice—though Waller is forced himself to admit its inadequacy for narrative purposes [35]—offered obvious advantages to the baroque sensibility.

> Draw the whole world, expecting who should reign,
> After this combat, o'er the conquer'd Main . . .
> Make thy bold pencil, hope, and courage spread
> Thro' the whole navy, by that Hero led:
> Make all appear, where such a Prince is by,

[35] In "Instructions," p. 170

> Painter, excuse me, if I have a-while
> Forgot thy art, and us'd another style:
> For, tho' you draw arm'd Heroes as they sit;
> The task in battel does the *Muses* fit.

In the whole of Europe at this time much attention was given to the comparison of poetry with painting. Dryden himself translated du Fresnaye, *De Arte Graphica*, with a preface on the parallel.

Resolv'd to conquer, or resolv'd to die.
With his extraction, and his glorious mind,
Make the proud sails swell, more than with the wind: . . .
Make him bestride the ocean, and mankind
Ask his consent, to use the sea, and wind:
While his tall ships in the barr'd Channel stand,
He grasps the Indies in his armed hand.   [pp. 161–162]

Painting was not the only art to provide matter for the baroque love of spectacle. As Waller sees the death of his three noble youths in terms of theatre, so Dryden talks of the several sorts of sculpture to be used in the varieties of epic poem: "But tho' the same images serve equally for the epic poesy, and for the historic and panegyric, which are branches of it, yet a several sort of sculpture is to be us'd in them. If some of them are to be like those of Juvenal, *Stantes in curribus Aemiliani,* heroes drawn in their triumphal chariots, and in their full proportion; others are to be like that of Virgil, *Spirantia mollius aera:* there is somewhat more of softness and tenderness to be shewn in them." [36]

A. A. Mendilow, in his *Time and the Novel* [37] has pointed out that "Classicism had developed the spatial sense and conceived even literature in terms of the plastic arts." Thus, too, had the neo-classicism of the Restoration. When in addition the insistence on the glory of the hero replaces investigation of his part in the process of historical forces, that glory comes increasingly to be presented in a series of tableaux, like those which decorated the city shows in honor of a royal visit.

The Reaction

The *Instructions* was followed by a whole spate of mock-imitations, what might almost be called a Martin Mar-Painter series, whose object was to debunk the heroics of the official or court panegyrists. The disappointments and disillusions of Charles II's glorious reign produced a response which was an exact reflex of baroque exaltation. The grandiose and super-

[36] "An Account of the Ensuing Poem," *Poetical Works,* ed. Noyes, p. 26.
[37] London (1952), p. 4.

human heroic, felt to be so cruelly inappropriate to the facts, was countered with mockery and derision. If we exclude Butler's *Hudibras* of 1663, whose satire is directed not against the court but against its Puritan enemies, the "Painter" satires may be said to constitute the first phase of the anti-heroic, or mock-heroic modes which gather momentum towards the end of the 1660's and throughout the following decades. These, the varieties of burlesque, have their own literary history and genealogy which will be discussed in subsequent chapters. It is worth noting here, however, that just as Dryden's baroque similitude can be related directly to Cleveland's hyperbolic conceit, so the burlesque similitude, so soon to come into fashion and be perfected by Butler for the purpose of satire, is also derivative from that same hyperbolic "metaphysical" manner of Cleveland. Cleveland was an extremely popular poet in his day, many times reprinted. The vigor and energy of his political pieces must have been what most caught attention. And it is not altogether surprising that he should have affected Dryden's baroque-heroic phase as much as he affected Marvell's or Butler's burlesque, for baroque and burlesque are akin as are the two sides of the same medal.[38] It requires no more than a shift in point of view to turn heroic into burlesque, as Buckingham's *Rehearsal* sufficiently witnesses. Such transvaluations of the attitudes of reverence and irreverence are universal human experience; they are also enshrined in classical and neo-classical doctrine regarding the separation of the "high" tragic or epic from the opposite "low" comic in style. And it is this which is registered by Dryden in his Preface to *Annus Mirabilis* at a time when he is himself rejecting his own "Clevelandesque" baroque manner in favor of an heroic style which shall be less precarious, less subject to the dangerous shafts of mockery. The "adequate delight of heroic poesy" he therefore finds to be "such well-wrought descriptions or images as beget admiration, which is its proper object; as the images of the burlesque, which is contrary to this, by the same reason beget laughter; for the one shews nature beautified, as in the picture of a fair woman, which we all admire; the other shews her deform'd, as in that

[38] See Chapters 7–8, below.

of a lazar, or of a fool with distorted face and antic gestures, at which we cannot forbear to laugh, because it is a deviation from nature. . . ." [39] and this "proper wit of an heroic or historical poem," these "well-wrought descriptions or images" consist, he claims, "in the delightful imaging of persons, actions, passions, or things. 'Tis not the jerk or sting of an epigram, nor the seeming contradiction of a poor antithesis (the delight of an ill-judging audience in a play of rhyme,) nor the jingle of a more poor *paronomasia;* neither is it so much the morality of a grave sentence, affected by Lucan, but more sparingly us'd by Virgil; but it is some lively and apt description, dress'd in such colors of speech that it sets before your eyes the absent object as perfectly and more delightfully than nature." [p. 25]

Thus, if the baroque heroic gave rise to, and was destroyed by, the mock-heroic—a mode as characteristic of the later Restoration as the heroic (in the drama, for instance) is of the earlier—it begins, as early as 1666, to be undermined from within by one of its chief practitioners. The year 1666 saw Dryden celebrating "the most Heroick Subject which any Poet could desire" in a manner which is quite different from that of his panegyrics of 1661 and 1662. E. N. Hooker has shown that *Annus Mirabilis* was undertaken for political purposes,[40] to counter three seditious pamphlets on the Great Fire which had exploited the popular terror of prodigies and portents associated with the promised Second Coming in order to stir up unrest against the King's restoration and the Dutch War.[41] The apologetic purpose of the poem is implicit in Dryden's *Account:*

". . . I have taken upon me to describe the motives, the beginning, progress, and successes, of a most just and necessary War: in it, the care, management, and prudence of our king; the conduct and valor of a royal admiral, and of two incomparable generals; the invincible courage of our captains and seamen; and three glorious victories, the result of all. . . . All

---

[39] "An Account of the Ensuing Poem," p. 25.

[40] E. N. Hooker, "The Purpose of Dryden's *Annus Mirabilis*," *Huntingdon Library Quarterly*, x (1940), pp. 49–67.

[41] *Annus Mirabilis, the Year of Prodigies; Annus Mirabilis Secundus; or the Second Year of Prodigies;* and *Mirabilis Annus Secundus: or the Second Part of the Second Years Prodigies.*

other greatness in subjects is only counterfeit; it will not endure the test of danger; the greatness of arms is only real: other greatness burdens a nation with its weight; this supports it with its strength. And as it is the happiness of the age, so is it the peculiar goodness of the best of kings, that we may praise his subjects without offending him. Doubtless it proceeds from a just confidence of his own virtue, which the luster of no other can be so great as to darken in him; for the good or the valiant are never safely prais'd under a bad or degenerate prince." [p. 23]

It may very well be that part of the reason for Dryden's abandonment of the baroque heroic mode of his earlier pane-gyrics was his keen sense of audience. He is addressing himself to public opinion, and must modify his style accordingly. The elaborate facade, the verbal panoply of baroque heroic was too static and too ceremonial for his present purpose; his mind turns towards the problem of presenting heroic actions, heroic mo-tions of mind or body, clear, swift, vivid, and unimpeded; and it is Virgil that he invokes as the master of this newly desired realism: "But when action or persons are to be describ'd, when any such image is to be set before us, how bold, how masterly are the strokes of Virgil! We see the objects he represents us with in their native figures, in their proper motions; but so we see them, as our own eyes could never have beheld them so beautiful in themselves . . . the very sound of his words has often somewhat that is connatural to the subject; and while we read him, we sit, as in a play, beholding the scenes of what he represents." [p. 25 f.]

Thus it is sufficient for him to state, of Rupert, with the utmost brevity, that:

> Heroic virtue did his actions guide,
> And he the substance, not the appearance chose;
>
> [st. 116]

and the way is clear for action to be described with all the spare vividness of logically uncomplicated and sensuously precise imagery—those "excellent images of nature" of which he has spoken:

Deep in her draught and warlike in her length,
She seems a sea-wasp flying on the waves. [st. 153]

And his loud guns speak thick like angry men . . .
[st. 120]

The broken air loud whistling as she flies . . . [st. 108]

Dryden's rejection, for this poem, of the couplet, is consistent
with his rejection of the baroque heroic *in toto*. The "heroic
stanza" of *Annus Mirabilis* is the stanza of the narrative *Gondibert*, and, significantly enough, of the poem to Cromwell,
man of action par excellence. Once again, as a critical crafts-
man, Dryden explains his choice: "But in this necessity of our
rhymes, I have always found the couplet verse most easy, (tho'
not so proper for this occasion,) for there the work is sooner
at an end, every two lines concluding the labor of the poet:
but in *quatrains* he is to carry it further on, and not only so,
but to bear along in his head the troublesome sense of four lines
together." [p. 24] The passages on the Great Fire show how
splendidly Dryden could bear along in his head the troublesome
sense of four lines together, when "such well-wrought descriptions or images as will beget admiration" were his objective.
Too long to quote, stanzas 218 to 234 are an incomparable
description of the activity and progress of the fire through
London.

Despite its excellences, however, the structure of the poem as
a whole is unsatisfactory. The level of style is heroic, but there
is no hero; the content is historical, but there is no over-all view
of history which could shape the material into a significant pattern. Emotions of praise, wonder, and gratitude towards the
Sovereign are certainly meant to be evoked by the handling of
the sea-battle, and by the presentation of the fire as impotent
to touch the King's palace or his naval magazines against the
power of the King's prayer. Yet these emotions do not constitute, nor are they associated with, a central unifying focus in
the poem. Dryden admits this himself.[42] Nevertheless, the

[42] "I have call'd my Poem *historical*, not *epic*, tho' both the actions
and actors are as much heroic as any poem can contain. But since the
action is not properly one, nor that accomplish'd in the last successes,
I have judg'd it too bold a title for a few stanzas . . ." (p. 24).

pattern of the baroque heroic is effectively shattered by the poem, and it will be through a very different approach to the heroic, and to history, after a decade during which burlesque and raillery have held the stage, that Dryden will find his next point of departure.

Meantime, in a work contemporary with *Annus Mirabilis,* Cowley concludes his career as a political poet with a review of the history of his time, inserted into a discursive work in six books, partly emblematic and partly botanical, called *Plantarum.*[43] In his preface Cowley defends his "defection" from the undertaking of "mighty matters" and great subjects, such as the *Davideis,* in favor of a poetry of "old Fables" and mere plants. The detractor of his poem, he says, may well express himself thus: "Your Muse is in this no less an Object of Shame and Pity, than if *Magdalen* should backslide again to the Brothel. Behold how the just Punishment does not (as in other Offenders) follow your Crime, but even accompanies it. The very Lowness of your Subject has retrenched your Wings, You are fasten'd to the Ground with your Herbs, and cannot soar as formerly to the Clouds; nor can we more admire at your Halting, than at your fabulous *Vulcan;* when he had fallen from the Skies." [44]

Cowley's reply to this charge is in the vein of ironic self-deprecation characteristic of much of his mood during these years—the years which produced the "mean estate" essays on liberty and retirement. He accuses his Muse—his disease—which, no matter how he struggles against the "frantick Fit," keeps him "chirping" in and out of season. His work is thus mere recreation, trifling, harmless wantonness which has nothing to do with the serious business of life.[45] Yet one can detect a note of serious intention beneath the irony as he outlines his purpose in the *Plantarum:* "There was a time when it did not misbecome a King to dance, yet it had certainly been indecent for him to have danced in his Coronation Robes. You are not

[43] References to the Dutch War make the date 1666–1667. The *Plantarum,* originally in Latin, was translated by several hands; Bk. 6, *Sylva,* in which the historical material was embedded, by Aphra Behn in Tate's edition (1721).
[44] *Works,* ed. Tonson, Vol. III, p. 232.
[45] *Ibid.,* p. 234.

therefore to expect, in a Work of this Nature, the Majesty of an Heroick Style, (which I never found any Plant to speak in) for I propose not here to fly, but only to walk in my Garden, for Health's sake, and partly for Recreation." [p. 233]

A comparison of *Sylva* with the *Poem on the Late Civil War* of twenty years before [46] is revealing not only of changes in the poet himself, already indicated, which account for his insistence upon the unheroic nature of his poem, but also of the general decline of, or retreat from, the baroque heroic, which is exemplified by *Annus Mirabilis*. The "three noble youths" passage is as strikingly different in temper and diction from its counterpart in Waller's *Instructions*, as it is from Cowley's own previous historical poem:

> Three noble Youths, by the same sudden Death,
> A brave Example to the World bequeath;
> Fam'd for high Birth, but Merits yet more high,
> All at one fatal Moment's Warning die,
> Torn by one Shot, almost one Body they,
> Three Brothers in one Death confounded lay.
> Who wou'd not Fortune *harsh* and *barbarous* call?
> Yet Fortune was *benign* and *kind* withal;
> For next to these—I tremble still with fear,
> My Joy's disturb'd while such a Danger near,
> Fearless, unhurt, the Royal Adm'ral stood
> Stunn'd with the Blow, and sprinkl'd with their Blood.
>
> [p. 470]

Neither Cowley's contemporaries nor his successors accepted the author's evaluation of his work. In 1683 the political parts of *Sylva* were found useful enough to be extracted and collected as *An Heroick Poem Upon the Late Horrid Rebellion, His Majesties Happy Restauration: and the Magnanimity and Valour of his Royal Highness James Duke of York, In the Late Dutch War, wherein he Exposed his Royal Person to the greatest Dangers for the Safety and Interest of this Nation.*[47]

Nahum Tate informs the reader in the preface to his edition

[46] See Chapter 1, above.
[47] London (1683).

that Cowley "enlarges on the History of the Late Rebellion, the King's Afflictions and Return, and the beginning of the Dutch Wars . . . in a Style, that (to say all in a Word) is equal to the valour and Greatness of the *English* Nation"; [48] and asks the impartial reader to judge "if *Virgil* himself has better design'd for the Glory of *Rome* and *Augustus*, than *Cowley* for his Country and the Monarch of his time." [49]

While the exigencies of political propaganda during the accession fever of the 1680's would claim any work as "heroic" that was grist to its mill, the plainness and perspicuity, the familiar Horatian level of the diction of *Sylva* was far more calculated to please the taste of the town in the time of Queen Anne than in the first years of the Restoration; and it may well mark the end of the florid and grandiloquent heroic which ushered in the reign of Charles II.

[48] London (1721), L2 v. (The *Third Part* of the *Works,* ed. Tonson).
[49] *Ibid.,* L4 v.

CHAPTER SEVEN

Iconoclasts and Prophets

COUNTERSTATEMENT

 DRYDEN's version of events during the wonderful year did not stem the tide of general dissatisfaction with the state of the nation. The year 1667 saw the publication of more bitter and scathing satire against the court of Charles II than any which had been produced in England during the century. In the light of the corruption of court and parliament, and the ignominious burning of the navy by the Dutch at Chatham, the rejoicing which had heralded the Restoration turned to gall, shame, and disillusion with a swiftness and completeness rivalled only by the scurrility and venom of the Painter poems which register it. Rochester's *History of Insipids*, of 1676, a lampoon which with flippant bitterness reviews most of the *causes célèbres* and the scandals of the previous ten years, sums up the situation with pungent brevity:

> Chast, pious, prudent, Charles the Second,
> The Miracle of thy Restauration,
> May like to that of Quails be reckon'd
> Rain'd on the Israelitick Nation;
> The wish't for Blessing from Heav'n sent,
> Became their Curse and Punishment.[1]

By that time, ten years later, the idea was common currency among critics of the regime from the ranks of Court and Country party alike, whose discontent was by then further exacerbated by the growing "Popish" disturbances. Rochester's biting nonchalance reflects the opinion of a decade which had survived the first shock and anger; the 1670's also saw the return to political verse of the crusading republican note. But in the

[1] *Poems*, ed. de Sola Pinto, Muses' Library (1953), p. 107.

[164]

1660's, the satires express not so much a zealous ideology as the contempt and indignation of a cheated people. The contemptuous indignation falls naturally into the form of counterstatement to the splendid confidences of 1660, as these were expressed in the Restoration panegyric. Public figures are pilloried. They are cruelly caricatured in their aspect as pretenders to the heroic; and what is caricatured is the awful discrepancy, not between "seeming" and "being," as in the older Elizabethan court satire, but between "ought to be" and "is."

The Painter poems [2] are the example and symbol of that counterstatement. So also is another group, the "Statue" poems,[3] of which there were many, by Marvell and others. In these can be seen again the impulse to contradict the ceremonial monuments to greatness which the baroque heroic had erected.[4] Thus the unknown author (or authors—judging from style, there would seem to be more than one hand at work) of the first four *Directions* seized, not by chance, upon the Waller panegyric with its grandiose conception of the painter of state triumphs. That the idea proved popular enough to give rise to continued imitations for something like twenty years would seem to indicate the centrality, for the period, of the "handy-dandy" of

[2] "Second Advice to a Painter For Drawing the History of our Navall Business; In Imitation of Mr. Waller" (1666), "Third Advice to a Painter" (1666), "Fourth Advice to the Painter" (1667), "Fifth Advice to a Painter (1667). These four were later issued together, with other anti-Clarendon verses, as *Directions to a Painter* (1667). Margoliouth deals with the difficult bibliography, in his notes to Marvell's "The Last Instructions" (1667), p. 267 ff., and to Savile's "Advice to a Painter to Draw the Duke by" (1679), p. 321. Page references are all from the collection of political verse—*Poems on Affairs of State*, 1697.

[3] Marvell's are "The Statue in Stocks Market," "The Statue at Charing Cross," and "A Dialogue between Two Horses," all, according to Margoliouth (pp. 300, 310, 317), dating from 1675.

[4] The description in *The London Gazette* for 29 May (1672) is interesting. "This day being the great Anniversary of His Majesties Birth, as well as of His Glorious Restauration, has been Celebrated in this City with all imaginable Demonstrations of publick Joy, and to add to the solemnity of the day, a new Conduit of a Noble and Beautiful structure was opened in the Stocks-Market-place near Lumbard street, plentifully running Claret for divers hours, adorned with an excellent Figure of His present Majesty on Horseback, having a Turk or Enemy under foot; the Figures all of the best white Genoua Marble, and bigger than the Life. . . ." Quoted by Margoliouth, p. 301.

attitudes involved. There is often a kind of obsessive sadism about their venomous scurrility. It is not an opposition faction which is being abused, but a sacred image which is being revengefully defiled.

Since the indictment is in terms of moral backsliding, the poems take their place naturally in the Juvenalian flaying tradition. One is reminded of Marston's self-consciously hysterical mingling of prurience and fulmination against another courtful of corruption and iniquity. The chief difference in each case lies in the closeness and specificity of the target. Where Marston's was primarily an "ideal" literary undertaking, enlivened, to be sure, by personalities under Roman *noms de plume*, the Painter diatribes are direct responses to actual political events and actual court politicians.

Though the disappointment and disillusion involve king-and-court together, the first *Directions* (and the others following suit) is accompanied by a poem to the King which attempts to save, as it were, the figurehead from the "swarms of insects" (Clarendon chief among them, in these years) which surround him. The loyal obeisance leaves the poet free, in the body of the text, to present his counter-image, his "mock-heroic," by every means at his disposal.

> Imperial Prince! King of the Seas and Isles!
> Dear Object of our Joys, and Heaven's smiles!
> What bootes it that thy Light doth gild our days,
> And we lie basking in thy milder Rays,
> While swarms of Insects, from thy warmth begun
> Our Land devour, and intercept our Sun? [5]
>
> Great Prince! and so much Greater as more Wise;
> Sweet as our Life, and dearer than our Eyes,
> What Servants will conceal, and Councels spare
> To tell, the Painter and the Poet dare . . .
> Here needs no Fleet, no Sword, no Forreign Foe;
> Only let Vice be damn'd, and Justice flow.
> Shake but, like Jove, they Locks divine, and frown,
> Thy Scepter will suffice to guard thy Crown. [6]

[5] *Directions I*, p. 35.
[6] *Directions II*, p. 48.

So his bold Tube, Man, to the Sun apply'd,
And Spots unknown to the bright Star descry'd;
Show'd they obscure him, while too near they please,
And seem his Courtiers, are but his disease.
Through Optick Trunk the Planet seem'd to hear,
And hurls them off, e're since, in his Career.
And you, *Great Sir*, that with him Empire share,
Sun of our World, as he the Charles is there.
Blame not the *Muse* that brought those spots to sight,
Which, in your Splendor hid, Corrode your Light . . .[7]

The first *Directions* is the one most nearly linked to Waller's panegyric, and adopts, therefore, the obvious method of parody. When one compares, however, Buckingham's parody of a passage in *The Conquest of Granada*[8] with the parody in *Directions* of Waller's courtly-romantic tribute to the ladies of the court, the particular function and direction of the latter will become clear.

Buckingham has:

> So Boar and Sow, when any storm is nigh,
> Snuff up, and smell it gath'ring in the sky;
> Boar beckons Sow to trot in chestnut Groves,
> And there consummate their unfinish'd Loves:
> Pensive in mud they wallow all alone,
> And snore and gruntle to each others' moan . . .[9]

He is applying his model's elevated treatment of "two kind turtles" to animals with less dignified associations, in order to ridicule the elevation. The author of *Directions* on the other hand deflates the romantic-courtly with a "low" interpretation of the same phenomenon, with the implication that the latter is the more applicable of the two. This method aims to bring into contempt, not so much Waller's heroic style, as the pitiful objects of it.

[7] Marvell, "Last Instructions," *Poems*, Margoliouth, pp. 141–165, l. 949.
[8] In *The Rehearsal* (1671), Buckingham's famous burlesque of heroic plays, Dryden's in particular.
[9] Quoted by V. C. Clinton-Baddeley, *The Burlesque Tradition* (London, 1952), p. 35.

> But Painter, now prepare t'enrich thy piece,
> Pencil of Ermins, Oyl of Ambergreece,
> See where the Dutchess with Triumphant trail
> Of numerous Coaches, *Harwich* does assail!
> So the Land-Crabs, at Natures kindly call,
> Down to ingender to the Sea do Crawl.[10]

This perfectly defines the nature of the mock-heroic in the Painter poems. That which *should* be heroic—and the animus springs from the strength of that expectation in the author—is found wanting; only language and imagery as "low," as degrading, as the proper heroic is "high" and idealizing, will serve to release and express the author's anguished sense of discrepancy. It is the dialectic of Hamlet, who found a king of shreds and patches where there should have been an Hyperion.

There was available for the satirist in the mid-seventeenth century a type of "mock-poem" which could well serve his purpose. It is to be found most frequently in those miscellanies of wit—*Wits Recreations, Musarum Deliciae, Wit Restor'd,*[11] so popular for their mixture of salacious ribaldry, cavalier gallantry, and political broadside. A characteristic example is Cleveland's *The Author's Mock Song to Mark Antony:*

> When as the night-raven sung Pluto's matins
> And Cerberus cried three amens at a howl,
> When night-wandering witches put on their pattens,
> Midnight as dark as their faces are foul;
> Then did the furies doom
> That the nightmare was come.
> Such a misshapen groom
> Puts down Su. Pomfret clean.
> Never did incubus
> Touch such a filthy sus
> As this foul gypsy quean.
>
> First on her gooseberry cheeks I mine eyes blasted,
> Thence fear of vomiting made me retire

[10] *Directions I,* p. 27. The Duchess of York, Anne Hyde, Clarendon's daughter, whose marriage to the Duke of York was generally regarded as a "stain and dishonour to the Crown."

[11] 1640, 1656, and 1658 respectively. These three were published as *Facetiae,* in two volumes (London, 1817).

Unto her bluer lips, which when I tasted,
My spirits were duller than Dun in the mire.
But then her breath took place
Which went an usher's pace
And made way for her face!
You may guess what I mean.
Never did, &c.

In this case the poem may be said to be travesty since it is specifically related to the author's own romantic *Mark Antony*, as a similar mock-poem in *Wits Recreations* is related to Carew's *Ask me no more*, by the substitution of strong images of repulsion for Carew's images of delight. In all such instances of the mock-poem the "mockery" consists in the substitution of obscenity for erotic romance; the mode reappears, linked more closely to satire proper, in the ribald sensualities of Rochester; and continues in fashion [12] as the obverse of gallantry until gallantry itself is displaced by the bourgeois ethic of the eighteenth century. While the psychology of profanation links these more generally libidinous mock-poems to the iconoclasms of the Painter satires, and both can trace their remote origins in a feast of fools or Bacchic licence from inhibition, the mockery of the Painter series is distinguished, by its purposeful and political venom, from any predecessors.

Thus, the bawdily scurrilous treatment of the "monkey Duchess," or of Aumerle in *Directions II:*

. . . But most with story of his Hand and Thumb,
Conceal (as Honour would) his Grace's Bum,
when the rude Bullet a large Collop tore
Out of that Buttock never turn'd before . . .
But should the Rump perceiv't, they'd say that *Mars*
Had now reveng'd them upon Aumarle's Arse. . . .
[p. 40][13]

or of Ann Hyde in Marvell's *Last Instructions:*

[12] The many eighteenth century poems in the manner of Swift's *Strephon and Chloe* will be remembered.
[13] George Monk, Duke of Albemarle, General-at-Sea, one time hero of the return of Charles. The fleet was divided between Albemarle and Rupert, and was severely defeated at the battle of the North Foreland.

Paint then again *Her Highness* to the life,
Philosopher byond *Newcastle's* Wife.
She, nak'd, can *Archimedes* self put down,
For an Experiment upon the *Crown*.
She perfected that Engine, oft assay'd,
How after Childbirth to renew a Maid.
And found how *Royal Heirs* might be matur'd,
In fewer months than Mothers once indur'd.
Hence *Crowder* made the rare Inventress free,
Of's *Highnesses Royal Society*.
Paint her with Oyster Lip, and breath of Fame,
Wide Mouth that Sparragus may well proclaim;
With *Chanc'lor's* Belly, and so large a Rump.
There, not behind the Coach, her Pages jump.   [l. 49][14]

This deliberately iconoclastic scurrility is the distinguishing characteristic of what may be called the first phase of mock-heroic. It is to be found, in the Painter poems, in conjunction with passages of straightforward indignant statement of the destruction of the nation's heroic image:

Here, Painter, let thine Art describe a Story
Shaming our warlike Islands ancient Glory:
A Scene which never on our Seas appear'd,
Since our first ships were on the Ocean steer'd;
Make the *Dutch* Fleet, while we supinely sleep,
Without Opposers, Masters of the Deep:
Make them securely the *Thames* mouth invade . . .
Draw Thunder from their floating Castles, sent
Against our Forts, weak as our Government . . .
Instruct then thy bold Pencil to relate
The saddest Marks of an Ill govern'd State.
Draw th' injur'd Seamen deaf to all command,
While some with Horror and Amazement stand:
Others will know no other Enemy but they
Who have unjustly robb'd them of their Pay:

[14] Newcastle's wife was the author of several works on natural philosophy. Crowder was the Duke's chaplain, who performed the secret marriage of 1660 between the Duke and Anne Hyde.

Boldly refusing to oppose a Fire;
To kindle which, our Errors did Conspire: . . .[15]

Between these two modes comes the fleering sarcasm with
which in the first *Directions*, the mournful inadequacy of the
fleet's heroes, the Duke of York, or Rupert, is revealed:

Now Painter, spare thy weaker Art; forbear
To draw her [the Duchess of York's] parting Passions and each
    Tear:
For Love, alas! hath but a short Delight;
The Sea, the *Dutch*, the King, all call'd to Fight.
She therefore the Dukes Person recommends
To *Brunker*, *Pen*, and *Coventry*, her Friends;
To *Pen* much, *Brunker* more, most *Coventry*;
For they she knew were all more fraid then he:
Of flying Fishes one had sav'd the Fin,
And hop'd by this he through the Air might Spin;
The other thought he might avoid the Knell,
By the invention of the Diving Bell;
The third had try'd it, and affirm'd a Cable
Coyled round about him, was impenetrable.
But these the Duke rejected, only chose
To keep far off; let others interpose.
Rupert, that knew no fear, but Health did want,
Kept State suspended in a Chair volant;
All save his Head shut in that wooden case,
He shew'd but like a broken Weather-glass;
But arm'd with the whole Lyon Cap-a-Chin,
Did represent the *Hercules* within. [p. 28][16]

---

[15] *Directions III*, pp. 51–52.
[16] Brunkar was Cofferer to Charles II, Groom of the Bed-Chamber to
the Duke of York. He was dismissed from court in 1667 and expelled
from parliament in 1668, one of the "troop of Clarendon" whom Marvell
calls "Gross bodies, grosser Minds, and grossest Cheats." (*Last Instructions*, l. 179.) Sir William Pen, the Duke of York's "Great Captain and
Commander," incurred censure for his conduct of the battle of Lowe-
stoft in 1665 and henceforth served in the Navy Office and not at sea.
Sir William Coventry was Commissioner of the Treasury and the Navy,
and Secretary to the Duke of York.

Now all conspire unto the *Dutchmens* loss;
The wind, the fire, we, they themselves do cross.
When a sweet sleep began the Duke to drown,
And with soft Diadems his Temples crown:
And first he orders all the rest to watch,
And *They* the Foe, whilst *He* a *Nap* doth catch:
But lo, *Brunker* by a secret instinct,
Slept not, nor needed; he all day had winkt.
The *Duke* in bed, he then first draws his steel,
Whose vertue makes the misled Compass wheel.
So ere He wak'd, both Fleets were innocent:
And *Brunker* Member is of Parliament. [p. 32]

Broken fragments of the heroic associations in heroic couplets
—used, however, more like a bludgeon than a rapier; virulent
indecency in the broadsheet medium of the short line or doggerel tetrameter (such as produced Marvell's *Clarindon's
House-Warming*, 1667; *The Kings Vowes*, 1670; and later
Rochester's *Insipids*, 1676)—these comprise the spectrum of the
philippic in the period during which Lord Chancellor Hyde
was almost universally regarded as the "burthen of the Earth,"
and his policies, and his peers, the ruin of the nation.

Curs'd be *the Man that first begat this War;*
In an ill *hour,* under a Blazing Star.
For *Others* sport two Nations fight a Prize;
Between them both, Religion wounded dies.
So of first Troy, *the angry Gods unpaid,*
Raz'd the Foundations which themselves had laid.

Men who in *England* have no other Lot,
Than what they by betraying it have got;
Who can pretend to nothing but Disgrace,
Where either Birth or Merit find a place.
Plague, Fire and War, have been the Nations Curse,
But to have these our Rulers, is a worse . . .[17]

[17] *Directions II*, pp. 48–49.

Iconoclasts and Prophets

MARVELL'S *Last Instructions*— A BID FOR EPIC

Marvell's *The Last Instructions*, written with the four *Directions* in mind, is, it would seem, a serious attempt to create a more fitting form for the complexities of the matter presented. The very fact that he deals with the same events in the Dutch wars as his predecessors lends color to the idea that he felt the need to shape their material, give it form and status. He was sufficiently a poet in the high Renaissance tradition, and of the highest creative gifts, to be dissatisfied with a mere polishing and sharpening of lampoon; moreover, he had lent his best energies to the analysis of the republican heroic during the Commonwealth, and, if only as parliament man and republican, had a wider and less intimately venomous view of court failures than his revengeful and anonymous colleagues in the Painter mode. Even in the Painter satires had been implicit the epic idea of a noble and puissant nation brought to shame and disaster. Constant references to Troy, to Nero's Rome, to Michaelangelo's painting of the Day of Judgment point to this. But the idea is submerged beneath the torrent of abuse. It is, therefore, a true instrument of epic satire that Marvell seeks, and his poem marks an intermediate stage upon the road to Dryden and the Augustans. In the *Anniversary*, at the high tide of his republican enthusiasm, Marvell had been able, in the "Chammish issue" passage on the Sects, for instance, to blend with his ardent panegyric a denunciatory, keen-witted satire:

> Accursed Locusts, whom your King does spit
> Out of the Center of th'unbottom'd Pit;
> Wand'rers, Adult'rers, Lyers, *Munser's* rest,
> Sorcerers, Atheists, Jesuites, Possest;
> You who the Scriptures and the Laws deface
> With the same liberty as Points and Lace;
> Oh Race most hypocritically strict!
> Bent to reduce us to the ancient Pict;
> Well may you act the *Adam* and the *Eve;*
> Ay, and the Serpent too that did deceive. [l. 311]

[173]

Now, however, the proportion of praise to blame is to be radically different, and he is not sustained by the republican vision which could raise the importance and significance of the target of his satire in proportion to the value of that which it threatens to destroy. And so, in *The Last Instructions* much of the piece remains at the level of the obscene and the gross characteristic of all the Painter satires, albeit with a finer turn of wit than their authors could command:

> Paint then *St. Albans* full of soup and gold,
> The new *Courts* pattern, Stallion of the old,
> Him neither Wit nor Courage did exalt,
> But Fortune chose him for her pleasure salt.
> Paint him with *Drayman's* Shoulders, butchers *Mien*,
> Member'd like Mules, with Elephantine chine.
> Well he the Title of St. *Alban's* bore,
> For never *Bacon* study'd Nature more . . .   [l. 29][18]

> Paint *Castlemaine* in Colours that will hold,
> Her, not her Picture, for she now grows old.
> She through her Lacquies Drawers as he ran,
> Discern'd Love's Cause and a new Flame began.
> Her wonted joys thenceforth and *Court* she shuns,
> And still within her mind the Footman runs:
> His brazen Calves, his brawny Thighs, (the Face
> She slights) his Feet shapt for a smoother race.
> Poring within her Glass she re-adjusts
> Her looks, and oft-try'd Beauty now distrusts:
> Fears lest he scorn a Woman once assay'd,
> And now first, wisht she e're had been a Maid.
> Great Love, how dost thou triumph, and how reign,
> That to a Groom couldst humble her disdain!
> Stript to her Skin, see how she stooping stands,
> Nor scorns to rub him down with those fair Hands;
> And washing (lest the scent her Crime disclose)
> His sweaty Hooves, tickles him 'twixt the Toes.

[18] St. Albans—Henry Jermyn, Ambassador to France, of whom there were rumors of an affair with the Queen.

But envious Fame, too soon, begun to note
More gold in's Fob, more Lace upon his Coat
And he, unwary, and of Tongue too fleet,
No longer could conceal his Fortune sweet.
Justly the Rogue was whipt in Porter's Den:
And *Jermyn* straight has leave to come agen.   [l. 79][19]

The *Last Instructions*, then, is sufficiently peppered with the
salacities of philippic in the mock-heroic vein of the middle
1660's. It is undertaken with spleen and opens with the announced intention to castigate "this race of Drunkards, Pimps,
and Fools." Nevertheless, it ends with a vision of Britannia
distressed which was to set off a chain reaction of prophetic
Harringtonian "vision" satires, and is the sole Painter poem in
which can be discerned, side by side with the lampoon material, verse of a level, kind, and quality which can only be
accounted for in terms of a serious epic intention. Taken as a
whole, the poem resolves itself not into a consistent caricature
of unheroic heroes, but into what is in effect an epic in reverse
—an epic of defeat and demoralization, not of triumph and victory. De Ruyter's progress up the Thames, for instance, is
given a quality quite unlike the self-searing flippancy of the
other passages through the serious imagery of violation; while
the epic value of the joys of conquest is presented, with a
tragic irony, through the eyes of the enemy:

Ruyter the while, that had our Ocean curb'd,
Sail'd now among our Rivers undisturb'd:
Survey'd their Crystal Streams, and Banks so green,
And Beauties e're this never naked seen.
Through the vain sedge the bashful *Nymphs* he ey'd;
Bosomes, and all which from themselves they hide.
The Sun much brighter, and the Skies more clear,
He finds the Air, and all things, sweeter here.

[19] Barbara Villiers, the notorious Countess of Castlemaine, created
Duchess of Cleveland in 1670, was favorite mistress to Charles till 1671.
It is amusing to contrast Dryden's gallant *To the Lady Castlemaine,
Poetical Works,* ed. Noyes, p. 20.

The sudden change, and such a tempting sight,
Swells his old Veins with fresh Blood, fresh Delight.
Like am'rous Victors he begins to shave,
And his new Face looks in the *English* Wave.
His sporting Navy all about him swim,
And witness their complaisence in their trim.
Their streaming Silks play through the weather fair,
And with inveigling Colours Court the Air.
While the red Flags breath on their Top-masts high
Terrour and War, but want an Enemy.
Among the Shrowds the Seamen sit and sing,
And wanton Boys on every Rope do cling.   [l. 523]

Comparison with an analogous passage in the first *Directions*
clearly brings out the difference:

By this time both the Fleets in reach dispute,
And each the other mortally salute:
Draw pensive *Neptune* biting of his Thumbs,
To think himself a Slave whoe're o'recomes.
The frighted *Nymphs* retreating to their Rocks,
Beating their Blue Breasts, tearing their Green locks . . .
Opdam . . .
Makes to the Duke and threatens him from far, . . .
But in the vain attempt, took fire too soon,
And flies up in his Ship to catch the Moon,
Monsieurs like Rockets mount aloft, and crack
In thousand sparks, then dancingly fall back.   [p. 30]

Here the author is concerned to create an effect of bathos by
devices of expression, whereas Marvell's passage on the progress
of de Ruyter up the Thames allows the actual truth of events
to provide their own comment on a narration which is—except
perhaps for the touch of wit in respect to the amorous victors
—consistently dignified in diction.

There are, of course, great difficulties in the way of an exact
assessment of the heroic in diction in any particular era. Dennis'
critical dialogues are sufficient witness to the difficulty en-

countered even by a contemporary.[20] And Marvell's vocabulary range is in any case closer to the more familiar Horatian, or witty metaphysical, than to the Latinised neo-classical which Augustan theory regarded as solely heroic. Nevertheless, if we allow the Painter series to provide their own scale of dignity, the heroic tenor of Marvell's style is incontestable. A conclusive instance, quite unequivocal in its successful "begetting of admiration"—the proper object of heroic imagery, one remembers—follows as comment on the de Ruyter passage:

> So have I seen in *April's* bud, arise
> A Fleet of Clouds, sailing along the Skies:
> The liquid Region with their Squadrons fill'd,
> The airy Sterns the Sun behind does guild;
> And gentle Gales them steer, and Heaven drives,
> When, all on sudden, their calm bosome rives
> With Thunder and Lightning from each armed Cloud;
> Shepherds themselves in vain in bushes shrowd.
> Such up the stream the *Belgick* Navy glides,
> And at *Sheerness* unloads its stormy sides.   [l. 551]

The marriage of the Thames and the Medway in *The Faerie Queene* is deliberately recalled, for the sake of its epic associations, in the description of the disgrace which overtook the fleet:

> Black Day accurs'd! On thee let no man hale
> Out of the Port, or dare to hoise a Sail . . .

[20] For instance in *The Impartial Critic* (1693). *Dialogue III*, in Spingarn, Vol. III, p. 171:

FREEMAIN: . . . the metaphor *Feed* is too gross for a ship, tho' I perfectly know what Mr. Waller means by it. But what think you of the word *Sped?* Is that an Heroicall word?

BEAUMONT: No, I must confess that *Sped* is something too mean.

FREEMAIN: Too mean! Why it is fit for nothing but Burlesque, man. Besides, the word heretofore seems too obsolete, nor is Fishes very Heroical.

Neo-classical restrictions upon vocabulary in the interests of the pure heroic are too well known to need reviewing. Davenant's Shakespeare is a case in point. But it is interesting to watch Marvell in practice working towards an Augustan phraseology—"liquid Region"—when his object is "admiration."

Thee, the Year's monster, let thy Dam devour.
And constant Time, to keep his course yet right,
Fill up thy space with a redoubled Night.
When aged *Thames* was bound with Fetters base,
And *Medway* chast ravish'd before his Face,
And their dear Off-spring murder'd in their sight;
Thou, and thy Fellows, held'st the odious Light.
Sad change, since first that happy pair was wed,
When all the Rivers grac'd their Nuptial Bed . . .

[l. 737]

The presence in the 1689 text of Douglas, the loyal Scot, the truly heroic and undefeated, is perhaps the conclusive indication of Marvell's underlying and incompletely realized intention in *The Last Instructions*.

But the question of decorum remains a vexed one. As the Caroline satirists wrestled with the question of "jest and reprehension," so Marvell has to find a way to modulate from heroic "admiration" through to the sting and jibe of contemptuous sarcasm. He does so by didactic passages and by invoking the Painter machinery. It is impossible to claim that he has succeeded in the total task, despite the wit which informs both the epic and the lampoon. The two elements, Douglas and Ann Hyde, tend to separate in the mind. There is no sufficiently unifying medium in which they can coexist and coalesce. It is interesting that Marvell himself removed Douglas from the *Instructions* and built round his heroic death a reflective political poem in the Denham manner, in which the description of Douglas is the baroque-heroic cornerstone.[21]

We shall have occasion to remember this intermediary work of Marvell when we come to consider Dryden's final fusion, through such "(nice) and most delicate touches of Satire (as) consist of fine Raillery," of epic with lampoon. The resultant blend is the perfected mock-heroic of a politer decade. Marvell's own later prose polemic, *The Rehearsal Transpros'd*, plays its part, as we shall see, in the genesis of Dryden's "fine Raillery," but for Marvell it represents a turning aside from the en-

[21] See Chapter 6, above.

deavor to create philippic which shall have the dignity of epic utterance as well as the salt of stinging wit.

THE VISIONARY BRITANNIA AND
THE SATANIC JESUIT

If Dryden fused the elements which were unreconciled in Marvell, the years between 1667 and 1680 saw the development of each element separately as the basis of different kinds of satire. The lampoon, more or less witty, continued to flourish. Its original impetus as the obverse of the grandiloquent heroic of the Restoration disappears, and it acquires, as it were, an independent life of its own as an effective weapon, for republicans as much as for disillusioned royalists. *The Dream of the Cabal*, 1672, pillories Shaftesbury thus:

> A little bobtail'd Lord, Urchin of State,
> A *Praise-God-bare-bone* Peer whom all men hate;
> Amphibious Animal, half Fool, half Knave;
> Begg'd silence, and this purblind Counsel gave . . .
> A mixt hodge podge will now no longer do,
> *Caesar* or nothing, You are brought unto: . . .
> We may unpolitick be judg'd, or worse,
> If we can't make the Sword command the Purse;
> No Art or Courtship can the Rule so shape
> Without a Force, it must be done by Rape . . .
> Phanaticks they'll to Providence impute
> Their Thraldom, and immediately grow mute . . .
> For they, poor pious Fools . . .
> When their Reason is abase'd to it,
> They forthwith think't Religion to submit . . .
> When bite they can't, what hurt can barking do?
> And, Sir, in time we'll spoil their barking too,
> Make Coffee-Clubs talk of more humble things
> Than State Affairs, and Interest of Kings.[22]

On the other hand, the prophetic note which Marvell had sounded in the Britannia passage with which he ended the *Last Instructions* began to form the staple of those satires of the

[22] *Poems on Affairs of State*, p. 148.

vision type by which the Painter satires were superseded.
The Vision satires can claim Piers Plowman as a remote ancestor, are strongly Puritan in tone, and, wherever sufficiently
articulate, republican in sentiment and doctrine. Their motivation is not iconoclastic, nor is their origin in a frustrated heroic
of the Restoration. They derive from the old reforming republican zeal which had slumbered since the death of Cromwell. Their motive is revolutionary rather than polemic or
punitive; and, since they spur to action rather than to reform,
they do not employ the flaying, railing Jacobean Juvenal, but
rather that Juvenalian vehemence of which Milton was a master,
and which Dryden admired when he said "his spirit has more
of the commonwealth genius; he treats tyranny, and all the
vices attending it, as they deserve, with the utmost rigor." [23]

An early satire of this type is Hodge's *Vision from the
Monument*, 1675:

> Like Chaos you [Rome] the tott'ring Globe Invade,
> Religion cheat, and War ye make a Trade.
> Next the lewd Palace of the Plotting King,
> To's Eyes new Scenes of Frantick Folly bring;
> Behold (says he) the Fountain of our Woe,
> From whence our Vices and our Ruin flow:
> Here Parents their own Of-spring prostitute,
> By such vile Arts t'obtain some viler Suit;
> Here blooming Youth adore Priapus's shrine,
> And Priests pronounce him Sacred and Divine.
> The *Gotish* God behold in his *Alcove*,
> (The secret Scene of Damn'd incestuous Love.)
> Melting in Lust, and Drunk like *Lot*, he lies
> Betwixt two bright Daughter Divinities: . . .
> Cease, cease, (O C——) thus to pollute our Isle,
> Return, return to thy long wish'd Exile . . .[24]

It is difficult to know why Charles tolerated these and similar
attacks, or for that matter the Painter poems, which constituted
lèse majesté when they were not open libel. True, Anthony à

[23] "Discourse Concerning Satire," p. 311.
[24] *Poems on Affairs of State*, p. 110.

Wood notes of one of the latter that "the printer that printed them, being discover'd, stood in the pillory for the same." [25] But this was evidently insufficient deterrent. The attacks were printed, and tolerated. But whether this was the toleration of a libertine monarch, or the dependence of a needy exchequer, or the King's fear of going on his travels again, is difficult to assess.

In 1671 appeared *Nostradamus's Prophecy*, with the Harringtonian reference in the last line to "Venetian Libertye," and in 1675 *Britannia and Rawleigh*, both attributed to Marvell.

A *Colony* of *French* posess the *Court;*
Pimps, Priests, Buffoons, in Privy Chamber sport;
Such slimy Monsters ne'r approacht a throne
Since *Pharaoh's Days*, nor so defil'd a Crown.
I'th sacred ear Tyrannick Arts they croak,
Pervert his Mind, and good Intention choak;
Tell him of Golden *Indies*, Fairy Lands,
Leviathan, and absolute Commands . . .
Tyrants, like Leprous Kings, for publick weal,
Should be immur'd, lest the Contagion steal
Over the whole. Th'Elect of the *Jessean* line
To this firm Law their Scepter did resign . . .
Till then, my Raleigh teach our noble Youth,
To love Sobriety and holy Truth . . .
Teach them how Arts and Arms in thy Young Days
Employ'd our Youth, not Taverns, Stews and Plays . . .
Greek Arts and Roman Arms, in her conjoyn'd,
Shall England raise, relieve opprest Mankind . . .
So shall my *England* in a Holy War
In Triumph lead chain'd Tyrants from a far,
Her true *Crusado* shall at last pull down
The *Turkish* Crescent and the Persian sun.
Freed by thy Labours, Fortunate Blest Isle,
The Earth shall rest, the Heaven shall on thee smile;
And this kind Secret for Reward shall give,
No Poyson'd Tyrants on thy Earth shall live.[26]

[25] Margoliouth, ed. *Poems*, Marvell, p. 269.
[26] *Ibid.*, p. 90 ff.

Oceana and Britannia, 1679, brings this series up to the time of the Exclusion Bill and the fixing of hopes upon Monmouth. Ocean gives birth upon Britannia's shores to a "Sweet smiling Babe" mightier in Heaven's scales than "Crowns, Crosiers, Scepters," who is given into the care of he who

> By's Sire rejected, but by Heaven call'd,
> To break my Yoke, and rescue the Enthral'd.
> He'll guide my People through the Raging Seas,
> To Holy Wars and certain Victories.[27]

The crusading republican note makes of these poems almost a genre, tracing back through the vision in *The Last Instructions* to the *First Anniversary*, and to Milton's *Defenses* themselves. Old Testament reference is prominent everywhere; Old Testament allegory lies, one feels, just below the surface, and breaks through explicitly in *An Historical Poem*, 1680, which was attributed to Marvell, but is more likely to be by the author of Hodge's *Vision from the Monument*, and the inserted anti-prelatical sections of *The Loyall Scot:* [28]

> Of a tall Stature and of sable hue,
> Much like the Son of Kish that lofty Jew,
> Twelve Yeares compleat he suffer'd in Exile
> And kept his Fathers Asses all the while.
> At length by wonderfull impulse of Fate
> The People call him home to helpe the State,
> And what is more they send him Mony too,
> And cloath him all from head to foot anew; . . .
> In a slasht doublet then he came to shoare,
> And dubd poore Palmer's wife his Royall Whore.[29]

Here is a cutting irony of biblical allusion used to deflate the enemy. Dryden must surely have had such a poem in mind when he outdid the anti-Stuart ironists, and the Bible-quoting City Puritans, with his own use of biblical allegory.

[27] *Ibid.*, p. 131.
[28] See Margoliouth, p. 325.
[29] *Poems on Affairs of State*, p. 201. Poor Palmer is of course the Earl of Castlemaine, Barbara Villier's husband.

This emergence of ironic biblical allegory, with the pressure
of the republican and Puritan ethos behind it, coming after the
anti-heroical lampooning of the Painter satires and Marvell's
abortive attempt at elevation, would seem to be the "penulti-
mate step" in the progress towards Dryden's master achievement in *Absalom*. The distinction has been claimed [30] for Oldham's *Satires Upon the Jesuits*, 1678. Dryden certainly admired
Oldham, finding that:

> For sure our souls were near allied, and thine
> Cast in the same poetic mold with mine.
> One common note on either lyre did strike,
> And knaves and fools we both abhorr'd alike.[31]

Nevertheless the alliance of his soul with the heroic intemper-
ance of Oldham's invective was overweighed by his conviction of the efficacy of a lighter touch, a subtler indirection of
irony. He has recorded this debate, the debate between what
the age called the Juvenalian and the Horatian, railing and raillery, in *The Discourse Concerning Satire*, 1693, which will be
discussed in the following chapter. Oldham's afflatus, at all
events, belongs to a school of satire which has affinities with
the impassioned zeal of the prophets against the court, lashed
to frenzied hyperbole by the excitements of the Exclusion Bill
period. *A Satyrical Poem* by W. M. Esquire, for instance, is
typical:

> A Plot! Heavens bless us! will the Romish *Whore*
> Never leave *Teeming?* will She ne'r give o're?
> But like Impraegnate *Aetna* fright the *World*,
> With fresh *Granados* from her *Entrails* hurl'd?
> Or, like her *Mother-Wolf*, bring forth a *Brood*
> Of *Miscreant Whelps*, t'be suckt with human *Blood?*
> T'ravage the Christian Lambs with griping Claws,
> A ravenous Stomach, and Blood Thirsty Jaws? [32]

[30] See Weldon M. Williams, "The Genesis of John Oldham's *Satires
Upon the Jesuits*," *PMLA*, Vol. LVIII (1943).
[31] "To the Memory of Mr. Oldham," *Poetical Works*, ed. Noyes, p. 174.
[32] London (1678), p. 1.

So is the Pindaric *Satyr against Vertue*, 1679, by Oldham himself:

> A greater crime befitted his [Nero's] high Power,
> Who sacrific'd a City to a Jest,
> And shew'd he knew the grand Intrigues of human Lust.
> He made at Rome a bonfire for Loud Fame,
> And Sung, and play'd and danc'd amidst the Flames;
> Bravely begun! yet pity there he stay'd,
> One step to Glory more, he should have made.
> He should have heav'd the noble frolic higher,
> And made the People on that Funeral expire,
> Or, providently, with their blood put out the Fire.[33]

When John Oldham searched for a model for his satires [34] he hit upon the old parodic device of the disingenuous or mock confession, and cast the vauntings of his satanic Jesuits into the mould of the period's Juvenalian railing—a superhyperbolic expression of outrage and execration. The ghost of Garnet, of Gunpowder Plot fame, thus curses Luther:

> Thrice damned be that apostate monk, from whom
> Sprung first these enemies of us and Rome;
> Whose poisonous filth, dropt from engendering brain,
> By monstrous birth did the vile insects spawn,
> Which now infest each country, and defile
> With their o'er spreading swarms this goodly isle.[35]

His own particular gift however, was an almost Marlovian flair for dramatic rhetoric; in the mouth, for example, of his archetypal Jesuit:

> Had you but half my bravery in sin,
> Your work had never thus unfinished been; . . .

[33] London (1679), p. 10. This satire was published together with the *Jesuits* and accompanied by an epilogue in which the author claims that he was attacking the vices of the age "in Masquerade."

[34] Weldon M. Williams, *loc. cit.*, has examined the manuscript records of Oldham's satiric experiments, and analyzed the genesis of his choice of form.

[35] *Poetical Works,* ed. Robert Bell (London, 1854), p. 89. Reference is to this edition.

. . . I would leap hell,
To reach his life, though in the midst I fell,
And deeper than before,—
Let rabble souls, of narrow aim and reach,
Stoop their vile necks, and dull obedience preach;
Let them with slavish awe (disdained by me)
Adore the purple rag of majesty,
And think't a sacred relic of the sky;
Well may such fools a base subjection own;
Vassals to every ass that loads a throne;
Unlike the soul, with which proud I was born,
Who could that sneaking thing a monarch scorn,
Spurn off a crown, and set my foot in sport
Upon the head that wore it, trod in dirt. [p. 87]

Each snivelling hero seas of blood can spill,
When wrongs provoke, and honour bids him kill; . . .
Give me your thorough-paced rogue, who scorns to be
Prompted by poor revenge, or injury,
But does it of true inbred cruelty;
Your cool and sober murderer, who prays
And stabs at the same time, who one hand has
Stretched up to heaven, the other to make the pass . . .
So they with lifted hands, and eyes devout,
Said grace, and carved a slaughtered monarch out.
                                              [p. 98]

Oldham's portraits of his latter-day Tamburlaines, the Jesuits,
are brought up to date by a neatness of couplet wit which only
Dryden could excell:

Two grains of dough, with cross, and stamp of priest,
And five small words pronounced, make up their Christ.
To this they all fall down, this all adore,
And straight devour, what they adored before. [p. 131]

Another frights the rout with rueful stories,
Of wild chimeras, limbos, purgatories,
And bloated souls in smoky durance hung,

Like a Westphalia gammon, or neat's tongue,
To be redeemed with masses and a song.

Here blessed Mary's milk, not yet turned sour,
Renown'd (like asses') for its healing power . . .   [p. 128]

In the extremism of statement which characterizes such a piece as *Loyola's Will* (Satire III), Restoration philippic reaches a climax of vehemence. Oldham certainly takes his opponents seriously, so seriously, indeed, as almost to preclude the possibility of "jest" with the "reprehension" altogether. This is diatribe, name-calling, epic perhaps in its scale and the degree of its virulence, but with no touch of reasonable reality, either in description or analysis. Loyola instructs thus:

If any novice feel at first a blush,
Let wine, and frequent converse with the stews,
Reform the fop, and shame it out of use,
Unteach the puling folly by degrees,
And train him to a well-bred shamelessness:
Get that great gift, and talent, impudence,
Accomplished mankind's highest excellence,
'Tis that alone prefers, alone makes great . . .   [p. 109]

Confession, our chief privilege and boast, . . .
'Tis this that spies through court intrigues, and brings
Admission to the cabinets of Kings;
By this we keep proud monarchs at our becks,
And make our footstools of their thrones and necks . . .
This is your harvest; here, secure and cheap,
You may the fruits of unbought pleasure reap;
Riot in free and uncontrolled delight,
Where no dull marriage clogs the appetite;
Taste every dish of lust's variety,
Which popes and scarlet lechers dearly buy
With bribes, and bishoprics, and simony.   [pp. 113–114]

During the decade 1660–1676 the note of harmony upon which the Restoration had opened had turned to discord. Whereas the disillusioned royalists lashed the failings of those who should have realized their ideal of royal heroic glory and might, turning like scorpions their stings upon themselves, the republicans revived their heroic vision of a reformed nation in prophetic denunciations of the same corrupt court. Meanwhile the Jesuits provided a scapegoat for all those Protestants who shared the general malaise of unrest, fear, and an almost hysterical suspicion. While all were at odds, they had one thing in common: the hyperbolic violence of their railing. It is a universal failing. Those who were to become the Tories, in their demoralization restricted their view to the grotesquely unheroic aspects of their leaders; those who were to become the Whigs in their fervor lost themselves often in the bogey-visions, the Frankenstein monsters conjured up by an inflamed moral imagination. It is the eve of the Popish Plot.

CHAPTER EIGHT

"Raillerie à la Mode Consider'd"

BURLESQUE WIT

IT IS often pointed out that among the skepticisms and levities which the courtiers brought back with them from exile was the burlesque genre, in the form, at first, of travesty. Now burlesque is a protean mode; it has its own spectrum of folly and laughter at folly; and of all moods or modes it is perhaps the most elusive of definition.[1] Upon a scale of intellectual detachment and indirection the Painter satires can be seen as standing at one extreme of burlesque, *Mac Flecknoe* at the other. Nevertheless, if Butler's *Hudibras* can be said to represent the heart and center of the mode in its historical seventeenth century sense, then it is clear that we have to deal with a distinct phenomenon, one which marks an important stage in the development of the style and the sensibility, the method and kind of criticism, which, under the blanket-term "mock-heroic," is recognized as a distinctive feature of late seventeenth century and early eighteenth century literature. A comprehensive account of the mock-heroic temper would have to include such major movements of thought as philosophical skepticism in its various forms, Hobbesian materialism and nominalism, Royal Society rationalism, religious latitudinarianism and toleration, and, in general, the spirit of doubt and free inquiry of the *ésprits forts* and the *libertins* of the period. The immediate concern of this study, however, is to trace the literary development of mock-heroic in the specific field of

---

[1] R. P. Bond, *English Burlesque Poetry 1700–1759* (Harvard, 1932), gives a valuable account of the various types of burlesque. D. Worcester, *The Art of Satire* (Harvard, 1940), has an excellent analysis of the varieties of satiric laughter.

literary-political comment and criticism as expressed in the poems on affairs of state of the time.

In France the vogue of burlesque had reached its height by the 1640's; the neo-classical separation of styles, and the consequent preoccupation with stylistic incompatibilities, flourished in France earlier than in England. But the *gamin* indecorum of the innumerable French travesties had been overdone,[2] and the word had come to be used so indiscriminately that, though centered upon a facetious and irreverent rendering of the classics, it had come to mean little more than any flippant doggerel. As late as 1693 Dryden, in *The Discourse Concerning Satire*, could refer to "the sort of verse which is called *Burlesque*, consisting of Eight Syllables, or Four Feet," though in 1683, in his translated version of Boileau's *Art Poétique*, he characterizes the burlesque (and clearly travesty is what is meant) as a work turning upon a general incongruity and liberty of style—"low Stuff," from the indictment of which he exempts only Butler:

> The dull burlesque appear'd with impudence,
> And pleas'd by novelty, in spite of sense.
> All, except trivial points, grew out of date;
> *Parnassus* spoke the cant of *Belinsgate:*
> Boundless and Mad, disorder'd Rhyme was seen:

[2] Paul Pellison, *Histoire de l'Académie Francaise* (1653), translated in 1656 as *The History of the French Academy*, complains: ". . . it (the word Burlesque) not onely passed in *France*, but . . . has overrun it, and made strange havock there . . . is it not the opinion of most men, that to write well in this kind, tis sufficient to speake things that have neither sense nor reason. Everyone thinks himself able enough for it, of what sex soever, from the Ladies and Lords at Court to the Chambermaides and Pages. This madnesse of Burlesque, which at last we begin to be cured of, went so far, that the Stationers would meddle with nothing that had not his name in the front; that whether out of ignorance, or the better to put off their wares, they fixt it upon things that were the most serious provided onely that they were short verses: whence it was that in the time of the war at Paris in 1639, they printed a piece, bad enough in deed, but yet serious, with this title, which strook with horror all those that read no more of it, The Passion of our Lord in Burlesque Verses, and the learned Monsieur Mandaeus who doubtlesse was of this number, reckons it amongst the Burlesque books of our times" (pp. 71–72).

Disguis'd *Apollo* chang'd to *Harlequin.*
This plague, which first in country towns began,
Cities and kingdoms quickly overran; . . .
But this low stuff the town at last despis'd,
And scorn'd the folly that they once had priz'd;
Distinguish'd dull from natural, and plain,
And left the Villages to Flecknoe's reign.
Let not so mean a style your Muse debase,
But learn from Butler the buffooning grace . . .[3]

This was written in the light of the reaction which, in France, had soon set in against "burlesque"; and it was a reaction which accorded perfectly with Dryden's own distaste for the form. However, the development of burlesque in Restoration England, now free for harlequinade after the tensions and conflicts of civil war and Commonwealth, is of the greatest importance, both in itself and because Butler's "buffooning grace" and the later more sophisticated forms of burlesque had the greatest influence, albeit inversely, upon Dryden's own style.

In 1663 Davenant registers the new Restoration mood, as well as the confusion of terminology which reigned at that date, in his *The Playhouse to be Lett:*

. . . the travesti,
I mean Burlesque, or more t'explain myself,
Would say, the Mock Heroique must be it,
Which draws the pleasant hither i'the Vacation,
Men of no malice who will pay for laughter . . .[4]

and he offers a definition most significant for the subject of this study:

Our Bullies the Burlesquers,
That show the wrong side of the Hero's outward.

Cotton's *Scarronides* appeared in 1664 and initiated a spate of classical travesty. The first two parts of *Hudibras* were pub-

---

[3] "The Art of Poetry," *Poetical Works,* ed. Noyes, pp. 916–925, l. 81.
[4] First published 1673. The passage is quoted in Clinton-Baddeley, *The Burlesque Tradition* (London, 1925), pp. 29–30.

lished in 1663 and 1664 respectively, and the first draft of Buckingham's *Rehearsal* dates from 1665, though it was not performed, on account of the plague, till 1671. These works cover a wide range of burlesque and show that, while the critical terminology remained confused throughout the century, the practice of the 1660's was exploring intensively the ways in which formal stylistic buffoonery could be turned to the purposes of social, political, or literary satire.

What in fact we have to deal with in these chapters can be subsumed under the seventeenth century term "raillery." It is a term of the widest, and often vaguest, application; it gained wide currency during the period of the genesis of the mock-heroic. An analysis of its emergence and significance, its relation to burlesque on the one hand, and to the growth of the attitudes of the Enlightenment on the other, throws a great deal of light, not only upon the nature of the philippic in our period, but also upon an important chapter of critical history.

Any description of the raillery of the period cannot but note the presence of what we may call the burlesque similitude as a constant distinguishing feature. These burlesque similitudes continue the tradition of the hyperbolic, "metaphysical," witty conceit as used by Donne in his satires, or by those hypercritical grotesques, the malcontents of Jacobean drama, in theirs. Bosola's vision of human existence as fantastical puff-paste, Flamineo's description of the Spanish ambassador carrying his face in his ruff like a serving man carrying glasses in a "cypress hatband, monstrous steady, for fear of breaking" and looking like "the claw of a blackbird, first salted and then broiled in a candle," Donne's affected courtier squeaking like a high-stretched lute string, Cleveland's Mixed Assembly and Madam Smec, whose truckling together would produce, not a child-birth, but a gaol-delivery, Marvell's *basso relievo* of a man—all bear the stamp of the hyperbolic, surrealistic, fantastic, and grotesque, coupled with the keenest powers of analysis and analogy, which made up the antic disposition of the time.[5]

[5] Saintsbury registers his sense of the burlesque in Cleveland but with a certain doubt whether he deliberately set out to burlesque the metaphysical manner, or was possessed of a "general burlesque personality."

The principle of such burlesque similitudes would seem to reside in a concertina-like expansion and contraction of dimensions. There might be a disparity between the quantitative treatment and the triviality of the thing treated: or between the magnitude of the simile's vehicle and the littleness of its tenor; or vice versa; or a battery of terms all clashing in their associations of size or importance.

A few instances should serve to show how such burlesque imagery passes along a line of wit from Donne through Cleveland, then Butler,[6] the Restoration wits (Marvell, Eachard, Buckingham), and on indeed to Sterne. "Between Error and Truth," wrote Butler, "li's [sic] the Proper Sphere of wit, which though it seems to incline to Falshood, do's it only to give Intelligence to Truth . . . wit by a certaine Slight of the Minde, deliver's things otherwise then they are in Nature, by rendring them greater or lesse than they really are . . . or by putting them into some other condition than Nature ever did."[7]

And thus indeed, Donne:

> Would not Heraclitus laugh to see Macrine,
> From hat to shooe, himselfe at doore refine,
> As if the Presence were a Moschite, and lift
> His shirts and hose, and call his clothes to shrift,
> Making them confesse not only mortall
> Great staines and holes in them; but veniall
> Feathers and dust, wherewith they fornicate . . .[8]

Thus Cleveland, among many other instances:

The Caroline Poets, Vol. III, p. 7. Sypher, *Four Stages of Renaissance Style*, gives a most illuminating account of Mannerism, in whose precarious, or shocking, or daring perspectives these images may well take their origin.

[6] Nethercot, "The Reputation of the Metaphysicals during the Age of Johnson," *S.P.* (1925), notes passages from Cleveland from which Butler took hints. Aubrey says "they had a clubbing every night." (*Brief Lives*, ed. Clark [1898], Vol. I, p. 175.)

[7] *Characters and Passages from Note-Books*, ed. A. R. Waller (Cambridge, 1908), p. 336.

[8] *Satire IV*, l. 197.

Had Cain been Scot, God would have changed his doom;
Not forced him wander but confined him home!
Like Jews they spread and as infection fly,
As if the Devil had ubiquity.
Hence 'tis they live at rovers and defy
This or that place, rags of geography.
They're citizens o'th'world; they're all in all;
Scotland's a nation epidemical.[9]

Thus Marvell:

> This *Basso Relievo* of a Man,
> Who as a Camel tall, yet easly can
> The Needles Eye thread without any stich,
> (His only impossible is to be rich)
> Lest his too suttle Body, growing rare,
> Should leave his Soul to wander in the Air,
> He therefore circumscribes himself in rimes;
> And swaddled in's own papers seaven times,
> Wears a close Jacket of poetick Buff,
> With which he doth his third Dimension Stuff . . .
> But were he not in this black habit deck't,
> This half transparent Man would soon reflect
> Each colour that he past by; and be seen,
> As the *Chamelion*, yellow, or green.[10]

> The Fish oft-times the Burger dispossest,
> And sat not as a Meat but as a Guest;
> And oft the *Tritons* and the *Sea-Nymphs* saw
> Whole sholes of *Dutch* serv'd up for *Cabillau*;[11]

> Or what a Spectacle the *Skipper gross*,
> A *Water-Hercules Butter-Coloss* . . .[12]

And finally Butler, also on Holland:

> A Country that draws fifty Foot of Water,
> In which Men live, as in the Hold of Nature;

[9] "The Rebel Scot," l. 63.
[10] "Flecknoe," l. 63.
[11] "The Character of Holland," l. 29.
[12] *Ibid.*, l. 93.

And when the Sea does in upon them break,
And drown a Province, does but spring a Lake; . . .
That feed, like Canibals, on other Fishes,
And serve their Cousin-Germans up in Dishes:
A Land, that rides at Anchor, and is moor'd,
In which they do not live, but go aboard . . .[13]

on an Anabaptist:

"His dipping makes him more obstinate and stiff in his Opinions, like a Piece of hot Iron, that grows hard by being quenched in cold Water . . ."[14]

on an Haranguer:

"His Measure of Talk is till his Wind is spent; And then he is not silenced, but becalmed . . . He is so full of Words, that they run over and are thrown away to no purpose: and so empty of things or sense, that his Dryness has made his leaks so wide, whatsoever is put in him runs out immediately";[15]

on a Proud Man:

"A Proud Man is a Fool in Fermentation, that swells and Boils over like a Porridge-Pot";[16]

on a Huffing Courtier:

"He rides himself like a well-managed Horse, reins in his Neck, and walks *Terra Terra*. He carries his elbows backward, as if he were pinioned like a trust-up Fowl, and moves as stiff as if he was upon the Spit. His legs are stuck in his great voluminous Britches . . . in which his nether Parts are not cloathed, but packt up. His Hat has been long in a Consumption of the Fashion, and is now almost worn to Nothing; if it do not recover quickly it will grow too little for a Head of Garlick."[17]

[13] "Description of Holland," *The Genuine Remains in Verse and Prose of Mr. Samuel Butler*, ed. Thyer (London, 1759), Vol. i, p. 270.
[14] *Characters, etc.*, ed. Waller, p. 163.
[15] *Ibid.*, pp. 61–62.
[16] *Ibid.*, p. 44.
[17] *Ibid.*, p. 37.

The family resemblance between Donne's bore, Marvell's Flecknoe, and Butler's Haranguer (fathered originally by Horace, it is important to note), and between Donne's Courtier,[18] and Butler's, is not solely a matter of tone, humorously martyred or exasperated, or of the systole and diastole of the burlesque similitude, but also of a shared trick of burlesque description whereby mockery is positively enacted by syntax and image. In Butler particularly, satiric exposure is above all sportive, embedded, as it were, in the vagaries of his jog-trot measure, his phonetic, syntactic, and metaphoric acrobatics. Aided by his doggerel measure and multiple rhymes, Butler makes the diction of *Hudibras* (and to a lesser extent, by sheer tempo and comic image, the diction of many of the *Characters*) perform or enact the antics of his absurd pair and their associates:

> But Ralpho (who had now begun
> Th'adventure resurrection
> From heavy squelch . . .)
> Looking about, beheld pernicion
> Approaching Knight from fell musician,
> He snatch'd his whinyard up, that fled
> When he was falling off his steed
> (As rats do from a falling house),
> To hide itself from rage of blows;
> And wing'd with speed and fury, flew
> To rescue Knight from black and blue.[19]
>
> When Gospel-trumpeter, surrounded
> With long-ear'd rout, to battle sounded;
> And pulpit, drum ecclesiastic,
> Was beat with fist instead of a stick: [i.i.9]
>
> So politic, as if one eye
> Upon the other were a spy; . . .
> Could turn his word, and oath, and faith,

---

[18] *Satire I.* See for instance ll. 72–77.
[19] *Poetical Works*, ed. Gilfillan (Edinburgh, 1854), i.ii.931. All citations of *Hudibras* from this edition.

As many ways as in a lath:
By turning, wriggle like a screw,
Int' highest trust, and out, for new.   [III.II.355, 375]

"If he can he will run a Man up against a Wall, and hold him
at a Bay by the Buttons. . . . When he finds him begin to sink,
he holds him by the Cloaths, and feels him as a Butcher does a
Calf, before he kills him." [20]

"He flutters up and down like a Butterfly in a Garden; and
while he is pruning of his Peruque takes Occasion to contemplate his legs, and the Symmetry of his Britches . . . When he
accosts a Lady he puts both Ends of his Microcosm in Motion,
by making Legs at one End, and combing his Peruque at the
other." [21]

The Exposure of Irrationality

Butler's *Hudibras* is often regarded as a thing *sui generis*,
unique and without progeny, if the innumerable pasquils and
lampoons claiming his title, but having little but grammatical
licence and a crude doggerel tetrameter to remind us of the
original, be excepted. The uniqueness of *Hudibras* will be
dealt with in the next chapter. Here it will be sufficient to show
that *Hudibras* and the *Characters* (known in manuscript though
not published until well into the eighteenth century) [22] had
a profound influence upon the later direction of polemical
satire. This influence was exercised in two main ways: through
the miming in language, by sound and syntax, of absurdities;
and through the exposure of irrationality, the satirical analysis
and presentation of unreason in all its forms.

For it was through Butler that the burlesque similitude, in
which in any case the element of logical analysis is strong,
and the pantomime, came to be turned towards the deflating
of argument. The clown grins and tumbles, not only in mockery of absurd behavior, but of those *ignes fatui* of the mind
which take the form of inconsistency, sophistry, equivocation,
rationalization, scholasticism, or the ubiquitous non-sequitur.

[20] "An Haranguer," *Characters*, etc. p. 61.
[21] "A Huffing Courtier," *ibid.*, pp. 35, 37.
[22] They were first published in 1759, in *Genuine Remains*, ed. Thyer.

The vexed question of Synods or Bears debated by the Knight and his Independent henchman may well stand as a paradigm:

> The question then, to state it first,
> Is, Which is better or which worst,
> Synods or Bears? Bears I avow
> To be the worst, and Synods thou . . .
>
> [I.III.1265]

> But yet we are beside the question,
> Which thou didst raise the first contest on;
> For that was, Whether Bears are better
> Than Synod-men? I say, *Negatur.*
> That Bears are beasts, and Synods men,
> Is held by all: they're better then;
> For Bears and Dogs on four legs go,
> As beasts; but Synod-men on two.
> 'Tis true, they all have teeth and nails;
> But prove that Synod-men have tails;
> Or that a rugged, shaggy fur
> Grows o'er the hide of Presbyter;
> Or that his snout and spacious ears
> Do hold proportion with a Bear's.
> A Bear's a savage beast, of all
> Most ugly and unnatural,
> Whelp'd without form, until the dam
> Has lick'd it into shape and frame:
> But all thy light can ne'er evict,
> That ever Synod-men was lick'd,
> Or brought to any other fashion
> Than his own will and inclination.   [I.III.1291]

Ian Jack has well said that "in Butler parody of a man's idiom is inseparable from satire on the cast of his mind." [23] And it was this element of critical analysis in the parodic burlesquing of false logic which Butler bequeathed to Eachard, for his *Contempt of the Clergy,*[24] and to Marvell, "the liveliest

[23] *Augustan Satire, 1660–1750* (Oxford, 1952), p. 29.
[24] *The Grounds and Occasions for the Contempt of the Clergy* (1670) in *An English Garner,* ed. Arber (1883), Vol. VII.

[197]

droll of his age, who writ in a burlesque strain, but with so entertaining a conduct, that from the king down to the Tradesman his book was read with great pleasure." [25]

Thus the line of burlesque wit in the service of a critical rationality runs clear from the mock-logic exhibited in the Synods and Bears passage, and from applications of the burlesque similitude to logical misbehavior, such as

> He had First Matter seen undress'd;
> He took her naked, all alone,
> Before one rag of form was on. [i.i.560] [26]

> He could raise scruples dark and nice,
> And after solve 'em in a trice;
> As if Divinity had catch'd
> The itch, on purpose to be scratch'd . . .
> [i.i.163]

to mockery of the opponent's logic such as is to be found in *The Rehearsal Transpros'd*. In reply to Bishop Parker's contention that "Public peace and tranquillity in itself is a thing so good and necessary, that there are very few actions that it will not render virtuous, whatever they in themselves, wherever they happen to be useful and instrumental to its attainment," Marvell drily remarks: "There is another [necessity], which may be termed the necessity of the neck, or Caligula's necessity, before spoke of; that is, that the whole body of the people would have but one neck. Do you mean this? for it is very useful and virtuous toward the attainment of 'publick tranquillity and the ends of government . . ." [27]

Parker's view that "there is no creature so ungovernable as a wealthy Fanatick" provokes Marvell to inquire whether "a dram of wealth mixed with a pound of conscience, or a scruple

---

[25] Said of *The Rehearsal Transpros'd* (1672). The quotation is from Burnett, *The History*, ed. Airy, Vol. i, pp. 467–468. Walton speaks of Marvell's "Hudibrastic jocularity" in the *Life*.

[26] Compare Cleveland's Diurnall which "smells out plots . . . while they are yet in their causes, before *Materia prima* can put on her smock." (p. 54 above)

[27] London (1672), p. 366.

of conscience infused in a thousand pounds a year, do compound a wealthy Fanatick?"[28] And the Bishop's theocratic doctrine, "there cannot be a pin pull'd out of the Church but the State immediately totters," is promptly christened by Marvell "Push-pin Divinity." Even where the sheer joy of mockery takes hold of him, one is constantly aware of the astringent underlying rationality, which had not been present in Marvell's earlier burlesque mode, in the *Character of Holland*, for instance, or the Clarendon satires, in which he had attempted a popular idiom. When one compares the *Butter-Coloss* captain of *Holland*, or the portraits in *Last Instructions*, or the Clarendon lampoons, with Marvell's presentation of his Ecclesiastical Politician, Bayes the second, it becomes evident that the distinguishing feature here is the dramatic or mimetic element, which was also so prominent in *Hudibras:*

"But yet he 'knows not which way his mind will work itself and its thoughts.' This is Bayes the second.—' 'Tis no matter for the plot—the intrigo was out of his head.—But you'll apprehend it better when you see't.' Or rather, he is like Bayes his actors, 'that could not guess what humour they were to be in: whether angry, melancholly, merry, or in love.' Nay, insomuch that he saith, 'he is neither prophet nor astrologer enough to foretell.' Never man certainly was so unacquainted with himself. And indeed, 'tis part of his discretion to avoid his acquaintance and tell him as little of his mind as may be: for he is a dangerous fellow." [29]

One or two instances from Eachard will suffice to show the similarity of his style and approach:

"Another, he falls a fighting with his text, and makes a pitched battle of it, dividing it into the Right Wing and Left Wing; then he rears it! flanks it! intrenches it! storms it! and then he musters all! to see what word was lost or maimed in the skirmish: and so falling on again, with fresh valour, he fights backward and forward! charges through and through! routs! kills! takes! and then 'Gentlemen! as you were!' " [30]

[28] *Ibid.*, p. 362.
[29] *Ibid.*, p. 12.
[30] "The Grounds and Occasions" . . . , p. 273.

"There is a great difference of Texts. For all texts come not asunder alike! For sometimes the words naturally fall asunder! sometimes they drop asunder! sometimes they untwist! and there be some words so willing to be parted that they divide themselves! to the great ease and rejoicing of the Minister. But if they will not easily come to pieces, then he falls to hacking and hewing! as if he would make all fly into shivers! The truth of it is, I have known, now and then, some knotty texts, that have been divided seven or eight times over! before they could make them split handsomely, according to their mind." [31]

Butler's gift for pure parody shows itself at its best in the masterpiece on Pryne.[32] But it is clear that the histrionic sense, the keen ear and eye and feeling for gesture required for successful parody is equally an ingredient of his style when it is not directly parodic. Marvell, too, produced a brilliant parody in his mock-speech of the King.[33] Marvell's comedy is richer and suaver than Butler's; it draws upon a higher level of urbane insinuation than Butler's deliberately plebeian coarseness (in *Hudibras*) allows. It is worth noting that Marvell's "comfortable importance" became a byword, and was taken up by Rochester, for instance, in a satirical passage on Bishop Parker [34]—a clear indication of the assimilability of his wit to the manner of sophisticated conversation. And this would be true of the *Characters* as well. It would seem to be the combination of the mimetic or histrionic with the keenly rationalistic in Butler's work which made possible for Marvell (and Eachard as well) the attainment of a level of style both playful and graphic, which would comprehend both popular appeal and serious controversy. Marvell's tribute to Butler is significant: "But, lest I might be mistaken as to the persons I mention, . . . I will assure the reader that I intend not Huddibras; for he is a man of the other robe, and his excellent wit hath taken a flight far above these whiflers: that whoever mis-

[31] *Ibid.*, p. 277.
[32] *Genuine Remains*, Vol. I, p. 382.
[33] "His Majesty's Most Gracious Speech to the Commons," in A. Birrell, *Andrew Marvell* (London, 1905).
[34] Satire LIII, "Tunbridge Wells," l. 64. And by Butler: "All Divines that marry, are (like Citizens) commonly Hen-peckt by their Comfortable Importances." (*Characters, etc.*, p. 453.)

likes the choice of his subject, cannot but commend his performance, and calculate if on so barren a theme he were so
copious, what admirable sport he would have made with an
Ecclesiastical Politician." [35] "Admirable sport" is perhaps the
key-phrase for the serious raillery which was the achievement
of the Restoration controversialists.

DECORUM—FROM THE CRITERION OF RANK
TO THE CRITERION OF REASON

Any discussion of the nature of the new "raillery à la mode"
during the Restoration would be incomplete without further
examination of its political or sociological significance. It is a
truly revolutionary significance, part indeed of the manifold
revolutionary transformations in attitudes of mind familiar to
students of the mid-seventeenth century in nearly every field.
In this particular field the change concerns the attitude of the
satirist of state affairs to his satirized opponent, and the grounds
of his attack. Butler, once again, will be seen to stand at the
very pivot of the swing, though he himself, as will be shown
in Chapter Nine, failed to realize fully the implications of his
own work.

The first point to notice is the easy assimilation of the burlesque similitude discussed at the beginning of this chapter with
those denigratory physical images with which the royalist
satirists [36] bombarded the vulgar multitude of their Puritan
opponents, or the vulgar pretensions of the upstarts within
their own ranks. These images are demeaning, gross, grotesque,
because the opponent was considered essentially too "low,"
socially or intellectually, to be taken seriously; or, taking himself seriously, required, it was felt, to have his low origins
forcibly brought home to him. The quotation from Butler's
Huffing Courtier (above, p. 194) is particularly a case in point,
though indeed in many of the instances of the burlesque
similitude already quoted the aristocratic scorn can be detected behind the analytic wit. It was quite natural, therefore,
that the burlesque manner should come to be adopted by the
court for its select, coterie audience, the *paucis lectores* which

[35] *The Rehearsal Transpros'd*, p. 35.
[36] See Chapter 2, above.

Horace found essential for the refinements of satiric wit; and for its own social intercourse, in conversation generally, as the contemporary *sprezzatura*, mark of the true gentleman. These points, centering upon the perennial attitude of aristocracy to the multitude, are excellently illustrated in Richard Flecknoe's *Diarium* . . . , "in Burlesque Rhime or Drolling Verse," which in 1657 was the earliest "Scarronesque" in English. In his preface he writes:

"Of this Kind [Burlesque] is the Poem I present thee here, which when its figures are lively, and representations naturall, is one of the delightfullest of all; where note, that as nations grow more polite and witty, they fall upon this strain, it being the luxuriant branches of a flourishing language, and the very interiour of it, beyond the access of vulgar wits . . . the vulgar . . . are properly the subject of ridiculousness . . . whose follies, abuses and vices are properly the subject of satire. . . ." [37]

and he goes on to complain that to satisfy all objections to the style

"were to think to peel a Bulbus root to its last rinde, or sweep an Earthen floor to its last grain of dust, especially here, where they understand *railing*, farre better than *Raillery*." [A4]

Flecknoe thus recognizes the affinity between burlesque in his time and the demonstrative attitude of superiority of court society towards its despised and ridiculous inferiors; and moreover he hints at something like a revolt of the court wit against the dogmatic enthusiasm—railing—of his political opponents.

The practice of this Flecknoe, Dryden's Prince of nonsense, is certainly uninspiring.[38] His poem is a trifling enough version,

[37] London (1657), A3 v.
[38] As his reference to the masters under whose aegis he will write is undiscriminating. "Whose genius," he asks, "shall I invite?" and mentions Aristophanes, Plautus, Cervantes, Scarron, the *Secchia Rapita*, Dr. Smith, and Sir John Mennis, the editors and part authors of *Wit Restor'd*. His final decision is:

> Faith, once Ile trust unto my own,
> For trifling yieldeth unto none . . .

which, one feels, is at least true of his own.

in tetrameters, of what has been the standard type of aristocratic denigration since *A Satire against Separatists* in 1642. His
conventicle, for instance, echoing many another, is

> . . . in form (you might discern)
> Betwixt a *Chamber* and a *Barn*,
> So narrow, one does thrash a *Cock*,
> Has not room to strike a stroke,
> They sitting (as in Oven heat)
> In summer stewing all with sweat,
> And chimney't had to keep them hot
> In winter when their zeals would not.
>
> > [p. 15]

But the poor quality of Flecknoe's performance need not blind
us to the fact that he is one of the earliest, if not the first, to
notice, however sketchily, the nature and origin of the raillery
of his time. And he uses, significantly the two terms which
were to become crucial in the debate—Railing vs. Raillery—
which accompanied the emergence of the new satire during the
remainder of the century and well on into the following era.

The practice of satire develops in the period under consideration from the crude, demeaning ridicule of Flecknoe and
his like—a safety valve for repressed resentments and hostilities
—to the subtler indirections of a later irony undertaken in the
name and under the influence of a positive or skeptical rationalism. The shift was gradual and complex, and there is much
oscillation in tone and vocabulary until a level of style which
is colloquial, serious, rational, and witty is attained. While
no one factor can fully account for the metamorphosis, mention must be made of what seem to be at least the most
important.

First perhaps is the high value that comes to be placed upon
the achievement of decorum. This places style, or styles, in the
forefront of consciousness, but whether the decorum be that
of mind or of manners, of logic or behavior, remains an open
question. Burlesque was polite society's rod of correction for
errors of decorum; but we have seen how, in a rationalistic
age, and in literary practice directly through the powerful

agency of Butler, burlesque came to be a main means for the scourging of the logically absurd. Thus, through the mediation of the passion for decorum, in style, in thought, the object of ridicule shifted gradually and unevenly from the improper or plebeian in manners or actions—from the standpoint of an aristocratic ruling class, to the improper in reason—from the standpoint of a dispassionate seeker after truth. Butler, as I shall try to show in the following chapter, is in this respect the completely transitional figure.

DOGMA AND IRONY

The transition outlined above is part of a greater, a more general, and a more lasting transition: from a belief in truth found and asserted through vehement dogma to a belief in truth found and asserted through skeptical irony.

The achievement of decorum, in all spheres of Restoration activity, tended to take precedence over the inculcation of virtue. One need not assume a necessary or irreducible incompatibility between the two; virtuous minds would find virtue to reside in a decorum of the mind itself, that is, in reason. But for the moment the shift is conclusive. The norm of Butler's comedy is reason, not virtue; its quarry is folly, not vice. And indeed only when "vice" begins to be seen under the aspect of folly, of Aristotelian error rather than Pauline sin, can it be burlesqued. One notes that Davenant, spokesman for the didactic view of heroic poetry, who said that the poet's task was "to figure virtue and disfigure Sin," [39] wrote no burlesque, no raillery, has nothing in this vein beyond the elementary travesty of the *Playhouse* already referred to. On the other hand stand a long line of satirists and critics who, in theory and practice, formulated the Enlightenment's defense of raillery.

The first to note the connection between raillery and rationality was Sprat, in his *History of the Royal Society*, 1667. Sprat's attitude to raillery was ambivalent, for reasons which should be clear when one remembers *The Elephant in the*

[39] "Poem to the King's Most Sacred Majesty" (1663).

Moon. Thus, though he chastises raillery, he nevertheless provides for the inclusion of the railleurs in the camp of the truth-seeking natural philosophers:

"I confess I believe that *New Philosophy* need not (as Caesar) fear the pale, or the melancholy, as much as the humourous, and the merry: For they perhaps by making it *ridiculous*, because it is *new*, and because they themselves are unwilling to take pains about it, may do it more injury than all the Arguments of our severe and frowning, and dogmatical *Adversaries*.

"And now I hope what I have here said will prevail something with the *Wits* and *Railleurs* of this *Age*, to reconcile their Opinions and Discourses to these Studies; . . . And indeed it has bin with respect to these terrible men, that I have made this long digression. I acknowledge that we ought to have a great dread of their power: But to gain their good will, I must acquaint them, that the Family of the Railleurs is deriv'd from the same Original with the *Philosophers*. The Founder of *Philosophy* is confess'd by all to be *Socrates;* and he also was the famous Author of all *Irony.*" [40]

In *The Rehearsal Transpros'd,* interwoven with the polemic against the intolerant and authoritarian Bishop Parker, is to be found a consistent exposition of Marvell's belief in the efficacy of raillery as against railing in the pursuit of truth. Of his opponent he says:

"But the Author's end was only railing. He could never have induced himself to praise one man but in order to rail on another. He never oils his hone but that he may whet his razor, and that not to shave, but to cut mens' throats. And whoever will take the pains to compare, will find that, as it is his only end, so his best, nay, his only talent is railing. . . . But it is a brave thing to be the ecclesiastical Draw-can-sir; he kills whole nations, he kills friend and foe." [pp. 32–34]

". . . And this he does for the most part in the most bitter manner that is possible: I know not whether I may properly call it satyrical, but let it go so for once; . . . where the conceit is deficient, he makes it out always with railing. He scarce

[40] London (1667), p. 417 ff.

ever opens his mouth but that he may bite; nor bites, but that from the vesicles of his gums he may infuse a venom. . . ." [p. 265]

and of his own practice, and its object:

"Yet I will not decline the pursuit, but plod on after him in his own way thorow thick and thin, hill or dale, over hedge and ditch, wherever he leads; till I have laid hand on him, and delivered him bound either to Reason or Laughter, to Justice or Pity. If at any turn he gives me the least opportunity to be serious, I shall gladly take it; but where he prevaricates or is scurrilous (and where is he not?) I shall treat him betwixt jest and earnest." [p. 295]

In a treatise on *The Different Wits of Men*, in 1669, Charleton uses a traditional Baconian distinction between Judgment and Imagination to make a point relevant to this matter. Whatever is written by way of analytic reason—that "perspicacity of the Mind, whereby it is able to compare things one with another, and discern the difference betwixt them, notwithstanding they appear very much alike"—is superior, as a vehicle of truth, in the field of polemic as in others, to the heightened rhetoric of persuasion which was the alternative instrument of controversy at the time. "By Imagination, on the contrary, we conceive some certain similitude in objects really unlike and pleasantly confound them in discourse: which by its unexpected Fineness and allusion, surprising the Hearer, renders him less curious of the truth of what is said. . . . In *Panegyrics*, and *Invectives*, Phansie ought to take place; because they have for their end not truth, but praise or dispraise, which are effected by comparisons illustrious, or vile and ridiculous. . . ." [41]

Here essentially is the theoretical basis for the unanimous neo-classical distinction, made most concisely by Dennis forty years later, between the two Roman satirists: "*Horace* argues, insinuates, engages, rallies, smiles; *Juvenal* exclaims, apostrophizes, exaggerates, lashes, stabbs. There is in *Horace* almost

[41] London (1669), pp. 19, 26.

everywhere an agreeable Mixture of good Sense, and of true Pleasantry. . . . And there is almost everywhere in *Juvenal*, Anger, Indignation, Rage, Disdain, and the violent Emotions. . . ." [42]

The railleurs chose Horace. Marvell indicates his preference with an admirable brevity: "For our Author seems copious, but is indeed very poor of expression; and, as smiling and frowning are performed in the face with the same muscles very little altered, so the changing of a line or two in Mr. Bayes at any time, will make the same thing serve for a panegyrick or a philippick." [43]

So does Mulgrave, in his elegant couplets:

Some think if sharp enough, they cannot fail,
As if their only business was to rail;
But 'tis mens *Foibles* nicely to unfold,
Which makes a Satyr different from a Scold.
Rage you must hide, and prejudice lay down:
A Satyr's Smile is sharper than his Frown.
So while you seem to scorn some Rival Youth,
Malice it self may pass sometimes for Truth. [44]

In 1709, Anthony Ashley Cooper, the grandson of Dryden's Achitophel, enunciated the principle established by the bantering controversialists of the Restoration: Ridicule is the Test of Truth: "Truth, 'tis suppos'd, may bear *all* Lights: and *one* of those principal Lights or natural Mediums, by which Things are to be view'd, in order to a thorow Recognition, is *Ridicule* it-self, or that Manner of Proof by which we discern whatever is liable to just Raillery in any subject." [45]

[42] *Upon the Roman Satirists* (1721). Letter to M. Prior, Esq. in *The Critical Works*, ed. Hooker (Baltimore, 1939), Vol. II, pp. 218–219.

[43] *The Rehearsal Transpros'd*, pp. 38–39.

[44] "Essay on Poetry" (1682), in Spingarn, Vol. II, p. 290.

[45] *Sensus Communis: An Essay on the Freedom of Wit and Humor* (1709). In *Characteristicks* (London, 1711), Vol. I, p. 61. This despite the plaintive objection of a Dennis, for example: ". . . when a laughing Critick condemns an Author, how can I know whether he has convicted him by the advantage of his Wit or the force of his Argumentation?" (*The Impartial Critick, Dialogue I*, in Spingarn, Vol. III, p. 157.)

If another victory of the Enlightenment was thus won, it had not been without strong opposition, especially since the twitting mode of an irreverent court had given rise to a spate of shamelessly scurrilous personal lampoons, and the indignant onlooker was not prepared to make fine distinctions as to the quality and content of the works of King Charles' mob of gentlemen. It will be noticed too that the controversy is confused by the use of the same terminology by both parties to the dispute. The same coins, however, "ridicule," "satire" etc., have different values. Only the context can make clear in each case to which of the two camps the writer belongs.

The forces against raillery were drawn up under the banner of Juvenalian rigor and morality. Oldham, for example, rejected raillery for his *Jesuits* in 1678 on the grounds that:

> 'Tis pointed satire, and the shafts of wit
> For such a prize are the only weapons fit;
> Nor need there art, or genius here to use,
> Where indignation can create a muse . . .
> . . . urge on my rank envenomed spleen,
> And with keen satire edge my stabbing pen,
> That its each home-set thrust their blood may draw,
> Each drop of ink like aquafortis gnaw.
> Red hot with vengeance thus, I'll brand disgrace
> So deep, no time shall e'er the marks deface;
> Till my severe and exemplary doom
> Spread wider than their guilt, till it become
> More dreaded than the bar, and frighten worse
> Than damning Pope's anathemas and curse.[46]

In 1684 one W. C., in the Preface to his *Poems on Several Occasions*,[47] expresses the very spirit of the opposition:

". . . so impious is the Age, and so deprav'd are the *Wits* thereof, that the most happy Book of *Morals* in the World is become the Subject of *Satyr*, *Burlesque*, *Jocularity*, and *Contempt*. . . .

"I would only beg the *Ingenious Satyrists* to divert their

[46] Prologue to *Satires Upon the Jesuits*, pp. 81, 84.
[47] London (1684). A4.

[208]

Strains, and represent *Vice* in its proper Figure. This Age affords Persons Excellent beyond Vulgar Capacity; would they undertake to depict *Vice*, what a Monster would She appear, when such bold Pencils had colour'd Her! And how beauteous a *Panegyrick* might they write upon Vertue! *Satyrs* upon *Vice* are very Influencing to a *Reformation*, the ridiculing of a Thing makes it immediately become Odious. Too sensibly may we fear this is the Devils Snicke (sic) to catch Atheists in, he hath laught and hist more out of their *Religion*, than by any down-right Temptation. If ever *Vice* be wrackt it must be upon this Coast: Make her once appear what really She is, ugly and ridiculous, and then 'tis an easie thing to hiss Her out of the world. . . ." [No. sig.]

Political passion is ever ready to see in the licence of laughter subversion and danger to manners and morals, and the 1680's were a period of high political passions. W. C.'s "ridicule"— the ridicule of moral indignation, of the dogmatic conception that virtue is to be equated with a particular truth or doctrine, coupled with the zeal to reform—is a very different phenomenon from the ridicule of the free-thinking railleurs.

In 1673 there appeared a tract which, while protesting against the bantering mocking spirit of the time, testifies to its prevalence: *Raillerie à la Mode Consider'd: or the Supercilious Detractor* is "A Joco-serious Discourse; shewing the open Impertinence and Degenerosity of Publishing Private Pecques and Controversies to the World." The author complains of "the lecherous itch to write slanders and lampoons" and finds:

"the *frantick* Age so intollerably pester'd with whimsical Pasquils, Railleries, and Rota's, that, in truth we have nothing else that's Novil; nor indeed is this *strictly* so, for it is no more than the old Mad Humor of the *Cobler* of *Gloucester new Vampt*. [pp. 1-2]

". . . Beside the smart *Itch* of Writing and *Replying* in this *New Canting Drolling* Way, . . . no better than downright Railing, Frenchifi'd into Raillerie à la Mode, . . . made up of a few *fugitive* Expressions, I am sure he that gives himself up to this, must at once licentiously let go the Rains of his *Sobriety*, *Reason*, and *Religion* . . . For let his *Rodomonta-*

does and Bombast be but unreachably Remote, or Far-sought, . . . and it will want nothing to make it off; . . ." [48]

The author finds the *Rehearsal Transpros'd* "all wire-drawing wit and Gingle Gangle," [49] notes the rash of "Rehearsals Transpros'd, Transprosers Rehears'd etc." or "everyone having a bob at Bayes—Whoops Bayes, hollo Bayes," and, most interestingly, suggests a clue to the essential value of raillery (which he insists on calling Railing—"Frenchified into Raillerie à la Mode") and its distinguishing stylistic feature: "One may observe a Sort of Natural Rhetorick, even among the *Common* Professors of the Art of Railing; they have their Figures, Graces, and Ornaments peculiar to their Kind of Speech, though they do not distinguish or use them Grammatically, by the Names of *Sarcasmus, Asteismus, Micterismus, Antiphrasis, Charientismus,* or *Ironia,* yet have they their Dry *Bobs,* their Broad *Flouts,* Bitter *Taunts,* their Fleering *Frumps,* and Privy *Nips.* Besides the use of their admirable Art of Canting, they have a cunning way of Jeering, accusing others by justifying themselves . . . by this evasive way of Abuse they will be sure to keep wide of the Law's Tenterhooks." [p. 54]

Much as he dislikes the mode, he is evidently aware of it as a distinct style, to describe the ironies of which he finds it necessary to draw upon Puttenham's terminology in *The Art of Poesie.* He accounts for these ironies in the way that Shaftesbury was later to do [50]—as evasions of the law; and he adds to his diatribe a *Character of a Detractor,* "a kind of *Monster* among *Men,* and hath a *double* Face, a *double* Heart, and a *cloven* Tongue," in which an ironic duplicity is clearly the distinguishing feature.

For, though the term "irony" is not frequently used, the

[48] London (1673), pp. 1-2, 6-7.

[49] Of his picking up *The Rehearsal Transpros'd* in a shop, he says: "I found myself very wittily beguil'd of both (time and money). But (believe me) I think I might as well have read *Tom of Lincoln,* or *Bevis of Southampton,* for ought I was edified by it" (p. 31).

[50] "If men are forbid to speak their minds seriously on certain subjects, they will do it ironically. Thus raillery is brought more in fashion. . . . 'Tis the persecuting Spirit has rais'd the *bantering* one. (*Characteristicks,* I, p. 72.)

question at issue between the Horatians and the Juvenalians is in fact the holding of that particular reserve, that awareness of other possibilities, which is an aspect of ironic detachment; and this both as a prerequisite for successful technique and as an attitude to the nature of truth. With regard to the cool reserve of the ironist in pursuit of truth, Butler and Marvell expressed a similar view of the inverse relation common between heat and light:

"The less he understands of his Religion, the more violent he is in it, which, being the perpetual condition of all those that are deluded, is a great Argument that he is mistaken." [51]

"For in my observation, if we meet with an argument in the streets, both men, women, and boys, that are the auditory, do usually give it on the modester side, and conclude that she that rails most has the least reason." [52]

But it is important to note that these dispassionate critics of unreason are not so dispassionate as to lose their capacity to be, in the modern jargon, engagé. Both Butler and Marvell were as deeply committed in the political and ideological struggle as they were influenced by that skepticism relating to the vanity of dogmatizing, so clearly stated by Abercrombie, whereby they were "forced to ballance (their) understanding in the middle by an almost equal Weight of counterpoizing Reasons." [53] Marvell's irony, that which enables him to be "merry and angry" at the same time, is emphatically defended in the peroration with which he closes his *Rehearsal Transpros'd*, a polemical contribution to an issue as close to his heart as any could be: "And now I have done. And I shall think myself largely recompensed for this trouble, if any one that hath been formerly of another mind shall learn by this example, that it is not impossible to be merry and angry as long time as I have been writing, without profaning and violating those things which are and ought to be most sacred."

[51] *Genuine Remains*, "A Catholic," p. 148.
[52] Marvell, *The Rehearsal Transpros'd*, p. 121.
[53] D. Abercromby, *A Discourse of Wit* (1686). "So as the greatest *Wit* of Angels, consists in Knowing; the greatest *Wit* in *Men* consists in doubting . . ." (p. 106).

"*Raillerie*

Such was the irony of the great Restoration railleurs. Such and similar ironies were the response of many a skeptic, a Trimmer or a Pyrronist, to the antinomies of libertine and zealot, epicurean and hypocrite, tyranny and toleration; antinomies whose perplexing transformations are characterized by the royalist Butler in his satire on the licentiousness of the court of Charles II, or by the libertine Rochester in his acid exposure of the Mountebank Politician. "Example," says Butler,

> Alters all Characters of Virtue and Vice,
> And passes one for th'other in Disguise,
> Makes all Things, as it pleases, understood,
> The Good receiv'd for Bad, and Bad for Good;
> That slyly counter-changes Wrong and Right,
> Like white in Fields of black, and black in white . . .[54]

"So you see," says Rochester, "*the Politician* is, and must be a *Mountebank* in State-Affairs, and the *Mountebank* (no doubt if he thrives) is an arrant *Politician* in Physick. . . . Consider, pray, the Valiant and the Coward, the wealthy Merchant and the Bankrupt, the Politician and the Fool; they are the same in many things, and differ but in *one* alone. The Valiant Man holds up his Head, looks confidently round about him, wears a Sword, courts a Lord's Wife, and owns it: So does the Coward; one only Point of Honour, and that's Courage, (which, like false Metal, one onely Trial can discover) makes the distinction. The Bankrupt walks the Exchange, buys Bargains, draws Bills and accepts them with the richest, whilst Paper and Credit are current Coin: That which makes the difference is real Cash, a great Defect indeed, and yet but one, and that the last to be found out, and till then the least perceiv'd." [55]

Fletcher, in his *The Perfect Politician*, 1660, had called the irony of his own account of the Great Protector's career— moderation: "My aim is Moderation, as the surest way to hit *Affection;* therefore have I chosen it before partiality or egre-

---

[54] *Genuine Remains*, p. 74.
[55] "Alexander Bendo's Bill," *Works*, ed. Rymer (1691). Quoted by de Sola Pinto, *Restoration Carnival* (1954), pp. 165–166.

gious Encomiums, which do not become an Historian: . . . Panegyricks must profit the maker, or else the same Quill will again drop Gall in a Satyrical strain up his [the subject's] reputation." [56]

One may think of such irony as a "moderating" between the assertions and certainties of either panegyric or philippic, towards a qualified truth. But those of the opposite camp, the "Dogmatical Heads," were never more active and voluble than in the 1680's. D'Urfey, in the Preface to *The Malcontent*, 1684, echoing the familiar distinction between the Horatian attack on follies and the Juvenalian attack on vice, makes sarcastically clear that the subtleties and reservations of irony are not for the major "crimes" of political opposition:

" 'Tis true there may be offences which no Poet is so much a Cynick always to treat at this blunt Rate; the surly Muse may be strok'd into good nature when the sin comes within the list of the Venial, as for example, Pride may be gloss'd over and call'd Presence of mind, or Courtly breeding; Fornication may be poetically styl'd the Errour of Licentious bloud, the Imperfection of irregular Youth . . . The railing Whig, or what's worse, the *Trimmer* (provided he speak no Treason) by the obliging Satyrist may be tenderly us'd, because he has a way with him, and expresses nothing but according to his Conscience; the Sordid Miser may be rendred a wise and provident Person, nay, even the crying sin Adultery, by the varnish and illustration of Poetry may be guilded o'er with Moral justice, provided the Wife be old and Bedrid, and the young Husband wants an heir for his Estate: But Parricide, privy Conspiracy, Rebellion, Incest, Murther and such like, must never expect such favour; the Satyr there should lash to the bloud, and make each stroke so terrible, and the shame so obvious, that the weakest judgement may comprehend, and feel the meaning: Neither am I of an opinion with them that affirm, that Satyr should tickle till it smarts; I rather, like a good Surgeon, would have it smart soundly at first, the wound will tickle enough when it is healing, and I am very apt to believe the undaunted

---

[56] London (1660), Preface.

Juvenal was in this mind, for I never read in any of his Satyrs where he was daubing any vice, with intent to lessen it, but, encouraged by his perfect honesty, and man-like bravery of soul, always painted it in its natural sables." [57]

It was a natural consequence of the Juvenalian fervor that burlesque, long ago, as we have seen, assimilated by the railleurs to the ends of rationality, continued to be conceived by the Juvenalians as a medium for the degrading caricature of aristocratic disdain, rather than for any kind of "sense"; indeed as something diametrically opposed to sense and argument. *A Satyr against Commonwealths,* 1684, is a case in point:

"If then anything will do, it must be *Satyr,* and we may if we observe, find in the dullest apprehension a quicker resentment of a Jest than of an Argument, the one renders that ridiculous, which the other perhaps cannot make appear to be false, and *Satyrs* are like those *Indian* Apes, of whom I have read, that when *Alexander* came into those parts, they straight rally'd their deformed Squadrons, rank'd themselves in Battalia, camp'd and decamp'd with all the moving Solemnities of a real Army, and brought greater affronts upon that all-conquering Army with their Martial Grimaces than all the force of *Darius* and *Parus.* . . .

". . . And who I pray would take the pains to convince a *Taylor* by a Syllogism, who perhaps after the consummation of a pair of Breeches, creeps into a Coffee-House, where after he has lin'd his Pallet with that factious juice, he looks upon his long and limber Fingers to have been contriv'd by Nature for the handling of a Scepter, and curses the bitter fates that had dwindled it into a Needle, away he goes home, and performs the Offices of distributive Justice upon his Apprentices shoulders, and fancies every piece of Parchment cut from an old Bond to make his measures withal, little less to be than a clipping from *Magna Charta.*" [58]

Practice accords with theory, and shows how primitive the conception of "low" ridicule, or burlesque, could remain when it was not emancipated from the moralistic-aristocratic view:

[57] London (1684), Preface.
[58] London (1684), A2 v.

All hail Geneva! to thy Lake all health,
Whom Calvin made a Commonwealth:
Calvin a Bishop grudg'd to see
Lord it in robes of soveragnty.
He push'd the Miter'd Moppet from his Throne,
He threw the mighty Lawn-sleeves down:
Bishop and Bible both believe me
Got a Translation at Geneva.
She cleansed away the filthy Rags of *Rome*,
Laundress she was to the Whore of *Babylon;*
With Gospel Soap she purg'd her Popish sins,
Stifn'd her Rites and starch'd her Disciplines.[59]

RAILING AND RAILLERY IN THE "DISCOURSE CONCERNING SATIRE"

From the Billingsgate of the *Satyr against Commonwealths* [60] to Dryden's "best and finest manner of Satire . . . that sharp, well-manner'd way, of laughing a Folly out of countenance" may seem a far cry. It is, indeed, only in the light of the long debate between Horatians and Juvenalians which preceded *The Discourse Concerning Satire*, that Dryden's position in the matter can be properly understood, and his contribution to the statement of it fully appreciated.

The truth of the matter is that Dryden is divided in his mind. Not, certainly, between Billingsgate and irony; for Billingsgate, and all kinds of "low" burlesque he unconditionally rejects—even Butler's which he respects for its good sense despite its "debased Style"; [61] but between the rival merits of Horace and of Juvenal themselves. He will not, for example, grant Holyday his criticism of Horace, that: "A perpetual Grin, like that of

[59] *Ibid.*, p. 8.

[60] ". . . It always seeming to me as disagreeable to see a Satyr, Cloth'd in soft and effeminate Language, as to see a Woman scold, and vent herself in Billingsgate Rhetorick in a gentile and advantageous Garb" (*ibid.*, B v).

[61] He was well aware of the relation between Billingsgate and the abuse "foul-mouth'd and scurrilous" of those who would "compass by railing what they had lost by reasoning"; though he naturally attributes this failing to the "Schismatics and Sectaries" alone. (Preface to *Religio Laici* [1682], *Poetical Works*, ed. Noyes, p. 161.)

Horace, rather angers than amends a man." He is far too keenly aware of the great gain for satiric technique inherent in the ironies of a "fine raillery":

"I cannot give him up the manner of *Horace* in low (i.e. familiar) satire so easily. Let the chastisements of *Juvenal* be never so necessary for his new kind of satire; let him declaim as wittily and sharply as he pleases; yet still the nicest and most delicate touches of satire consist in fine raillery. . . . How easy it is to call rogue and villain, and that wittily! But how hard to make a man appear a fool, a blockhead, or a knave, with-out using any of those opprobrious terms! . . . There is still a vast difference betwixt the slovenly butchering of a man, and the fineness of a stroke that separates the head from the body, and leaves it standing in its place. A man may be capable, as Jack Ketch's wife said of his servant, of a plain piece of work, a bare hanging; but to make a malefactor die sweetly, was only belonging to her husband." [62]

Nevertheless he insists that, if the manner of Horace is best for amending manners, being a pleasant cure, Juvenal's performance of his more painful kind of operation was better. "Juvenal," he says, "has rail'd more wittily than Horace has rallied"; and again: "Horace means to make his Reader laugh; but he is not sure of his experiment. Juvenal always intends to move your Indignation, and he always brings about his purpose." [p. 316]

The reason for Dryden's preferring Juvenal despite the "better instruction" of Horace's manner is to be inferred from several well-known passages in *The Discourse Concerning Satire*:

"But, after all, I must confess that the delight which Horace gives me is but languishing. . . . His urbanity, that is, his good manners, are to be commended, but his wit is faint; . . . Juvenal is of a more vigorous and masculine wit; he gives me as much pleasure as I can bear. His spleen is rais'd and he raises mine: I have the pleasure of concernment in all he says. . . ." [p. 310]

---

[62] "Discourse Concerning Satire," p. 313.

"Horace . . . is commonly in jest, and laughs while he instructs; . . . Juvenal . . . was as *honest* and *serious* as Persius,
and more he cou'd not be." [p. 307]

"His thoughts are sharper; his indignation against vice is more
vehement; his spirit has more of the commonwealth genius; he
treats tyranny, and all the vices attending it, as they deserve,
with the utmost rigor: and consequently, a noble soul is better
pleas'd with a zealous vindicator of Roman liberty, than with
a temporizing poet, a well-manner'd court slave, and a man who
is often afraid of laughing in the right place; who is ever decent,
because he is naturally servile. Juvenal had a larger field than
Horace: Little follies were out of doors, when oppression was
to be scourg'd instead of avarice: it was no longer time to turn
into ridicule the false opinions of philosophers, when the
Roman liberty was to be asserted." [p. 311]

Nothing could be more revealing. Dryden, past-master himself of the art of fine raillery, cherishes in his heart, has always
indeed cherished, through the early panegyrics and the heroic
drama—the epic ambition. Hence his delight in what he calls
Juvenal's elevation of thought and expression, his sublimity and
loftiness, his sonority and nobility. And therefore it was
Boileau's mock heroic *Le Lutrin*, where "the Subject is trivial
but the Verse Noble," which kindled in him the idea of his two
finest satires, one mock-heroic lampoon in the Virgilian idiom,
the other dramatic narrative, in which he will turn to magnificent account the heroic myth and ethos of his opponents themselves, the heirs in his time to "the commonwealth genius." [63]

"This, I think, my lord," he says of *Le Lutrin*—and the words
may well be applied to *Mac Flecknoe* and to *Absalom*—"to be
the most beautiful and most noble kind of satire. Here is the
majesty of the heroic, finely mix'd with the venom of the other;
and raising the delight which otherwise would be flat and vulgar, by the sublimity of the expression . . . (for) beautiful
turns of words and thoughts . . . are as requisite in this, as in
heroic poetry itself, of which satire is undoubtedly a species."
[p. 319]

[63] This aspect of *Absalom and Achitophel* will be dealt with in Chapter
10.

[217]

If Dryden's witty heroic, or mock-heroic, was one result of raillerie à la mode in theory and practice, another was the vindication of burlesque. Butler's *Hudibras* came, by the 1690's, to be recognized as a watershed in the history of seventeenth century satire, and Butler himself to be seen as the father of "good sense" as well as a "gentleman's manner" in satire, notwithstanding the "impurities" and licence of his doggerel style. Dennis, defending burlesque against Boileau and Dryden in 1693, says:

"Scarron's Burlesque has nothing of a Gentleman in it, little of good sense, and consequently little of true Wit. . . . But Hudibras shows wit and good sense and reason, vivacity and purity of language (where ever such is fit), and a 'just design, which was to expose Hypocrisie.'

"Dryden allows *Butler* to have shewn a great deal of good Sense in that way of writing; so that we have here gain'd one considerable Point, which Boileau seem'd not to allow us, which is that good Sense is consistent with Burlesque. . . ." [64]

Peter Motteux, reviewing the *Miscellanies* in the *Gentleman's Journal*, disparages mock-heroic and insists upon a cultivated rationality as the distinguishing virtue of properly constituted burlesque:

"He (Dennis) hath shew'd us the difference between *Butler's* and *Scarron's* Burlesque, and judiciously defended the manner of the first. And indeed the Grace and Beauties of Burlesque do not consist only in a disproportion between the style in which we speak of a thing and its true Idea; tho' that is the distinguishing mark of *French* and *Italian* Burlesque. . . .

"Good Sence and a Gentleman's manner ought to be preserv'd, or Burlesque dwindles to Buffoonery, and the Dialect of the Mob. As for the way of describing small things in pompous terms, tho' it admits of more sence and fine expressions, and is also for some time pleasant to the Reader by the Air of Gravity and ridiculous Affectation, with which Trifles are related as mighty matters; yet he soon grows weary with it, as with most long-winded Poems. . . ." [65]

[64] *Miscellanies in Verse and Prose* (1693), A6 v–A7.
[65] *The Gentleman's Journal*, January (1693), pp. 26–27.

In the *Advertisement to Pendragon*, 1698, we find the fullest and liveliest account of the stylistic vagaries and caprices of burlesque in the seventeenth century. When this account is compared with Dryden's note on burlesque in the Preface to *Annus Mirabilis* [66] it will be seen that the author of *Pendragon* is drawing upon Dryden's conception, unless he derives his view directly from classical sources common to both, where the relationship between the heroic and the comic is defined. But what stands out as significant in the comparison between the two is the easy acceptance by the author of *Pendragon* of the instrumentality of burlesque in the achievement of the ends of reason—good manners, justice, good established government:

"Refining and Polishing, which give Beauty to other *Poetry*, spoils this: As if the Printer should leave out the Flat Nose, Goggle Eyes, Hump Back, and Distorted Limbs, and call it the Picture of Aesop . . .

"As true *Heroick*, may be compar'd to a Beautiful Well-dress'd Lady, who, when she pays her Visit, lets down her Train at length, and advances with an even and graceful Motion, so Burlesque may be liken'd to her wanton Chamber-maid, with her Petticoats tuck'd up . . . who walks, runs, shambles, stops, looks about, and laughs, and perhaps all in less than a Minute. Among many other Comparisons (which are Odious) one of the worst Things *Burlesque* may be likened to, is Mr. Bay's fierce Heroe in the Rehearsal; who frights his Mistriss, *shubbs* up Kings, baffles Armies, and does what he will, without regard to Numbers, Good Manners, or Justice: And yet after all, this frightful Thing does no more harm, when set upon proper Subjects, than Dogs that kill Vermin.

"If the author of *Hudibras* had a Right or took liberty to ridicule particular Factions and Perswasions, as he thought

---

[66] "Such descriptions or images, well wrought . . . are the adequate delight of heroic poesy; for they beget admiration, which is its proper object; as the images of the burlesque, which is contrary to this, by the same reason beget laughter; for the one shews nature beautified, as in the picture of a fair woman, which we all admire; the other shews her deform'd, as in that of a lazar, or of a fool with distorted face and antic gestures at which we cannot forbear to laugh, because it is a deviation from nature." (*Poetical Works*, ed. Noyes, p. 26.)

them faulty, sure another Man must needs have the same privilege to expose those who are apparently mischievous to Society, and destructive to good Establish'd Government. Though I doubt whether ever any Man will arise with so transcendant a Genius and happy Talent for this purpose, as Mr. Butler. . . ." [67]

As in previous decades there emerge once more two main opposing streams. But now their advocates have become more conscious of themselves, their intentions, and their media, as the quantity of critical discussion and theory, at this date, witness. Several pairs of opposing terms which conveniently name the tendencies referred to have come up in the course of the discussion; iconoclastic-prophetic; reprehension-jest; railing-raillery; Juvenal-Horace; dogma-irony; vice-folly. Burlesque, when turned towards, or used by, the first in any case of these pairs, remained a primitive expression, in a "Billingsgate" idiom, of aristocratic contempt; when towards the second, and chiefly through the agency of Butler, it became an urbane and sophisticated instrument of rationalistic criticism. The polarity indicated by the pairs is most acutely felt and understood by Dryden. He preferred the style adumbrated by the second terms, but he was deeply drawn to the potential sublime, the seriousness of purpose, the "commonwealth genius," implicit in the first. His solution of the problem was to become a major landmark in the history of satire.

[67] London (1698), A2–A4 v. Quoted by Bond, *English Burlesque Poetry*.

CHAPTER NINE

"The Wrong side of the Heros Outward . . ."

HUDIBRAS

ᔥ BUTLER's *Hudibras* is a satire different in kind from any produced before or since. Nevertheless, it is generically related to the development of raillery in two respects. Its author is preoccupied on the one hand with the problem of decorum in style and reasoning and, on the other, with that critical reappraisal of the nature of heroes and hero worship which characterized the Restoration.

It must at once be recognized that what Butler is essentially mocking in his absurd pair is their aspiration, "low" as they are, to gentility, honor, knighthood, or, in general, to the status of heroic seriousness which throughout the Renaissance had been conceived of as the characteristic and prerogative of rank. This places him squarely in the tradition of the aristocratic, Cavalier satirists, who had quite naturally used a denigrating, low, grotesque ridicule for their vulgar opponents, implying, at bottom, a refusal or inability to take them seriously at all.

Spenser's Hudibras was "more huge in strength than wise in works." It would certainly be impossible to claim that Butler's Hudibras is the latter. But then neither is he the former. Indeed, the poem exists in order to reduce his pretensions to "hugeness" of stature of any kind, and most especially in respect to the traditional heroic nobilities of character and conduct. Nowhere, before Butler, has aristocratic denigration been so skillfully conveyed. For he has conceived the idea, not of directly describing the vulgarity of his adversary—superciliously indeed, and by way of caricature, but in the latter's natural habitat—as had his predecessors; but of clothing his

[221]

quarry in the garments and accoutrements of the station in life to which he impudently aspires, so that it may be evident to all how badly they fit him. Seen in this way, the low diction and doggerel measure of *Hudibras*, with its occasional incongruous pompousness, form a style which, so far from being lower than its subject (as is often claimed), is exactly on a par with the lowness of its subject.[1]

Ralph's origin as a tailor is insistently recalled, not only directly but in such allusions as the "cross-legg'd Knights" [1.1.471] descended from his great ancestor, and his ability to unriddle deep mysteries as easily as thread a needle [1.1.500]. More subtle is the description of the Knight's steed and his costume. It is full of suggestions of a low bourgeois background, through the clash of knightly associations with those of domestic economy or trade. Coarse common fare and the values of thrift are constantly referred to. The whole passage is built upon the ridiculous incongruity of the Knight's use of ritual chivalric accoutrements for the most prosaic and utilitarian of purposes:

> To poise this equally, he bore
> A paunch of the same bulk before,
> Which still he had a special care
> To keep well-cramm'd with thrifty fare;
> As white-pot, butter-milk, and curds,
> Such as a country-house affords:
> With other victual, which anon
> We further shall dilate upon,
> When of his hose we come to treat,
> The cupboard, where he kept his meat.
> His doublet was of sturdy buff,
> And tho' not sword, yet cudgel-proof;
> Whereby 'twas fitter for his use,

[1] Ian Jack has come to a similar conclusion regarding the absence of discrepancy between style and subject, but I find I must differ from him as to the grounds of this judgment. For instead of the satiric scope of *Hudibras* being as general as in the *Ship of Fools*, as he claims, it would seem to be entirely specific and class-determined. (See Jack, *Augustan Satire*, p. 18.)

Who fear'd no blows but such as bruise.
His breeches . . .
Thro' they were lined with many a piece
Of ammunition bread and cheese,
And fat black-puddings, proper food
For warriors that delight in blood . . . [1.1.295]

His puissant sword unto his side,
Near his undaunted heart, was ty'd;
With basket-hilt, that would hold broth,
And serve for fight and dinner both: . . . [1.1.295]

His sword is rusty, his dagger

When it had stabb'd, or broke a head,
It would scrape trenchers, or chip bread;
Toast cheese or bacon, tho' it were
To bait a mouse-trap, 'twould not care:
'Twould make clean shoes, and in the earth
Set leeks and onions, and so forth:
It had been 'prentice to a brewer,
Where this and more it did endure . . . [1.1.381]

Thus clad and fortified, Sir Knight sets forth to fight. The mounting of his horse is the most inept and awkward of performances:

But first, with nimble active force,
He got on th'outside of his horse;
For having but one stirrup tied
Th'is saddle, on the further side,
It was so short, h'had much ado
To reach it with his desp'rate toe:
But, after many strains and heaves,
He got up to the saddle-eaves,
From whence he vaulted into th'seat,
With so much vigour, strength, and heat,
That he had almost tumbled over
With his own weight, but did recover,
By laying hold on tail and mane,
Which oft he used instead of rein. [1.1.405]

The horse itself (one remembers the characterizing function of the mounts in Chaucer's pilgrimage) is a sorry jade, wall-eyed, in the single eye that it has, draggle-tailed, saddle-galled. With characteristic economy, the Knight possesses but one spur, knowing that if he can manage to stir one side of his steed to a trot, the other will certainly follow suit.

In the battle scenes, no means is neglected to expose the Knight's conduct as a travesty of the code of knighthood.

> And, placing Ralpho in the front,
> Reserved himself to bear the brunt,
> As expert warriors use; . . .   [I.III.481]

> For Colon, choosing out a stone,
> Levell'd so right, it thump'd upon
> His manly paunch with such a force,
> As almost beat him off his horse.
> He loosed his whinyard and the rein,
> But laying fast hold on the mane,
> Preserved his seat: And as a goose
> In death contracts her talons close,
> So did the Knight, and with one claw
> The trigger of his pistol draw.   [I.III.519]

> . . . he spurr'd his steed,
> to run at Orsin with full speed,
> While he was busy in the care
> Of Cerdon's wound, and unaware.
> But he . . .
> Drew up, and stood upon his guard:
> Then like a warrior right expert
> And skilful in the martial art,
> The subtle Knight straight made a halt,
> And judged it best to stay the assault . . .
> [I.III.701]

The knightly passions—honor, despite, revenge, shame— which fire him when taunted, mark you, by Trulla the Amazon, do not suffice to save him from ignominious defeat at the hands of a woman, a virago, with the language of Billingsgate on her lips. The whole battle sequence ends with the stocks—humiliating punishment—and with some of Butler's most brilliant rationalizations, on the part of the defeated pair, on the subject of heroic prowess:

> The ancients make two sev'ral kinds
> Of prowess in heroic minds,
> The active and the passive valiant;
> Both which are *pari libra* gallant:
> For both to give blows and to carry,
> In fights are equi-necessary . . . [1.III.1029]

These rationalizations, it will be noticed, are once more cast in terms which are irreducibly bourgeois in their reference to litigation and property applied to that most immaterial of chivalric values, honor:

> Tho' we with blacks and blues are sugill'd,
> Or, as the vulgar say, are cudgell'd;
> He that is valiant, and dares fight,
> Though drubb'd, can lose no honour by't.
> Honour's a lease for lives to come,
> And cannot be extended from
> The legal tenant: 'tis a chattel
> Not to be forfeited in battle.
> If he that in the field is slain
> Be in the bed of honour lain,
> He that is beaten may be said
> To lie in honour's truckle-bed . . . [1.III.1039]

The bourgeois theme is evident again in the treatment of Hudibras' love affair. "Honor" says Hudibras, illuminating that curious concept by reference to more familiar experience, "is like a widow, won With brisk attempt and putting on" [1.1.913]; and, indeed, the lady of his heart is a widow, suitably furnished with the essential attribute. Cupid, aiming at the Knight's heart

> took his stand
> Upon a widow's jointure land;

"The Wrong side of the

(For he, in all his am'rous battles,
No 'dvantage finds like goods and chattels) . . .
[1.III.311]

This advantage, however, sufficient to ignite the flames of passion in the heart of the Knight, does not suffice to bring his
brisk attempt to a successful conclusion. For the proud lady is
possessed, in addition to her jointure land, of a strange freak—
the inability to love any but those who scorn and hate her.
These qualms on the lady's part give Butler the opportunity
for a double-edged treatment of the pair's courtship. The lady
suspects Hudibras' protestations of love as being a blind for his
desire for her property. He, in return, seizes the opportunity to
counter her aversion to love by admitting that it is indeed not

> your person
> My stomach's set so sharp and fierce on;
> But 'tis (your better part) your riches
> That my enamour'd heart bewitches:
> Let me your fortune but possess,
> And settle your person how you please;
> Or make it o'er in trust to th'Devil,
> You'll find me reasonable and civil.   [II.I.473]

This is offered, as it were, as a feint to overcome the lady's
excessive coyness; yet it is, of course, nothing but what has
from the start been the simple abject truth.

The lady's reply is again a travesty of knightly testing, made
to sound suspiciously similar to an unequivocal and fishwifely
"Go and drown yourself." Hudibras suggests that a better test
of his truth will be to make over

> In trust, your fortune to your lover:
> Trust is a trial; if it break,
> 'Tis not so desp'rate as a neck:
> Besides th'experiment's more certain; . . .   [II.I.508]

But the lady insists on the proper test of his affections—the
whipping. The whipping is a complex notion. It is at once a
reduction of the knightly test to the punishment of the lowest

classes; a hint at Puritan mortifications of the flesh as opposed
to Cavalier gallantry and wickedness:

> Who would not rather suffer whippin'
> Than swallow toasts of bits of ribbon?
> Make wicked verses, treats, and faces,
> And spell names over, with beer-glasses?   [II.I.857]

and a reminiscence of the mental and emotional aberrations of
fanatical flagellants of all creeds.[2]

All in all, the lady's caprice and the farcical wooing in II.I.
clearly bear the same relation to the coy disdain of a sonneteer's
courtly mistress as does Hudibras' conduct in the battle to the
standards of chivalric valor.

But that relationship itself is an ambiguous one. There is in
it an unresolved ambivalence which points to the transitional
character of Butler's burlesque. His mockery hovers at the very
crossroads between aristocratic contempt for vulgar manners
and rationalistic criticism of unreasoning and unreasonable
habits of thought. Butler mocks Hudibras for aspiring to chivalry, but at the very same time he mocks the object of that
aspiration itself.

This emerges clearly in passages involving the knightly machinery, for instance, the parenthesis to the description of the
Knight's carefully assembled provisions:

[2] The sardonic query in Butler's notes is illuminating: "Why should
not getting of Clap's or Bastards, pass for as sufficient a Penance for
Incontinence, as whipping dos in the Monasterys, especially of their own
Laying on?" (*Characters, etc.,* p. 464.) The whipping serves also as a
point of departure for some of Hudibras' most agile rationalizations on
the subject of oaths and the free-born consciences of Saints:

> He that imposes an oath makes it,
> Not he that for convenience takes it; . . .   [II.II.377]

> 'Tis the temptation of the Devil
> That makes all human actions evil:
> For Saints may do the same things by
> The spirit, in sincerity,
> Which other men are tempted to,
> And at the Devil's instance do;
> And yet the actions be contrary,
> Just as the Saints and Wicked vary.   [II.II.233]

And tho' knights-errant, as some think,
Of old did neither eat nor drink,
Because when thorough deserts vast,
And regions desolate, they pass'd,
Where belly-timber, above ground,
Or under, was not to be found,
Unless they grazed, there's not one word
Of their provision on record;
Which made some confidently write,
They had no stomachs but to fight.
'Tis false; for Arthur wore in hall
Round table, like a farthingal,
On which, with shirts pull'd out behind,
And eke before, his good knights dined . . .

[1.1.327]

Here the alleged superiority of knights over material circumstances is compared with Hudibras' all-too-obtrusive concern with material circumstances and the inner man. But the language can hardly be said to enhance the dignity of the knightly asceticism, and it may well be asked which, in truth, is the more reasonable position? When Spenser set out to "fashion a gentleman or noble person in vertuous and gentle discipline"—that is to say, in the duties of his class to govern a kingdom virtuously and well—he used the apparatus of chivalry as an allegorical vehicle for conveying the principles and insights of Christian humanism. Even the knight of la Mancha owes his origin to Christian humanism, though nowhere are the ideal illusions of humanity treated with greater irony—with greater realism— than in the pages of Cervantes. But Butler's temper is vastly different. His underlying values have no Platonic idealism, no element of the transcendental. He is in fact himself, by outlook and temperament a rationalistic critic of these very ways of thought, much closer to the materialism of a Hobbesian analysis of society.

Thus, for instance, he can point out with an acerbity equal to that he devotes to Hudibras, that

Certes our authors are to blame,
For to make some well-sounding name
A pattern fit for modern knights
To copy out in frays and fights
(Like those that a whole street do raze,
To build a palace in the place),
They never care how many others
They kill, without regard of mothers,
Or wives, or children, so they can
Make up some fierce dead-doing man,
Composed of many ingredient valours,
Just like the manhood of nine tailors . . . [I.II.11]

or, in a passage on Talgol which may serve as a paradigm, he
demolishes heroics at one stroke:

For he was of that noble trade,
That demi-gods and heroes made;
Slaughter, and knocking on the head,
The trade to which they all were bred;
And is, like others, glorious when
'Tis great and large, but base if mean:
The former rides in triumph for it;
The latter in a two wheel'd chariot,
For daring to profane a thing
So sacred with vile bungling. [I.II.321]

This kind of analysis informs the long passage on marriage as
well.

For what do lovers, when they're fast
In one another's arms embraced,
But strive to plunder, and convey
Each other, like a prize, away?
To change the property of selves,
As sucking children are by elves?
And if they use their persons so,
What will they to their fortunes do?
Their fortunes! the perpetual aims

Of all their ecstasies and flames.
For when the money's on the book,
And *all my worldly goods* but spoke
(The formal livery and seisin
That puts a lover in possession),
To that alone the bridegroom's wedded,
The bride a flam, that's superseded.   [III.I.949]

Indeed, the whole marriage debate between Hudibras and the
Widow, though interwoven with motifs familiar in such de-
bates since the Middle Ages, is firmly grounded, in both parties
to the debate, upon the assertion of the economic nature of the
institution. The economic motivation, moreover, acquires a
general validity which goes beyond the immediate purpose of
the satire. The effect is as of a penetration through the conven-
tional masks of society to the true, the real, and the rational
underlying dynamic. The implied tolerance, however, is strictly
limited. Butler uncompromisingly maintains his traditional disdain, and is of course quite free to do so where the proletariat
as distinct from the middle class is concerned.

As the whole poem is based upon a contemptuous refusal to
take even his middle-class opponents seriously as realistically
conceived individuals, so "the people" who rise in revolt against
the Puritanical interdict on bear-baiting are regarded as a negli-
gible rabble and share in the general automatic contempt for
the lower orders which informs this satire as well as many of
the pieces in *Characters*. The attitude receives unequivocal and
undisguised expression in the almost brutal contumely of the
Character of a Clown. In *Hudibras* too, far from any attempt to
portray "this wilde monster, the People" with any insight, or
serious realism, they are described in the traditional style of low
comic grotesque:

I' th' head of all this warlike rabble,
Crowdero march'd, expert and able.
Instead of trumpet and of drum,
That makes the warrior's stomach come,
Whose noise whets valour sharp, like beer
By thunder turn'd to vinegar . . .

[230]

A squeaking engine he apply'd
Unto his neck, on north-east side,
Just where the hangman does dispose,
To special friends, the knot of noose: . . .
His warped ear hung o'er the strings,
Which was but souse to chitterlings: . . .
His grisly beard was long and thick,
With which he strung his fiddlestick;
For he to horse-tail scorn'd to owe
For what on his own chin did grow.   [I.II.105]

In order to point up the ridiculous triviality of this warlike host, Butler criss-crosses his description with a mock-heroic style, in which terms of resounding nobility and classical association are employed upon subject matter of the lowest kind:

Next these the brave Magnano came,
Magnano, great in martial fame:
Yet when with Orsin he waged fight,
'Tis sung he got but little by't.
Yet he was fierce as forest boar,
Whose spoils upon his back he wore,
As thick as Ajax! seven-fold shield,
Which o'er his brazen arms he held;
But brass was feeble to resist
The fury of his armed fist;
Nor could the hardest iron hold out
Against his blows, but they would thro't.   [I.II.331]

Yet it must be noticed that even here Butler's is a mixed style, not a pure mock-heroic, since passages indubitably low, both in diction and matter, are juxtaposed cheek by jowl with the heroic. Of Orsin,[3] for instance, we are told:

Thus virtuous Orsin was endued
With learning, conduct, fortitude,
Incomparable: and as the prince
Of poets, Homer, sung long since,

[3] The name is probably a pun on "Whoreson."

A skilful leech is better far
Than half a hundred men of war;
So he appear'd, and by his skill,
No less than dint of sword, could kill. [1.11.241]

But we have already been informed thus of the nature of this leech-craft:

For, as when slovens do amiss
At others' doors, by stool or piss,
The learned write, a red-hot spit
Being prudently apply'd to it,
Will convey mischief from the dung
Unto the part that did the wrong; . . . [1.11.233]

The passage on Talgol the butcher is the most successful in this mixed style, the true reference of the high-flown diction— the pursuit of a wasp haunting a butcher shop—being concealed with the most skillful irony:

Yet Talgol was of courage stout,
And vanquish'd oft'ner than he fought:
Inured to labour, sweat, and toil,
And, like a champion, shone with oil:
Right many a widow his keen blade,
And many fatherless had made;
He many a boar and huge dun cow
Did, like another Guy, o'erthrow:
But Guy, with him in fight compared,
Had like the boar or dun cow fared.
With greater troops of sheep h'had fought
Than Ajax, or bold Don Quixote;
And many a serpent of fell kind,
With wings before and stings behind,
Subdued; . . . [1.11.299]

Hudibras' long speech to the rabble, in which he harangues them about bear-baiting subverting the ends of Reformation, is significantly not "in character" for Hudibras in any dramatic-realistic sense. Rather, it serves the ends of the author's irony

regarding the folly of a rabble-inspired "Reformation." This
is achieved by the details of a contemptuous genre realism
juxtaposed with the slogans of the grand enterprise:

> No sow-gelder did blow his horn
> To geld a cat, but cry'd, Reform!
> The oyster-women lock'd their fish up,
> And trudged away to cry, No Bishop!
> The mouse-trap men laid save-alls by,
> And 'gainst Ev'l Counsellors did cry;
> Botchers left Old Clothes in the lurch,
> And fell to turn and patch the Church . . .
> And some for brooms, old boots, and shoes,
> Bawl'd out to purge the Common-House:
> Instead of kitchen-stuff, some cry
> A Gospel-preaching Ministry: . . . [I.II.537]

For the most part, of course, the economic realities underlying the Puritan bourgeois rise to power of Hudibras and his
like, and the economic utilitarianism of the reasoning involved
with that rise, can be treated under the heading "hypocrisy,"
as part of the usual anti-Puritan indictment. In the masquerade
of Furies and Hobgoblins, for instance, in Part III:

> What makes a knave a child of God,
> And one of us?—A livelihood.
> What renders beating out of brains,
> And murder, godliness?—Great gains . . .
> What's orthodox and true believing
> Against a conscience?—A good living . . .
> What makes all doctrine plain and clear?—
> About two hundred pounds a year.
> And that which was proved true before,
> Prove false again?—Two hundred more. [III.I.1263]

And yet, as we have seen, Butler himself takes these economic
realities more seriously than the heroic knightly standards
against which his upstart Hudibras is allegedly measured. His
thought, in its own realism and rationality, runs close to the
very principles he exposes as those which animate his ridiculed

butts. This is the submerged reef, as it were, upon which
Butler's mock-heroic runs aground. Bond has said that, in both
"caricaturing Hudibras as a low rascal and placing him in an
heroic framework," Butler has adopted "a procedure both
antithetical and dangerous." Antithesis and danger there certainly are, but Bond's formulation seems just to miss the mark.
The antithesis and the danger lie in that compromising of the
heroic frame which results from the degree of seriousness with
which Hudibras and what he stands for, at least as Economic
Man,[4] and as Rational Man, is really taken.

Butler has achieved a great advance in polemical satire in that
he has dramatized his protagonist. It is a step forward in realism.
And he has at the same time seen the advantage for satire of the
implied contrast between a generally accepted standard of the
heroic (Spenserian Christian knighthood), and the behavior of
his True-blue Presbyterian militant. But he has blurred the
effect by double exposure. He is debasing his heroic currency.
And this is at least partly due to the fact that that currency is
already debased in his time—inflated by baroque heroic splendors not commensurate with real facts or values.[5] The crucial
moral symbol of political life in the seventeenth century—the
hero—has, as we have seen in preceding chapters, already been
radically compromised by doubt as to the hero's true efficacy,
and by a growing sense of historical and social forces. Thus it is
no wonder that Butler's mirror of knighthood is an oddly distorting one, which shows, in a truer sense than Davenant could
have meant, "the wrong side of the Heros outward." For, to
continue the previous metaphor, the gold standard of knighthood, the Spenserian epic, is no longer taken sufficiently seriously by Butler himself to inform the style and provide a posi-

[4] One might compare the unstable and ambivalent poise of Butler's
view of Economic Man with the approval of Defoe, a non-conformist
descendant of Butler's very Hudibras, whose *Robinson Crusoe* can serve
as a textbook for economists.

[5] Quintana, in an illuminating essay, notes that "*Hudibras* is a thing
peculiar to the Enlightenment" and goes on to point out that Butler had
"witnessed two living Burlesques in his time—the Saints' Romance of
Commonwealth, and the epic of Restoration, full of heroical poetry but
without heroical action." ("Samuel Butler—A Restoration Figure in a
Modern Light," *ELH*, Vol. xviii, 1951.)

tive norm of conduct, attitude, and evaluation. It has lost its validity. Butler comments in *Characters:*

"A Satyr is a kind of Knight Errant that goe's upon Adventures, to Relieve the Distressed Damsel Virtue, and Redeeme Honor out of Inchanted Castles, And opprest Truth, and Reason out of the Captivity of Gyants or Magitians: and though his meaning be very honest, yet some believe he is no wiser than those wandring Heros usd to be, though his Performances and Atchievments be ever so Renownd and Heroicall. . . ." [6]

or

"A Hero was nothing but a fellow of a greate Stature, and strong Limbes, who was able to carry a heavier Load of Armes on his Back, and strike harder Blows, then those of a lesser Size. And therefor since the Invention of Guns came up, there can be no true Hero in great Fights, for all mens Abilitys are so leveld by Gun-shot, that a Dwarf may do as heroique Feats of Armes that way as a Gyant." [7]

In such remarks he stands self-confessed. For knighthood is present in *Hudibras* to provide Butler with a mechanism of satiric contrast between superior and vulgar; but it remains a mechanism, since his underlying attitude is profoundly antiheroic.

In fact, the true heirs of Red Cross Knight and Guyon and their fellows are Christian and Mr. Standfast and theirs. It is a significant pointer to the course of history in the seventeenth century that the inheritors, in Christian epic, of Gloriana and her court of nobles are now Bunyan's wayfaring tinkers. If Butler and Bunyan both spent time in the employment of Sir Samuel Luke, it is an accident of history which adds a certain piquancy to one's observation of the polarity of the two works. *The Pilgrim's Progress* deals with the "low life" of humble people, traditionally the object of more or less contemptuous grotesquerie, or buffooning comedy, or at best a supercilious

---

[6] *Characters, etc.,* p. 469.
[7] *Ibid.,* p. 468.

genre particularity, but never of serious attention as significant or "real" or problematic. Bunyan's treatment, however, has that utter seriousness which makes of his unstylized prose a sublime style. If the source of the sublime is a vision of the grandeur of man's destiny, it is just such a vision which animates Bunyan's way-faring Christians and creates an epic vehicle for the new heroic demanded and formed by revolution and the times.

EXPERIMENTS IN MOCK-HEROIC

Hudibras, then, is Butler's chief essay in the mixed style of mock-heroic, but imperfectly conceived because of the dubiety of the heroic standard. That Butler was an inveterate experimenter in the art of satire, the pieces in the *Remains* amply show. These cover the whole range of contemporary method from the broadside ballad to the seriously familiar Horatian epistle, and include a brilliant parody of Prynne. It is interesting to notice that among his chief concerns was evidently the problem of the differing effects of the short and the long couplet line. The prosody of the fragment on *The Imperfections and Abuse of Human Learning* is the nearest Butler could force his drolling Muse to the heroic couplet used by Denham, for example, on a similar theme: [8]

> So some *Polemics* use to draw their Swords
> Against the Language only and the Words:
> As he, who fought at Barriers with *Salmasius*,
> Engag'd with nothing but his Stile and Phrases;
> Wav'd to assert the Murther of a *Prince*,
> The Author of false *Latin* to convince;
> But laid the Merits of the Cause aside,
> By those, that understood them, to be try'd.
> And counted *breaking Priscian's Head* a thing
> More capital, than *to behead a King* . . .[9]

and it is characteristic that even in the serious *Satyr on the Licentiousness of the Age of Charles II*, 1666, he cannot resist the temptation to "doggerelize" the rhyme and rhythm:

[8] "The Progress of Learning" (1641).
[9] *Genuine Remains*, Vol. I, p. 220.

Twice have Men turn'd the *World* (that silly Blockhead!)
The wrong Side outward, like a *Jugler's* Pocket,
Shook out Hypocrisy, as fast and loose,
As e're the Dev'l could teach, or Sinners use,
And on the other Side at once put in
As impotent Iniquity, and Sin.[10]

Indeed, he announces specifically that heroical poetry has nothing to do with satire,[11] for "Heroicall Poetry handle's the slightest, and most Impertinent Follys in the world in a formall Serious and unnaturall way: And Comedy and Burlesque the most Serious in a Frolique and Gay humor which has always been found the more apt to instruct, and instill those Truths with Delight into men, which they would not indure to heare of any other way." [12]

Despite his burlesque bent, however, Butler took the trouble to write his *Elephant in the Moon* in two versions—the short and the long line. The poem, by virtue of its comic situation and its neatly mimicked character, is a highly successful dramatization of a learned contretemps. What is significant in the change of prosody is that the long line clearly shifts the burlesque in the direction of mock-heroic though the comic imagination responsible for choice of words and arrangement of details remains irreducibly grotesque.

That Butler had Homer's mock-heroic consciously in mind is shown by the note on the infamous mouse which he added to this version:

A *Mouse*, whose martial Valour has so long
Ago been try'd, and by old *Homer* sung,
And purchas'd him more everlasting *Glory*
Than all his *Grecian*, and his *Trojan* Story;
Though he appears unequal matcht, I grant,
In Bulk and Stature by the *Elephant*,
Yet frequently has been observ'd in Battle
To have reduc'd the proud and haughty Cattle,

[10] *Ibid.*, p. 70.
[11] *Characters, etc.*, p. 330.
[12] *Ibid.*, p. 278.

[237]

When having boldly entered the Redoubt,
And storm'd the dreadful Outwork of his Snout,
The little *Vermin*, like an *Errant-Knight*,
Has slain the huge gigantick *Beast* in Fight.[13]

Had he sought a vernacular model, he would have found in
Spenser's *Muiopotmus* an exquisitely graceful example of epic
style, appropriate to "mighty ones of great estate" used to describe the fate of a butterfly. His own *Repartees between Cat
and Puss at a Caterwalling in the modern heroic way* transposes
the grand manner of contemporary tragedy to a crisis in the
love-life of Cat and Puss; but it is clear that for the most part
Butler was too wedded to the low mock style, and, moreover,
too critical of the heroic itself, to be able to give himself to the
development of a consistent mock-heroic medium. His best
attempt among the other pieces is the pindaric *Du Val*, in
which the highwayman does become a mock-heroic hero
through the application of an inflated heroic style to the preda-
tory activities of a common, if glamorous, lady-killing thief: [14]

And yet the brave Du-val, whose Name
Can never be worn out by Fame,
That liv'd, and dy'd, to leave behind
A great Example to Mankind; . . .
Ought not, like vulgar Ashes, rest
Unmention'd in his silent Chest,
Not for his own, but public Interest.
He, like a pious Man, some Years before
Th'Arrival of his fatal Hour,
Made ev'ry Day he had to live,
To his last Minute a Preparative;
Taught the wild *Arabs* on the Road

[13] *Genuine Remains*, Vol. I, p. 52.

[14] 1671. "The Reader may be pleased to note, that the said Mr. Du-val,
. . . had been a notorious Highwayman in *England;* and having been
a brisk, smart, gay, and handsome Fellow, and of about Twenty-Seven
Years of Age, when he was hang'd at Tyburn (which was on the 1st of
January 1669) did draw the loves of many Females in *London* towards
him. . . ." (From Wood's *Athenae*, quoted by Thyer in his Notes to the
Poem, *Genuine Remains*, Vol. I, p. 146.)

To act in a more gentee Mode,
Take Prizes more obligingly than those
Who never had been bred *Filous;*
And how to hang in a more graceful Fashion,
Than e'er was known before to the dull *English* Nation.

[pp. 147–148]

The juxtapositions are allowed to make their own effect without comment:

From these first Rudiments he grew
To nobler Feats, and try'd his Force
Upon whole Troops of Foot and Horse,
Whom he as bravely did subdue; . . .
In every bold Affair of War
He had the chief Command, and led them on;
For no Man is judg'd fit to have the Care
Of others Lives, until h'has made it known,
How much he does despise, and scorn his own.   [p. 150]

Social satire is insinuated without lowering of tone or diction; in such a passage as that which describes Du Val's French attainments:

To understand Cravats and Plumes,
And the most modish from the old Perfumes;
To know the Age and Pedigrees
Of Poynts of *Flandres* or *Venise;*
Cast their Nativities, and to a Day
Foretel how long they'll hold, and when decay.

[p. 148]

We are almost in the world of the *Rape*, and no more than a further twist of the irony will turn Du Val into Jonathan Wild. It is significant, however, that the effectiveness of the poem lies in its critical common sense, rather than in stylistic virtuosity. Its motive is to expose, more or less directly, the irrationality of behavior and evaluation displayed by the ladies who were so affected by Du Val's fate. Its mock inflation sets out to correct

[239]

their faulty sense of proportion, and the nature of their illusion is defined in a generalizing maxim:

> For as those Times the Golden Age we call,
> In which there was no Gold in Use at all,
> So we plant Glory and Renown,
> Where it was ne'er deserv'd, nor known, . . .
>
> [p. 146]

The remark includes, characteristically, the heroic standards and associations which have been used as the amplifying medium.

Nothing could better illustrate the peculiar neutrality of Butler's critical skepticism. He was, as has been said, truly transitional. He inherited no stable world of confident values. Among the innumerable follies ranged between the irrational licentiousness or vanity of the courtier, and the irrational enthusiasm and ignorance of the sectarian, his mind darted in derisive and non-committal images. To be capable of the mock-heroic, one must be capable, by aspiration, and conviction, as well as literary power, of the heroic. It was to a poet of a narrower vision, a more vigorous temperament, a readiness for intellectual commitment, and an Augustan reverence for classical literary culture, that the perfected art of mock-heroic is indebted.

Mac Flecknoe

Dryden's debt to Boileau's *Le Lutrin* is too prominent and too well known to require more than reference here. Dryden must have known *Le Lutrin* since the time of its publication in France—1674. He pays tribute to its mock-heroic as the finest sort of satire in *The Discourse Concerning Satire*, as opposed both to the "the Lowness of Style, and the Familiarity of Words," or "meanness of Words and vulgarity of Expression" of the Horatian way, and to the Hudibrastic burlesque, which, even at its best (in Butler), "turns earnest too much to jest, and gives us a boyish kind of pleasure." [15] Against these Boileau's is, Dryden finds, "the most beautiful and most noble kind

---

[15] "Discourse Concerning Satire," p. 318.

of satire. Here is the majesty of the heroic, finely mix'd with the venom of the other; and raising the delight which would otherwise be flat and vulgar, by the sublimity of the expression. . . ." [p. 319]

He places the source of the nobility of the verse in Virgilian allusion. "I doubt not but he had Virgil in his eye, for we find many admirable imitations of him, and some parodies. . . ." Virgil and Ovid, Dryden concludes, are the two principal fountains in Latin poetry of "the beautiful turns of words and thoughts . . . which are as requisite in this, as in heroic poetry itself, of which satire is undoubtedly a species." [p. 319]

Thus the Dulness of Shadwell is elevated to the status of an heroic attribute itself, and "the scourge of wit, and flail of sense" appears beside his venerable prince of Nonsense as the young Ascanius—"Rome's other hope, and pillar of the State." [l. 108]

The technique is magnification, not diminution. It is a refinement of mock-heroic as previously understood, which operates through the incongruity of stately language and trivial theme. Here the theme is of monumental magnitude; it is but just that Virgilian splendors should be lavished upon it; it is hardly to be regarded as the author's fault that the heroic quality possessed by Shadwell is not one conventionally regarded as such! And since the author is not prevaricating, not disguising in any way the quality in question, but on the contrary lauding it as that which confers upon Shadwell the well-deserved mantle of the prophet, he is enabled to dilate upon it at length, and by its proper name, as in the roundly definitive assertions of the proud sire:

> Sh— alone my perfect image bears,
> Mature in dulness from his tender years:
> Sh— alone, of all my sons, is he
> Who stands confirm'd in full stupidity.
> The rest to some faint meaning make pretense,
> But Sh— never deviates into sense. [l. 15]

Thus the convention of heroic attributes provides the ironic flattery of

His brows thick fogs, instead of glories, grace,
And lambent dulness plaid around his face . . .

[l. 110]

And so too, the piles of superfluous scribblers' stationary which, in lieu of Persian carpets, deck the imperial way for the royal pair, are made to serve the double purpose of epic amplification and a characteristically defamatory impudence. [l. 98]

Spence's anecdotes represent Dryden as saying: "If anything of mine is good, 'tis Mac Flecknoe, and I value myself the more upon it because 'tis the first piece of ridicule written in heroics."

The exact effect of the gain in obliquity, ironic duplicity, and hence triumphantly elegant superiority over the victim can be gauged by a comparison with Butler's masterly portrait of his true-blue Presbyterians, where the power and cogency of the analytic wit is no less than in any satire of Dryden's:

> Such as do build their faith upon
> The holy text of pike and gun;
> Decide all controversies by
> Infallible artillery;
> And prove their doctrine orthodox
> By apostolic blows and knocks;
> Call fire, and sword, and desolation,
> A godly, thorough Reformation,
> Which always must be carried on,
> And still be doing, never done;
> As if Religion were intended
> For nothing else but to be mended:
> A sect whose chief devotion lies
> In odd perverse antipathies;
> In falling out with that or this,
> And finding somewhat still amiss:
> More peevish, cross, and splenetic,
> Than dog distract, or monkey sick;
> That with more care keep holiday
> The wrong, than others the right way;
> Compound for sins they are inclined to,
> By damning those they have no mind to. [I.I.195]

[242]

Perhaps it would be true to say that the difference is ultimately due to the joy of battle in Dryden. Butler's was a more purely reflective mind. Polemic was the very air Dryden breathed. His genius lay in his ability to yoke his ideals and capacities as excellent poet to his animus as controversialist. *Mac Flecknoe*, written four years before its publication in 1682, was good preparation for the masterpiece among the century's poems on affairs of state: *Absalom and Achitophel*.

CHAPTER TEN

"That kingly power, thus ebbing out, might be Drawn to the dregs of a Democracy."

THE USE OF DRAMA
AND THE USE OF SCRIPTURE

❧ DRYDEN's triumph, in *Absalom and Achitophel*, lies in his having found a way to take his opponents with perfect seriousness. He has perfected a complex literary instrument which can at once place and present in the most compromising light the rascally lowness of his opponent's pretensions to power, while at the same time giving that lowness itself an epic quality. The poem is densely packed with reference and allusion, operating in different, if complementary, directions and at different levels of response; for this reason the task of analyzing the separate strands which go to its making is a difficult one. There are, however, certain cardinal points crucial to an understanding of the way in which Butler's similar idea is here bettered.

The latest and fullest attempt to account for the excellence of *Absalom* is Ian Jack's valuable *Augustan Satire*. He there joins issue with Weldon Williams, who had said that while both Oldham and Dryden were searching for a dignified vehicle for satire, "Oldham's poems are in a falsely inflated style. . . . Dryden's stayed much closer to the idiom and atmosphere of the lampoon or libel, even while reacting against it as a form." Jack finds this misleading. "Oldham," he says, "used an unsuccessful heroic style, while Dryden scored a signal success with an original blending of the heroic with the witty." [1] It

[1] *Augustan Satire*, p. 59, fn. 2.

[244]

would seem that while there is little disagreement as to the quality of Absalom, the peculiar source of its effectiveness has yet to be fully accounted for. Jack sums up his view of the poem thus: "It was because Charles was a witty man that Dryden was free to use for his poem a new alloy—a skilful blend of heroic panegyric, satire, 'discourse' and witty commentary." [2]

But this "alloy" as such, was not new. It had existed in Marvell's *Last Instructions*,[3] and before Marvell in Cowley's *Poem on the Civil War*,[4] a piece which Dryden evidently admired and which was included in the *Third Miscellany*, the *Examen Poeticum*, published by Tonson in 1693. Both those poems, however, had lacked (as well as the elegant turn of the couplet) a form, an action into which the alloy could be cast. Dryden's poem produces the effect of a self-contained whole in which the structure is organic, growing from within, and not a mere formal pattern imposed from without. Indeed the weakness of Cowley, Marvell, and Butler is that they lack even the latter. The *Civil War*, the *Last Instructions*, and *Hudibras* have no inevitable beginning, middle, and end, let alone an inner curve of climax, crisis, and resolution, or an organized variation of tension and tempo.

Yet it was Butler and Oldham, each in his own way, who set political satire moving in the direction of dramatization. Each provides an at least rudimentary dramatic action through which the satire can be exhibited. Dryden admired both poets greatly, with certain reservations, and it is probable that it was their work, coupled, of course, with his own experience in the theater subsequent upon the exercise in heroic narrative which had been his last long poem, that opened his eyes to the possibility of dramatic character, as opposed to the formal "character," as a medium for both the satiric and the panegyric content he had in mind. What had been held in suspension, as it were, by Cowley, Marvell, Oldham, and Butler, Dryden was exactly equipped to condense, through his command of dra-

[2] *Ibid.*, p. 75.
[3] See Chapter 7, above.
[4] See Chapter 2, above.

matic oratory and through the agency of his allegorical fable, into the hard gem that is *Absalom and Achitophel.*

The fable is all-important. Without it he could not have exercised his forensic art of ironic sophistry, not lifted the witty analytic lampoon to the level of dramatic significance. It is through the fable that the conflict is projected in terms of opposing characters and the forces represented by them, to produce the dialectical suspense and the dynamic forward-moving impetus of drama. Even more important than the casting of his satire into the form of a fable is the stereoscopic effect of the allegory in the fable. This generates the intellectual interest of reading on two distinct but parallel planes at once, each well known but novel in the stimulating juxtaposition, so that each becomes charged with the emotional associations and energies of the other.

The significance, moreover, of this particular choice of allegory is far from fully accounted for, or fully interpreted by a check-list of forerunners from whom he might have taken the hint.

Jack has drawn attention to the use in John Caryl's *Naboth's Vineyard,* 1679, on the "Popish" side, and in D'Urfey's *The Progress of Honesty,* 1680, of biblical allegory in the treatment of the Popish Plot. R. F. Jones, in "The Originality of Absalom and Achitophel," [5] has shown that sermons written as early as 1627 present Achitophel as the idea of a Wicked Politician, with contemporary reference, and has gathered numerous instances during the Restoration (when the analogy of Charles' exile and return with David's had become a commonplace) of the allegorical use, in a contemporary context concerning disloyal advisors, of Absalom, David and Achitophel. As we have seen in the satires reviewed in previous chapters, biblical analogy becomes more and more prevalent, especially, of course, in the hands of republicans, dissenters and Whigs, as the shadow of the accession crisis darkens and the consequent sense of a crisis in world history—a moment when Providence is present and manifest—returns. Scriptural ammunition however was no monopoly and in 1680 Monmouth was finally iden-

[5] *MLN,* Vol. XLVI (1931), p. 211.

tified as Absalom and Shaftesbury specifically as Achitophel in *Absalom's Conspiracy*, or *The Tragedy of Treason*.[6] Several months before Dryden's poem appeared, a tract called *The Badger in the Fox-Trap* announced in doggerel but unambiguous terms:

> Some call me Tony, some Achitophel,
> Some Jack-a-Dandy, some old Machiavel.[7]

Thus biblical allegorizing at the time of the Popish Plot was frequent, but sporadic and not consistently pursued. And no one had seized with such brilliant aptness and generality the biblical types in the present situation. *Naboth's Vineyard* is a case in point.[8] It comes nearer than any previous poem to Dryden's treatment (even the phrasing is echoed by Dryden at times).[9] It contains the "character" projected in a dynamic situation, and dramatically exposing himself in what is in effect a development of satiric parody:

> *Malchus*, a puny Levite, void of sence,
> And Grace, but stuft with Noise and Impudence,
> Was his prime Tool; so *venomous a Brute*,
> That every place he liv'd in, spued him out;
> Lyes in his Mouth, and Malice in his Heart,
> By Nature grew, and were improv'd by Art. [p. 9]

> "In great Designs it is the greatest Art,
> To make the Common People take your part:
> Some words there are, which have a Special Charm
> To wind their *Fancies* up to an *Alarm*.
> *Treason, Religion, Liberty*, are such;
> Like *Clocks* they strike, when on those points you touch."
>
> [p. 7]

---

[6] Harleian MS 1811, VII. In Dryden, *Works*, ed. Scott-Saintsbury, Vol. IX, pp. 206–208.

[7] Quoted by Jones, *loc. cit.*

[8] J. Caryl, *Naboth's Vineyard; or, The Innocent Traytor*: Copied from the Original of Holy Scripture, in Heroick Verse, (London, 1679), p. 9.

[9] "In the first rank of Levites Arod stood" (p. 11), for instance, as well as the "striking clocks" passage quoted.

Caryl turns the couplet neatly to the uses of acid comment:

> Ahab distrest, bow'd to his Lord, and pray'd;
> Ahab victorious, proudly disobey'd; . . . [p. 2]

Yet the choice of the poor man's vineyard as emblem does not offer the same scope for political generality, complexity, and penetration as the story of Absalom and Achitophel, even taking into consideration the fact that Caryl is not dealing with the Monmouth aspect of the Plot, but only with the plight of the unjustly treated Catholics.

It is, in fine, not so much the choice of this or that biblical character or circumstance for the allegory, as the unwavering and detailed consistency of the total allegory Israel-England that is the very root and heart of *Absalom's* success. Unlike Butler, who had placed his unheroic hero against a standard of the heroic not only outdated but by definition inimical to middle-class pretensions, Dryden has chosen to pay the enemy in his very own coin. It was his genius to exploit the perception that scripture, while no monopoly of a single class or party, is nevertheless the fundamental well-spring of the epic view of life as it existed in his day in Puritan myth and republican ethos, as opposed to the classicizing, strongly Epicurean tendencies of the court culture.[10] The mock-heroic element in the poem is in the exercise of that ironic duplicity whereby, while speaking to an entire (literate) nation in a language available to all, he is enabled subtly to undermine his opponent's position by evoking the latter's own sacred and incontrovertible text. Thus the triumphantly conclusive effect of such passages as

> True, they petition me t'approve their choice:
> But Esau's hands suit ill with Jacob's voice. [l. 981]

> The Jews, a headstrong, moody, murm'ring race,
> As ever tried th'extent and stretch of grace;
> God's pamper'd people, whom, debauch'd with ease,

[10] T. M. Mayo, *Epicurus in England 1650–1725* (Texas, 1934), analyzes and documents at length the influence and effect of neo-Epicureanism upon court literature, politics, and thought during the period.

No king could govern, nor no God could please; . . .
Those very Jews, who, at their very best,
Their humor more than loyalty express'd,
Now wonder'd why so long they had obey'd
An idol monarch, which their hands had made;
Thought they might ruin him they could create,
Or melt him to that golden calf, a State. [l. 45]

In the *Discourse Concerning Satire*, Dryden, as we have seen, while insisting upon the virtue of Horace's "delicate touches of fine raillery," bases his preference for Juvenal upon the serious vehemence of his morality—the condition for the "pleasure of concernment in all he says." In the significant passage which has already been noticed he says: "His thoughts are sharper; his indignation against vice is more vehement; his spirit has more of the commonwealth genius; he treats tyranny, and all the vices attending it, as they deserve, with the utmost rigor: and consequently, a noble soul is better pleas'd with a zealous vindicator of Roman liberty, than with a temporising poet, a well-manner'd court slave, and a man who is often afraid of laughing in the right place; who is ever decent, because he is naturally servile . . . it was no longer time to turn into ridicule the false opinions of philosophers, when the Roman liberty was to be asserted." [p. 311]

It is possible that this nostalgia for the sturdy Roman "commonwealthsman" was rooted in Dryden's perception that the truly heroic view of life had indeed passed from court to city in his day. His own increasing Toryism, his conversion to Rome—the extreme reaction from wayfaring Christianity—and the mood of disillusionment expressed finally in the *Secular Masque* may all be interpreted as confirmatory of such a view of his emotional progress: the growing feeling, that is, that his party had fallen behind in the historical race for predominance and leadership in the nation and its culture. It is at all events sufficiently established that his constant aspiration was towards the writing of epic. And it therefore seems not improbable that in his own deepest insight into the contemporary situation lay the origin of his idea—the turning of the tables upon those who held the key to epic in his day by the appropriation to his scheme of their authoritative myth, and the triumphant vindication, on his terms, of the great biblical hero as Charles, and of his "small but faithful band of worthies." Nor is it improbable that it is his own emotional though perhaps scarcely recognized "concernment" in the matter which lends such zest to the performance.

Ostensibly Dryden had ample and adequate motive (apart from royal command) for his enterprise in *Absalom and Achitophel.* He would bring to bear upon the "Hot distempered State" the sovereign remedy of cool reason. He will be in the long and honorable line of gentlemen wits serving the cause of a well-conducted rationalism. Spectator's qualifications for the writing of Horatian epistles seem exactly to fit this side of Dryden's achievement: "He that would excell in this kind must have a good Fund of strong Masculine Sense: To this there must be joined a thorough Knowledge of Mankind, together with an Insight into the Business, and the prevailing Humours of the Age. Our Author must have his Mind well seasoned with the finest Precepts of Morality, and be filled with nice Reflections upon the bright and dark sides of human Life; He must be a master of refined Raillery, and understand the Delicacies, as well as the Absurdities of Conversation. He must have a lively turn of Wit, with an easie and concise manner of Expression; Everything he says, must be in a free and disengaged manner. He must be guilty of nothing that betrays the air of a Recluse, but appear a Man of the World throughout." [11] This is an admirable description of the style, and yet not quite enough, one feels, to account for the inimitable, calculated, nonchalant insolence of such passages as the opening:

> In pious times, ere priestcraft did begin,
> Before polygamy was made a sin;
> When man on many multiplied his kind,
> Ere one to one was cursedly confin'd; . . .
> Then Israel's monarch after Heaven's own heart,

[11] No. 618.

His vigorous warmth did variously impart
To wives and slaves; and, wide as his command,
Scatter'd his Maker's image thro' the land . . .

or

(Gods they had tried of every shape and size,
That god-smiths could produce, or priests devise:) . . .

[1.49]

No description of Horatian raillery, however perspicacious, can quite cover this unless the ironic element outlined above —the sense of the opponent being hoist with his own petard— is taken into account. Of all Dryden's critics, Reuben Brower [12] has perhaps done the greatest justice to what he calls the "imaginative union of tones and levels," the "blend of manners" which is the essence of Dryden's witty heroic or mixed style. It is the exact stance or poise of the sophisticated court spokesman,[13] supremely aware of the social nuance of language, supremely aware of the reactions and assumptions of his heterogeneous audience, and confident, at least then, in the heat of the battle in which his poem played no insignificant a part, of an alternative structure of values to stand against those he deflates with such consummate and impudent irony.

A comparison with *The Medal*, on the one hand, and the satirical passage in *The Hind and the Panther*, on the other, will make clear the great gain in ironic deflation which the scriptural mechanism allows.

In *The Medal*, for instance, Shaftesbury,

. . . A vermin wriggling in th'usurper's ear
Bart'ring his venal wit for sums of gold,
. . . cast himself into the saintlike mold;
Groan'd, sigh'd and pray'd, while godliness was gain,
The loudest bagpipe of the squeaking train. [l. 31]

In *The Hind and the Panther* the "*wolfish* race"

[12] "An Allusion to Europe—Dryden and Tradition," *ELH*, Vol. xix (1952).
[13] Hence the jibes at the "Hebrew priests"—the Anglican clergy, as well as at the Levites (ll. 104, 126).

"That kingly power,
Appear with belly gaunt, and famish'd face:
Never was so deform'd a beast of grace.
His ragged tail betwixt his legs he wears,
Close clapp'd for shame; but his rough crest he rears,
And pricks up his predestinating ears . . .

With teeth untried, and rudiments of claws,
Your first essay was on your native laws;
Those having torn with ease, and trampled down,
Your fangs you fasten'd on the miter'd crown,
And freed from God and monarchy your town.
What tho' your native kennel still be small,
Bounded betwixt a puddle and a wall;
Yet your victorious colonies are sent
Where the north ocean girds the continent.
Quickn'd with fire below, your monsters breed
In fenny Holland, and in fruitful Tweed:
And like the first, the last effects to be
Drawn to the dregs of a democracy.
As, where in fields the fairy rounds are seen,
A rank sour herbage rises on the green;
So, springing where these midnight elves advance,
Rebellion prints the footsteps of the dance. [l. 160]

The perfect articulation of the verse, the variety, copiousness, and distinction of the language does not alter the fact that this is a variety of the direct vilification and abuse with which royalists had been belaboring their presumptuous inferiors on the republican or Presbyterian or Puritan side since the early 1630's. The traditional approach is once more directly stated in the *Epilogue to Amboyna:*

Well may they boast themselves an ancient nation,
For they were bred ere manners were in fashion;
And their new commonwealth has set 'em free
Only from honour and civility.[14]

In *Absalom and Achitophel*, on the other hand, the obliquity made possible by the biblical characterization allows a far

[14] *Poetical Works,* ed. Noyes, p. 71.

[252]

greater keenness and density of irony, and, paradoxically perhaps, a greater realism of treatment. The "if the cap fits" effect of Dryden's keen analysis of the "malcontents of all the Israelites" is due both to the apparent objectivity and to the witty aptness of the applications:

> The best, (and of the princes some were such,)
> Who thought the pow'r of monarchy too much;
> Mistaken men, and patriots in their hearts;
> Not wicked, but seduc'd by impious arts.
> By these the springs of property were bent,
> And wound so high, they crack'd the government.
> The next for interest sought t'embroil the State,
> To sell their duty at a dearer rate;
> And make their Jewish markets of the throne,
> Pretending public good, to serve their own.
> Others thought kings an useless heavy load,
> Who cost too much, and did too little good.
> These were for laying honest David by,
> On principles of pure good husbandry . . .
> Who follow next, a double danger bring,
> Not only hating David, but the king:
> The Solymaean rout, well-vers'd of old
> In godly faction, and in treason bold;
> Cow'ring and quaking at a conqu'ror's sword;
> But lofty to a lawful prince restor'd; . . .
> Hot Levites headed these; who, pull'd before
> From th'ark, which in the Judges' days they bore,
> Resum'd their cant, and with a zealous cry
> Pursued their old belov'd Theocracy: . . .
> Where Sanhedrin and priest enslav'd the nation,
> And justified their spoils by inspiration: . . .
>
> [l. 495]

In the individual portraits the biblical mask enables Dryden to exhibit the qualities the royalists constantly satirized—meanness of birth or behavior, hypocrisy or pharisaism, mercenary motivation, not, as Butler had done, through burlesque logic and burlesque action, but by sly reference to the scripture-

reader's own consecrated tenets of behavior. It is as if Dryden
is not criticizing his victims as falling short of his standards; on
the contrary, he is ironically commending them for maintain-
ing their own standards, or, at least, their version of those
standards. Shimei, for instance

> Did wisely from expensive sins refrain,
> And never broke the Sabbath, but for gain;
> Nor ever was he known an oath to vent,
> Or curse, unless against the government.
> Thus heaping wealth, by the most ready way
> Among the Jews, which was to cheat and pray,
> The city, to reward his pious hate
> Against his master, chose him magistrate . . .
> During his office, treason was no crime;
> The sons of Belial had a glorious time;
> For Shimei, tho'not prodigal of pelf,
> Yet lov'd his wicked neighbor as himself . . .
> If any leisure time he had from pow'r,
> (Because 'tis sin to misemploy an hour,)
> His bus'ness was, by writing, to persuade
> That kings were useless, and a clog to trade; . . .
> Cool was his kitchen, tho' his brains were hot.
> Such frugal virtue malice may accuse,
> But sure 'twas necessary to the Jews;
> For towns once burnt such magistrates require
> As dare not tempt God's providence by fire,
> With spiritual food he fed his servants well,
> But free from flesh that made the Jews rebel;
> And Moses' laws he held in more account,
> For forty days of fasting in the mount.   [l. 587]

Thus aristocratic disdain for the "rascal rabble . . . whom
kings no titles gave, and God no grace" is both objectified and
sanctioned by such travesty of Holy Writ.

THE TWO ANCIENT WORLDS

The values against which these ironies are set can in general
be labelled Augustan and divided under the heads Church,

King, and classical culture. It is, however, the latter, with its
aspirations towards neo-classical sublimity and nobility, which
is most clearly and closely woven into the texture of the verse.
In the panegyric passages, though these are kept within the
framework of biblical reference, the Virgilian allusions [15] are
most marked, and the values evoked are significantly the
familiar attributes of the life of the man of honor—magnanimity and the liberal profession of arts and arms. Barzillai, for
instance, "practic'd the court,"

> . . . not the courtier's art:
> Large was his wealth, but larger was his heart,
> Which well the noblest objects knew to choose,
> The fighting warrior, and recording Muse.   [l. 825]

The elegy upon his son is closely Virgilian and diametrically
opposed to any mood of biblical elegiac in such a way as to
place the maximum distance between the two ancient worlds so
subtly employed by Dryden to focus and evaluate contemporary affairs:

> His eldest hope, with every grace adorn'd,
> By me (so Heav'n will have it) always mourn'd,
> And always honor'd, snatch'd in manhood's prime
> B' unequal fates, and Providence's crime;
> Yet not before the goal of honor won,
> All parts fulfill'd of subject and of son:
> Swift was the race, but short the time to run . . .
> O ancient honor! O unconquer'd hand,
> Whom foes unpunish'd never could withstand!
> But Israel was unworthy of thy name;
> Short is the date of all immoderate fame.   [l. 831]

Indeed, all the panegyrics to the small but faithful band are
thus dexterously touched and flavored with classical echo,
myth, image, or concept. The tour de force is the greater for
the ostensible consistency with the biblical frame of reference.
Thus Amiel, chief of the Sanhedrin, and enjoying at the end

[15] The exact allusions have been noted by Noyes, p. 962.

"That kingly power,

"the sabbath of his toils," emerges unmistakably as an antique rhetor:

> Of ancient race by birth, but nobler yet
> In his own worth, and without title great:
> The Sanhedrin long time as chief he rul'd,
> Their reason guided, and their passion cool'd:
> So dext'rous was he in the crown's defense,
> So form'd to speak a loyal nation's sense,
> That, as their band was Israel's tribes in small,
> So fit was he to represent them all.
> Now rasher charioteers the seat ascend,
> Whose loose careers his steady skill command:
> They, like th'unequal ruler of the day,
> Misguide the seasons, and mistake the way; . . .
> [l. 900]

It is in the light of these perceptions that the crowning achievement of the poem—the character of Corah [16]—can best be appreciated. For it is in this character that the two great rival systems of evaluation, which, through subtle repetition throughout the poem have attained a wide symbolic significance, are simultaneously brought to bear, in a kind of double battery, upon the exposure of the arch-hypocrite, the arch-pretender to importance. Classical monumental fame, Mosaic redemption, perjury and prophecy all combine to articulate the inimitable, densely packed scorn of the following lines:

> Yet, Corah, thou shal from oblivion pass:
> Erect thyself, thou monumental brass,
> High as the serpent of thy metal made,
> While nations stand secure beneath thy shade.
> What tho' his birth were base, yet comets rise
> From earthy vapors, ere they shine in skies.
> Prodigious actions may as well be done

[16] I am indebted to R. Brower's article in *ELH*, mentioned earlier, and to his analysis of the Corah passage in terms of its battery of metaphors for presumptuous "rising" in *The Fields of Light* (Toronto, 1951), for illumination of many of the subtleties his able exposition discovers.

By weaver's issue, as by prince's son.
This arch-attestor for the public good
By that one deed ennobles all his blood.
Who ever ask'd the witnesses' high race,
Whose oath with martyrdom did Stephen grace?
Ours was a Levite, and as times went then,
His tribe were God Almighty's gentlemen . . .
His long chin prov'd his wit; his saintlike grace
A church vermilion, and a Moses' face . . .
Some future truths are mingled in his book;
But where the witness fail'd, the prophet spoke: . . .
Let Israel's foes suspect his heav'nly call,
And rashly judge his writ apocryphal;
Our laws for such affronts have forfeits made;
He takes his life, who takes away his trade.   [l. 632]

The utter rascality and presumption of this counterfeit are
themselves raised to epic proportions; given a sheer magnitude of audacity by words charged with the dignity of classical association. Oblivion, monument, brass, prodigious actions,
shining comets, and ennobled blood, are responsible for inflat-
ing the dimensions of the arch-attestor. On the other hand, the
sarcastic biblical reference to Mosaic serpents, prophecies, calls,
apocrypha, with the additional echoes of Deuteronomy and
Shylock in the last line, are responsible for the deflating effect
which punctuates the whole passage. Dryden is as it were constantly setting up his ninepins only to knock them down immediately. Any possible comic sympathy for the sheer size
of the audacity (such as Jack claims [17] is aroused for Mac
Flecknoe in somewhat the same manner as for Falstaff) is instantly neutralized here. For, in addition to the clashing associations indicated above, Corah's irredeemable social inferiority is
constantly kept in mind—by the nonchalant contempt of the
colloquialisms ("the Lord knows where," "as times went
then"), the lip-curled scorn of "God Almighty's gentlemen"—
which are given for the particular delectation of the cultivated

---

[17] *Augustan Satire*, pp. 51–52.

élite [18] among whom this weaver's issue will never *rise* to belong.

THE STRUGGLE FOR POWER

The subtly denigrating purpose of the satire is thus achieved, but it does not exhaust the full intention with which Dryden went to work. There remains to be considered the way in which he places his contemptibly vulgar opponents in the context of the struggle for power in the state. For this is no less the object of his enterprise than that manipulation of anger, laughter, and scorn which is the aim of satire. These successors of Hudibras are to appear as pretenders, not to an outworn code of chivalry, but to real political power. Dryden's view of this aspect of the political disturbances he dealt with is very clear and decisive. In *The Medal* he defines the succession issue as the conflict between "Property and Sovereign Sway." It is Harrington's perception of the politics of property, but Dryden, of course, unlike the republican author of *Oceana*, interprets the sway of property as anarchic, and sees behind the Whig "princes," themselves misled, leading and using others, that bugbear of the conservative mind, the "Almighty crowd."

> Almighty crowd, thou shorten'st all dispute;
> Pow'r is thy essence; wit thy attribute!
> Nor faith nor reason make thee at a stay,
> Thou leaps't o'er all eternal truths in thy Pindaric way!
> [l. 91]

Dryden's satire constantly reiterates the connection between property, money interest, the merchant classes, and sedition. These are presented as proliferating varieties of self-interest—low, grasping, mercenary, and hypocritical—in opposition to faith, reason, and the eternal verities. It is the linking of these motifs which characterizes the livelier parts of *The Medal*, and it is worth noticing that it is to be found, in *Absalom Part II*, only in Dryden's section—the part dealing with the "troop of busy spirits." There is none of it in Tate's, which is largely de-

[18] "Satire is of a difficult nature in itself," says Dryden in the "Discourse," "and is not written to vulgar readers."

voted to generalized argument upon the rights and wrongs of
the situation. In *Absalom and Achitophel* the problem of power
in the state is the essential significance of the last and inmost
sphere of allusion—the Miltonic—with which we have now to
deal.

Miltonic echoes in the poem have frequently been noticed.
Shaftesbury as Tempter is deliberately reminiscent of Milton's
arch-tempter. In *The Medal* he becomes "a vermin wriggling
in the'usurper's ear" [l. 31]. Here

> Him he attempts with studied arts to please,
> And sheds his venom in such words as these: . . .
>
> [l. 228]

and, conclusively, in the characteristic Miltonic inversion
which follows the susceptible Absalom's fatal rationalization
"Desire of greatness is a godlike sin":

> Him staggering so when hell's dire agent found,
> While fainting Virtue scarce maintain'd her ground,
> He pours fresh forces in, and thus replies: . . .
>
> [l. 373]

If, as Dryden well knew, and as he points out in the preface
to *Religio Laici*, the Bible is a magazine for Papist and Sectary
alike to furnish themselves with the weapon of authority for
whatever disobedience and rebellion their interests dictate,
Milton was a source nearer home both of epic sublimity and
of republican argument. "And 't is to be noted by the way,"
Dryden continues in the same preface, "that the doctrines of
king-killing and deposing, which have been taken up only by
the worst party of the Papists, the most frontless flatterers of
the Pope's authority, have been espous'd, defended, and are
still maintain'd by the whole body of Non-conformists and
Republicans. 'Tis but dubbing themselves the people of God,
which 'tis the interest of their preachers to tell them they are,
and their own interest to believe; and after that, they cannot
dip into the Bible, but one text or another will turn up for
their purpose; if they are under persecution, (as they call it,)
then that is a mark of their election; if they flourish, then God

works miracles for their deliverance, and the saints are to possess the earth." [19]

The allusion to *Paradise Lost* puts a further double edge upon Dryden's rapier. Through the identification of Achitophel with Satan, the historical struggle between "Property and Sovereign Sway" can be seen as the epic and eternal struggle between the forces of good and evil. At the same time, through the subtle sophistry of the temptation itself, he is enabled to dramatize the very characteristics of argument which he attributes in the preface to *Religio Laici* to "the whole body of Non-conformists and Republicans" when they rationalize the scriptures in the light of Calvinist theology. The equation is: sophistical prevarications based on the sanctimonious forcing of texts to ulterior purposes equals the republicans' lust for power equals the ultimate evil that menaces the ordered state, and threatens to set up in its stead the Golden Calf of Commonwealth.

Thus Achitophel's first attempt upon Absalom consists of the classic Machiavellian appeal to *virtu*, diametrically opposed, in its assertion of the pre-eminence of Fortune and heroic will, to the idea of supreme Providence.

> How long wilt thou the general joy detain,
> Starve and defraud the people of thy reign?
> Content ingloriously to pass thy days
> Like one of Virtue's fools that feeds on praise;
> Till thy fresh glories, which now shine so bright,
> Grow stale and tarnish with our daily sight.
> Believe me, royal youth, thy fruit must be
> Or gather'd ripe, or rot upon the tree.
> Heav'n has to all allotted, soon or late,
> Some lucky revolution of their fate;
> Whose motions if we watch and guide with skill,
> (For human good depends on human will,)
> Our Fortune rolls as from a smooth descent,
> And from the first impression takes the bent:
> But, if unseiz'd, she glides away like wind,

[19] *Poetical Works,* ed. Noyes, p. 161.

thus ebbing out . . ."

And leaves repenting Folly far behind . . .
Had thus old David, from whose loins you spring,
Not dar'd, when Fortune call'd him, to be king,
At Gath an exile he might still remain,
And Heaven's anointing oil had been in vain.

[l. 244]

The seed planted, and duly taking root, Achitophel then, in
his second encounter, parries the wavering Absalom's pangs of
conscience with a neat shift of premise. His fresh forces consist of an argument from Providence, not against it:

Th'eternal God, supremely good and wise,
Imparts not these prodigious gifts in vain:
What wonders are reserv'd to bless your reign!
Against your will, your arguments have shown,
Such virtue's only giv'n to guide a throne.

[l. 376]

One is reminded of Butler's Hypocritical Non-Conformist,
who "does not care to have any thing founded in Right, but
left at large to *Dispensations* and *Outgoings* of Providence, as
he shall find Occasion to expound them to the best advantage
of his own Will and Interest." [20] But this is far from the only
source of prevarication in the tempter's onslaught. The speech
is, of course, a tissue of sophistry, a shining example of the
art of having one's cake and eating it. Thus Absalom is told
not to let his father's love for him enchant his generous mind,
since that love is merely

. . . Nature's trick to propagate her kind.   [l. 424]

In the subsequent breath, however, he is urged to put that love
to the proof.

God said he lov'd your father; could he bring
A better proof, than to anoint him king?

[l. 429]

[20] *Characters, etc.,* p. 18.

From the Dispensations and Outgoings of Providence to "women's lechery"—all is grist to Achitophel's sophisticated mill—as all, indeed, is grist to Dryden's sophisticated audience.

> If so, by force he wishes to be gain'd;
> Like women's lechery, to seem constrain'd.
> Doubt not: but when he most affects the frown,
> Commit a pleasing rape upon the crown . . .
>
> [l. 471]

It was perhaps less "because Charles was a witty man" that Dryden was able to write his masterpiece than because Dryden belonged to Charles' party, and thus could share the supreme self-assurance that is the prerogative of the privileged class.

Whether it was the lack of this self-confidence or simply the lack of requisite ability which made effective reply to *Absalom and Achitophel* or *The Medal* so difficult, it would be hard to say—most likely the latter, since the Tory satire of the time is no more distinguished than the Whig efforts at defence. These fall into two chief kinds. One group, the most numerous, casts indignant, at times positively hysterical, abuse at the author, denigrating his wit, reminding him, with ample reference to Judas Iscariot, of his panegyric to Cromwell, and flatly denying, though with pathetically transparent literal-mindedness, the relevance of his matter. Too many instances would be tedious; one or two will serve to show the state of impotent fury to which Dryden's ironic effectiveness reduced his adversaries:

> Near to the King he falls on Monmouth next,
> Makes the Story of proud Absalom his Text.
> This Noble Duke he makes his Absalom,
> As if a Traitor to the King and Crown;
> Oh thou Incongruous Fool, what parallel
> Thats congruous twixt these two canst thou tell?
> (Absalom was . . .)
> A compleat Rogue, Ambitious, Arrogant,
> Ungrateful, Lying, a Dissembling Wretch, . . .
> And must brave Monmouth be his parallel,

By renegado Wits of Old Cromwell.
Five hundred Guinnies makes him sell his sense,
His King and Country, and his Conscience.[21]

"He has an easiness in Rime, and a knack at versifying, and can make a slight thing seem pretty and clinquant; and his Fort is, that he is a indifferent good Versificator. If at any time he has wit of his own, tis in Rayling, when the venome of his malice provokes his fancy. His Panegyricks are full of such nauseous flattery, that they are Libels; and he is now become so infamous, that his Libels will be thought Panegyricks." [22]

Thou stil'st it Satyr, to call Names, Rogue, Whore,
Traytor, and Rebel, and a thousand more.
An Oyster-wench is sure thy Muse of late,
And all thy Helicons at Billingsgate.
Good humour thou so awkwardly put'st on,
It fits like Modish Clothes upon a Clown . . .[23]

Clearly Dryden had nothing to fear from his colleagues. And the one adversary who apparently went too far on the subject of "wretched mercenary Bayes . . . Pied thing! half Wit! half Fool!" and coward and slave to boot, received his proper punishment in due time.[24]

The second type of reply borrows the apparatus of *Absalom* and applies it to the Papists, to the tyranny, lust, and pride of Rome, or to the desire for arbitrary power of the Tories, who "have tryed all ways imaginable, to push on the people to a Rebellion, that (they) might have a pretence to cut their throats." [25] *Azaria and Hushai* may stand as an example:

[21] *A Key (with a Whip)* to open the Mystery, and Iniquity of the Poem called Absalom and Achitophel (London, 1682), p. 19.
[22] Shadwell, *The Medal of John Bayes:* A Satyr against Folly and Knavery (London, 1682), A v.
[23] *Ibid.,* p. 2.
[24] Shadwell, author of *The Medal of John Bayes*, Og in *Absalom and Achitophel*, Part II, and the hero of *Mac Flecknoe*, which was published in an unauthorised edition in 1682.
[25] S. Pordage, *The Medal Revers'd:* A Satyre against Persecution (London, 1682), p. 5.

In impious Times, when Priest-craft was at height,
And all the Deadly Sins esteemed light;
When that Religion only was a Stale,
And some bow'd down to God, and some to Baal; . . .
These subtil Priests, in Habit black and grave;
Each man a Saint in shew, in Heart a Knave,
Did in Judea swarm, grew great withall,
And like th'Egyptian Frogs to Court they crawl:
Where, like them, too, they never are at rest;
But Bed and Board of Kings with Filth infest.[26]

Even Dryden himself could not repeat the achievement of *Absalom and Achitophel.* By 1688 the tide had turned. The alliance between landed wealth and city wealth which changed the nature of the monarchy in England made its repetition impossible. The revolution changed completely, or signalized the change in, the alignment of social forces from which Dryden's satire had drawn its strength. Since the long battle between court and city was now virtually over, the state poem which reflected it largely disappears. The characteristic political poetry of the eighteenth century—Whig panegyric and Tory satire—are works of quite another color.[27]

Though perhaps no eighteenth century satire or panegyric, Whig or Tory, can be fully appreciated without a knowledge of the works dealt with in these chapters, nevertheless, in respect to poems on affairs of state, *Absalom and Achitophel* is the last of its kind. For the division between Whig and Tory was never again as momentous, radical, or fateful as the struggle between republican and royalist for the future of the nation. The literature of affairs of state in the seventeenth century, of whatever quality or tendency, had been nourished upon that sense of destiny, and upon the inflamed passions, and passionately held ideologies, which had sprung from it. Thenceforth the tendency would be towards a generalized didacti-

[26] S. Pordage, *Azaria and Hushai* (London, 1682), p. 24.
[27] See C. A. Moore, "Whig Panegyric Verse," *PMLA*, Vol. XLI (1926); and L. I. Bredvold, "The Gloom of the Tory Satirists," *Pope and his Contemporaries:* Essays presented to George Sherburn (Oxford, 1949).

cism; in Tory satire, for instance, on the vanity of human wishes, or the baseness of man; or towards the excoriation of an individual personality robbed of his significance as representative in a struggle between great opposing forces, upon the issue of which the destiny of the entire nation depends. Or, in Whig panegyric, a similar tendency would take the form of the heroic hypostasized as Britannia, or Empire, or Commerce.

After a brief continuation of the older epic and historic presentation of great personality in the shape of the Benevolent Monarch, William of Orange, and Marlborough, none of the Georges seemed able to fill the role of hero; the court yielded its powers to a managed parliament, manipulated by a small circle of political oligarchs, and the glorification of mercantilism and trade came more and more to take the place both of the princely heroic of a court culture, and the redemptive, or messianic, heroic of a Puritanism newly aware of itself, newly surging up from the once inarticulate depths of the nation. It is not by chance that the Augustan peak of literary achievement is a mock-heroic satire, in which the heroic standard has receded from the contemporary scene to the remote Imperia of Rome, and the content, though splendidly and seriously general, is nevertheless the characteristic concern of a social, literary, and cultural Establishment.

BIBLIOGRAPHY

A. Major Authors

Butler, S. *Poetical Works*, ed. Gilfillan, 2 vols, Edinburgh, 1854
Genuine Remains, ed. Thyer, 2 vols, London, 1751
Characters and Passages from Notebooks, ed. Waller, Cambridge University Press, 1908
Cleveland, J. *Poems*, ed. Berdan, Yale University Press, 1903
Poems, ed. Saintsbury, The Caroline Poets, Vol. 3, Oxford, The Clarendon Press, 1921
The Character of a London, Diurnall, London, 1647
Cowley, A. *Works*, ed. Tonson, 3 vols, London, 1721 (12th. ed.)
Poems, ed. Waller, Cambridge University Press, 1905
Essays and Plays, ed. Waller, Cambridge University Press, 1906
The Puritan and the Papist, 1643, in *Wit and Loyalty Reviv'd*, London, 1682
Poem on the Late Civil War (printed fragment 1679), in *Examen Poeticum*, Vol. 3 of *Dryden's Miscellany Poems*, ed. Tonson, London, 1716
An Heroick Poem upon the Late Horrid Rebellion; His Majesty's Happy Restauration; and the Magnanimity and Valour of His Royal Highness James Duke of York . . . London, 1683
Denham, Sir J. *Poetical Works*, ed. Banks, Yale University Press, 1928
Dryden, J. *Poetical Works*, ed. Noyes, Harvard University Press, 1950

⌊ 267 ⌋

Bibliography

Essays, ed. Ker, Oxford, The Clarendon Press, 1926

Plays, ed. Saintsbury, 2 vols, Mermaid series, London, Ernest Benn, 1949

Marvell, A. *Poems*, ed. Margoliouth, Oxford, The Clarendon Press, 1927

    The Rehearsal Transpros'd; opr, animadversions upon a late book (by S. Parker, later Bishop of Oxford) *intituled A Preface to Bishop Bramhall's Vindication of himself and the episcopal clergy, shewing what grounds there are of fears . . . of Popery*, etc., London, 1672

    Mr. Smirke; or, The Divine in mode, being certain annotations upon the animadversions (by F. Turner, Bishop of Ely) *on the Naked Truth* (by H. Croft, Bishop of Hereford), London, 1676

Milton, J. *Complete Prose Works*, ed. Don M. Wolfe, Yale University Press, 1953

    The Works of John Milton, ed. F. A. Patterson, Columbia University Press, 1931–1938

Oldham, J. *Poetical Works*, ed. Bell, London, 1854

Waller, E. *Works*, ed. Fenton, London, 1730 (1st. ed. 1729)

    Works, ed. Thorn Drury, 2 vols., The Muses' Library, London, Routledge, 1905

B. Contemporary Works

Abercromby, D. *A Discourse of Wit*, London, 1686

Anonymous: *Absalom's Conspiracy; or, The Tragedy of Treason*, London, 1680

    Anglia Rediviva; or, England revived. An Heroick Poem, London, 1658

    A Key (with the whip) to open the mystery, and iniquity of the poem called Absalom and Achitophel, London, 1682

    Raillerie à la Mode Consider'd; or, The Supercilious Detractor, London, 1673

    Satyre against the Cavaliers: penned in opposition to the Satyre (by A. C.) against Separatists, London, 1643

    A Satyr against common-wealths, London, 1684

[268]

Bibliography

A Satyr against Vertue, London, 1679

The Unparalleled Monarch, London, 1656

Beeston, H. *A Poem to His Most Excellent Majesty Charles the Second*, London, 1660

Birkenhead, Sir J. *The Character of an Assembly Man*, London, 1647

Blount, T. *Glossographia; or, a dictionary interpreting all such hard words, . . . as are now used in our refined English tongue*, London, 1656

Caryl, J. *Naboth's Vinyard; or, The Innocent traytor: copied from the original of Holy Scripture, in heroick verse*, London, 1679

Charleton, W. *Two Discourses. I. Concerning the different Wits of Men; II. Of the Mysterie of Vintners*, London, 1669

Cooper, A. A. (Lord Shaftesbury) *Sensus Communis: an Essay on the Freedom of Wit and Humour*, in *Characteristicks*, London, 1711.

Cotton, C. *A Panegyrick to the King's most Excellent Majesty*, London, 1660

Scarronides: or Virgil travestie, London, 1664

Daniel, S. *A Panegyrike Congratulatory delivered to the Kings most excellent maiesty . . .* London, 1603

Davenant, Sir W. *Gondibert: an heroick poem.*
With "The Author's Preface to his much-honour'd Friend Mr. Hobs" and "The answer of Mr. Hobbes to Sr Will. D'Avenant's Preface before Gondibert . . ." London, 1651

Poem, upon his Sacred Majesties most Happy Return to his Dominions, London, 1660

Poem, to the King's Most Sacred Majesty, London, 1663

Davyes, T. *The Tenth Worthy. Or, Several anagrams in Latine, Welsh and English, upon the name of . . . Oliver late Lord Protector. Together with some elegeical (sic) verses upon his much lamented death . . .* London, 1658

Dawbeny, H. *Historie & Policie re-viewed, in the heroick transactions of his Most Serene Highnesse, Oliver, late Lord protector; from his cradle, to his tomb: declaring his steps to princely perfection; as they are drawn in lively parallels to the ascents of the great patriarch Moses, in thirty degrees, to the height of honour.* London, 1659

Dennis, Sir J. *Critical Works,* ed. Hooker, Baltimore, The Johns Hopkins Press, 1939

Miscellanies in Verse and Prose, London, 1693

D'Urfey, T. *The Progress of Honesty: or, a view of a court and city,* London, 1681.

The Malcontent: a satyr: being the sequel of the Progress of Honesty: or, a view of Court and City, London, 1684

Eachard, J. *The Grounds and Occasions for the Contempt of the Clergy and Religion inquired into,* 1670, in *An English Garner,* ed. Arber, Vol. 7, London, 1877

Fenton, E. *The Works of Edmund Waller,* London, 1729

Flecknoe, R. *The Diarium, or Journall: divided into 12 jornadas in burlesque rhime, or drolling verse* . . . London, 1656

The Idea of His Highness Oliver, late Lord Protector, With certain brief reflexions on his life, London, 1659

Heroick Portraits, London, 1660

Fletcher, H. *The Perfect Politician,* London, 1660

"Generosus, A. C." *A Satyre against Seperatists,* or, the Conviction of chamber-preachers and other chismatickes . . . London, 1642

Harrington, J. *The Common-Wealth of Oceana,* London, 1656

Higgons, Sir T. *A panegyrick to the King,* 1660

Hobbes, T. *Answer to the Preface to Gondibert,* 1651, in *Critical Essays of the Seventeenth Century,* ed. Spingarn Vol. 3, Indiana University Press, 1957

Hyde, E. (Earl of Clarendon) *The History of the Rebellion and Civil Wars,* ed. Huehns, Selections, World's Classics, Oxford, 1955

Lloyd, D. *Memoires of the Lives, Actions, Sufferings and Deaths of those noble, reverend and excellent personages that suffered by death, sequestration, decimation or otherwise for the protestant religion, and the great principle thereof, allegiance to their soveraigne, in our late intestine wars,*

. . . *With the life and martyrdom of King Charles I*, London, 1668

Lluelyn, M. *To the Kings most excellent Majesty*, London, 1660

Machiavelli, *The Prince*, trans. Marriott, Everyman's Library, London, J. M. Dent, 1916

Manley, T. *Veni; Vidi; Vici; The Triumphs of . . . Oliver Cromwell . . . done into English heroicall verse*, London, 1652

Mennis, Sir J. *Musarum Deliciae; or, The Muses Recreation*, London, 1655

Wit Restor'd, London, 1658

Nedham, M. *The True Character of a rigid Presbyter. To which is added, A short history of the English Rebellion: compiled in verse*, London, 1661

Pellison, P. *The History of the French Academy*, translated by H.S., London, 1657

Phillips, J. *A Satyr against Hypocrites*, London, 1655

Pordage, S. *Heroick Stanzas on his Majesties Coronation*, London, 1661

The Medal Revers'd. A Satyre against Persecution, London, 1682

Azaria and Hushai, a poem, London, 1682

Quarles, J. *Rebellion's Downfall*, London, 1662

Reynell, C. *The Fortunate Change: being a panegyrick to his sacred majesty king Charles the second, immediately on his coronation*, London, 1661

Settle, E. *Absalom Senior; or, Achitophel transpos'd: a poem*, London, 1682

Shadwell, T. *The Medal of John Bayes: a satyr against folly and knavery*, London, 1682

Sheffield, J. (Earl of Mulgrave) *Essay on Poetry, 1683*, in *Critical Essays of the Seventeenth Century*, ed. Spingarn, Vol. 2, Indiana University Press, 1957

Smith, G. *God's Unchangeableness . . . wherein is demonstrated that Oliver Cromwell is by the Providence of God, Lord Protector of England, Scotland and Ireland*, London, 1655

Bibliography

Sprat, T. *A Poem to the happie memory of the most Renowned Prince, Oliver, Lord Protector*, London, 1659
The History of the Royal Society of London . . . London, 1667
Villiers, G. (Duke of Buckingham) *The Rehearsal*, ed. Summers, Stratford, Shakespeare Head Press, 1914
Wilmot, J. (Earl of Rochester) *Poems*, ed. de Sola Pinto, London, Routledge, 1953
à Wood, A. *Athenae Oxonienses*, London, 1691

C. Miscellanies and Collections

Cavalier Poets, ed. Lindsay, New York, the Abbey Press, 1901
The Cavalier Songs and Ballads of England 1642–1684, ed. Mackay, 1863
A Collection of Poems on Affairs of State, London, 1689, 1697, 1698, and 4 vols, 1703–1707
Critical Essays of the Seventeenth Century, ed. Spingarn, 3 vols., Indiana University Press, 1957 (first published Oxford, The Clarendon Press, 1908)
Fugitive Tracts, ed. Hazlitt, London, 1875
The Loyal Garland, London, 1678
Loyal Poems and Satyres, London, 1685
The Muses' Farewell to Popery and Slavery, London, 1689
Political Ballads of the Seventeenth and Eighteenth Centuries, ed. Wilkins, London, 1860
Wit and Loyalty Reviv'd, 1682, ed. Scott, Somers Collection of Tracts, Vol. 5, London, 1811

D. Critical Studies

Allen, D. C. *Image and Meaning*, Baltimore, The Johns Hopkins Press, 1960
Auerbach, E. *Mimesis*, trans. Trask, Princeton University Press, 1953 (first published Berne, 1946)
Beljame, A. *Men of Letters and the English Public in the Eighteenth Century*, ed. Dobree, London, Routledge, 1948 (first published 1881)

[272]

Bibliography

Birrell, A. *Andrew Marvell*, London, Macmillan, 1905

Bond, R. P. *English Burlesque Poetry, 1700–1750*, Harvard University Press, 1932

Bradbrook, M. C. & Lloyd-Thomas, M. G. *Andrew Marvell*, Cambridge University Press, 1940

Bredvold, L. I. *The Intellectual Milieu of John Dryden: Studies in Some Aspects of Seventeenth Century Thought*, Michigan University Press, 1934

"The Gloom of the Tory Satirists" in *Pope and his Contemporaries: Essays presented to George Sherburn*, Oxford, The Clarendon Press, 1949

Brooks, C. "Marvell's Horatian Ode," *Sewanee Review*, Vol. 61, 1953

Brower, R. *The Fields of Light: an Experiment in Critical Reading*, Oxford, (Toronto), 1951.

"An Allusion to Europe-Dryden and Tradition," *ELH*, Vol. 19, 1952

Bullit, J. M. *Jonathan Swift and the Anatomy of Satire: a Study of Satiric Technique*, Harvard University Press, 1953

Bush, D. *English Literature in the Earlier Seventeenth Century*, Oxford, The Clarendon Press, 1945

Clinton-Baddeley, V. *The Burlesque Tradition in the English Theatre after 1660*, London, Methuen, 1952

Courthope, W. J. *History of English Poetry*, Vol. 3, London, Macmillan, 1895

Danby, J. F. *Poets on Fortune's Hill*, London, Faber, 1952

Eliot, T. S. *Homage to John Dryden*, London, Hogarth Press, 1924

Gibson, D. "Samuel Butler," in *Seventeenth Century Studies*, ed. Shafer, Princeton University Press, 1933

Haller, W. *The Rise of Puritanism, 1570–1643*, Columbia University Press, 1947

Hazard, P. *The European Mind: The Critical Years (1680–1715)*, trans. May, Yale University Press, 1953

Hook, S. *The Hero in History: a Study in Limitation and Possibility*, New York, Dial Press, 1946

Hooker, E. N. "The Purpose of Dryden's Annus Mirabilis," *Huntingdon Library Quaterly*, Vol. 10, 1940

Bibliography

Hughes, M. Y. "The Christ of Paradise Regained and the Renaissance Heroic Tradition," *SP*, Vol. 35, 1938

Jack, I. *Augustan Satire, 1660–1750*, Oxford, The Clarendon Press, 1952

Jones, R. "The Originality of Absalom and Achitophel," *MLN*, Vol. 46, 1931

Jordan, W. K. *The Development of Religious Toleration in England*, Harvard University Press, 1932

Kermode, F. "Milton's Hero," *RES*, Vol. 4, 1953

Krutch, J. W. *Comedy and Conscience after the Restoration*, Columbia University Press, 1924

Legouis, S. *André Marvell, Poet, Puritain, Patriot*, Oxford, The Clarendon Press, 1928

Lerner, L. "Marvell: an Horatian Ode," in *Interpretations*, ed. Wain, London, Routledge, 1955

Mayo, T. B. F. *Epicurus in England, 1650–1725*, Texas, Southwest Press, 1934

Moore, C. A. "Whig Panegyric Verse," *PMLA*, Vol. 41, 1926

Nethercot, A. R. *Abraham Cowley: The Muses' Hannibal*, Oxford, The Clarendon Press, 1931

Pinto, V de Sola, *Restoration Carnival*, London, Folio Press, 1954

Previté-Orton, Sir C. W. *Political Satire in English Poetry*, London, Macmillan, 1910

Quintana, R. "Samuel Butler—a Restoration Figure in a Modern Light," *ELH*, Vol. 18, 1951

Richards, E. S. *Hudibras in the Burlesque Tradition*, Columbia University Press, 1937

Ross, M. M. *Poetry and Dogma*, Rutgers University Press, 1954

Røstvig, M. S. *The Happy Man; Studies in the Metamorphoses of a Classical Ideal 1600–1700*, Oslo University Press and Oxford, Basil Blackwell, 1954

Russel, T. W. *Voltaire, Dryden and Heroic Tragedy*, Columbia University Press, 1946

Russell Smith, H. F. *Harrington and his Oceana*, Cambridge University Press, 1914

Shafer, R. *The English Ode to 1660; an Essay in Literary History*, Princeton University Press, 1918

Bibliography

Stebbing, W. *Some Verdicts of History Reviewed. Three Essays*, Oxford, 1887

Sypher, W. *Four Stages of Renaissance Style: Transformation in Art and Literature, 1400–1700*, New York, Doubleday (Anchor), 1955

Trilling, L. "Dr. Leavis and the Moral Tradition," in *A Gathering of Fugitives*, Boston, Beacon Press, 1956.

Tuve, R. *Elizabethan and Metaphysical Imagery*, Chicago University Press, 1947

Wallerstein, R. *Studies in Seventeenth Century Poetic*, Wisconsin University Press, 1950

Walton, C. *Metaphysical To Augustan: Studies in Tone and Sensibility of the Seventeenth Century*, London, Bowes, 1955

Wedgewood, C. V. "Cavalier Poetry and Cavalier Politics," *English Critical Essays, Twentieth Century*, 2nd. Series, Oxford (World's Classics), 1958

"A Cavalier Satirist," *The Listener*, May 8, 1958

Wasserman, E. *The Subtler Language*, Johns Hopkins, 1959

Werblovsky, Z. *Lucifer and Prometheus: a Study of Milton's Satan*, London, Routledge, 1952

Whitfield, F. *Beast in View: a Study of the Earl of Rochester's Poetry*, Harvard Honor Theses in English No. 9, 1936

Wiley, M. L. *The Subtle Knot: Creative Scepticism in Seventeenth Century England*, Harvard University Press, 1952

Willey, B. *The Seventeenth Century Background*, London, Chatto, 1934

Williams, W. M. "The Genesis of John Oldham's Satires Upon the Jesuits," *PMLA*, Vol. 58, 1943

Wilson, J. H. *The Court Wits of the Restoration*, Princeton University Press, 1948

Worcester, D. *The Art of Satire*, Harvard University Press, 1940

INDEX

Abercromby, D., *A Discourse of Wit*, 211
Advice to a Painter, see Directions to a Painter
Allen, D. C., 110n
Anglia Rediviva, 76, 84
Aubrey, 44n, 192n
Auerbach, E., 7n, 13, 94n
Augustan, 9, 146, 240, 254, 265

Badger in the Foxtrap, The, 247
baroque, *see under* style
Beeston, H., 142
Beljame, A., 3
Birkenhead, Sir J., *Character of an Assembly Man*, 54n
Birrell, A., 200n
Blount, *Glossographia*, 24
Boileau, 41, 72, 189–190; *Le Lutrin*, 217, 218, 240
Bond, R. P., 220n, 234
Bradbrook, M., 97
Brooks, Cleanth, 79, 107n
Brower, R., 251, 256n
Brunker, 171–172
Buckingham, Duke of, *see* Villiers, G.
Bunyan, 15, 235
burlesque, *see under* style
Burnett, the *History*, 198n
Bush, D., 18
Butler, S., 19, 189–204, 212, 218, 221–240, 245, 261; and Cleveland, 44, 157, 189–204, passim; and Cowley, 245; and Denham, 236; and Dryden, 16, 215, 220, 245, 248, 253; and Marvell, 10, 189–204 passim, 211, 248; and Oldham, 245; *Characters*, 194–195, 201,

227n, 230, 235; *Description of Holland*, 194; *Du Val*, 238–240; *Elephant in the Moon*, 204, 237; *Hudibras*, 10, 16, 157, 188, 195–198, 218–219, 221–236, 240, 242, 245, 258; *Imperfection and Abuse of Human Learning*, 236; *Repartee between Cat and Puss*, 238; *Satyr on the Licentiousness of the Age*, 236

C. W., *Poems on Several Occasions*, 208–209
Caryl, J., *Naboth's Vineyard*, 246–248
Cervantes, 228, 202n
Charleton, W., *The Different Wits of Men*, 206
Charles I, King of England, 12, 21, 22, 25, 26, 31, 36, 38, 46, 74, 75, 76, 79, 102, 105–106, 142
Charles II, King of England, 14, 15, 30, 74, 138, 148, 156, 163, 164, 175n, 180–181, 245, 250, 262
Chaucer, 224
class-consciousness, *see under* style
Clarendon, Earl of, *see* Hyde, E.
Cleveland, J., 19, 42–48, 56–61, 64; and Butler, 44, 157, 191–193; and Cowley, 42, 61; and Dryden, 4, 73, 151, 157; and Marvell, 69, 71, 72, 73, 191–193; and Milton, 9, 56; *Character of London Diurnall*, 45, 54; *Dialogue between Two Zealots*, 52, 64; *Epitaph on the Earl of Strafford*, 59; *General Eclipse, The*, 59–61; *Hue & Cry after Sir John Presbyter*, 61; *King's Disguise, The*, 45–47;

[277]

Index

Index

imagery (*continued*)
146, 147–156, 157, 166, 169, 191–206

Jack, I., 197, 222n, 244, 257
James, I, King of England, Jacobean, 10, 20, 59, 147
Jermyn, H., Earl of St. Albans, 174
Johnson, S., 37n, 147n
Jones, R. F., 246
Juvenal, 10, 51, 168, 166, 180, 183–184, 206, 208, 211, 213–214, 215–217, 220, 249

Kermode, F., 91n
A Key (with a Whip) to open the Mystery . . . (Anon), 262
To the King, Upon His Majesty's Happy Return (Anon), 149

Lucan, *Pharsalia*, 100
Leavis, F. R., 105n
Lerner, L. D., 97–98, 107n
L'Estrange, Sir Roger, 127

Lindsay, ed., *Cavalier Poets*, 13
Llevelyn, M., *To the King's Most Excellent Majesty*, 143
Lloyd, D., 4, 7, 45
Lovelace, R., 59, 127

M. W., *A Satyrical Poem*, 183
Machiavelli, 80–81, 82; machiavellian, 66, 75, 76, 82, 94, 109, 133, 260
Mackay, ed., *Cavalier Songs & Ballads*, 74n
Manley, T., *Veni; vidi; vici;* 82; *To the most Excellent, The Lord Generall of Great Brittayne, O.C.,* 83
Marlowe, C., 185
Marston, J., 7, 166
Marvell, A., 5n, 14, 19, 69–73, 77, 95–119, 132–133, 167–182 passim; 191–207 passim; and Butler, 10, 157, 191–200, 211, 245; and Cleveland, 69–73, 191–200; and Cowley, 26n, 71, 95, 103–105, 120, 123, 125, 127, 131, 132–133, 245; and Denham, 32, 33n, 35, 71, 178; and Dryden, 72–73, 134n, 178; and

Milton, 51, 91, 99, 112; and Waller, 26n, 110, 134n; *Upon Appleton House,* 109, 110; *On Blake's Victory,* 114–115; *Character of Holland,* 69–72, 193, 199; *Clarindon's House Warming,* 172, 199; *Upon the Death of Lord Hastings,* 97, 105, 117, 134n; *Dialogue between Two Horses,* 165; *First Anniversary,* 9, 109–114, 116, 119, 131, 173, 182; *The Garden,* 110; *Horatian Ode, An,* 5, 35, 36, 91, 97–109, 147; *King's Vowes, The,* 172; *Last Instructions,* 154n, 167, 169, 171n, 173–178, 179, 182–183, 199, 245; *Loyal Scot, The,* 150, 154, 178, 182; *To his Noble Friend, Mr. Lovelace,* 97, 104; *Rehearsal Transpos'd, The,* 5n, 51, 118, 178, 198–201, 205–206, 207, 210; *Statue at Charing Cross,* 165; *Statue in Stocks Market,* 165
    Attributions: Britannia & Rawleigh, 181; *An Historical Poem,* 182; *Nostradamus' Prophecy,* 181; *Oceana & Britannia,* 182
Mayo, T. M., 248
Mendilow, A. A., 156
metaphysical conceit, 42, 44, 147, 157, 177, 191
Milton, J., 19, 48–52, 88–91; and Cleveland, 9, 56; and Dryden, 73, 180, 259; and Marvell, 51, 91, 99n, 112n; *Apology against a Pamphlet,* 49; *Defense of the People of England,* 88–91, 182; *On the new Forcers of Conscience,* 49; *Ready & Easy Way, A,* 89–90; *Tetrachordon,* 49
mock-heroic, *see under* style
Monk, G., Duke of Albemarle, 169
Monmouth, 182, 246, 248
Montaigne, 119n
Motteux, P., 218
Mulgrave, Earl of, see Sheffield, J.

Netherot, A. H., 119n, 192n
Newcastle, 170
Newton, *Opticks,* 151n

Index

110–134n; *Of the Danger His Majesty Escaped*, 21–24; *Instructions to a Painter*, 150, 154–155, 156, 162, 165; *To the King upon His Majesty's Happy Return*, 141, 148; *Upon His Majesty's Receiving the News*, 25; *Upon His Majesty's repairing of St. Pauls*, 25, 27, 28, 36; *The Maid's Tragedy*, 117; *Panegyric to my Lord Protector*, 116–117, 136, 139; *Of a War with Spain & a Fight at Sea*, 115

Wallerstein, R., 97
Wasserman, E., 31, 33n, 35n
Wedgewood, C. V., 3n, 5n, 59n
Werblowsky, Z., 89n
Wild, Jonathan, 239

Wilkin, W. W., ed. *Political Ballads*, 74n
Williams, Weldon M., 183n, 184n, 244
Willey, B., 122–123
Wilmot, J., Earl of Rochester, 19, 164, 169, 200, 212; *Alexander Bendo's Bill*, 212; *History of Insipids*, 164, 172; *Satire Liu: Tunbridge Wells*, 200
wit, 9, 42, 48, 56–57, 61, 62, 63, 68, 70, 71, 73, 174, 177–179, 185, 191–201, 208–212; miscellanies, 168–169, 202n
à Wood, A., 4, 6, 44, 180–181
Worcester, D., 188n

York, Duke of, 170–171